Just Curious, Jeeves

Just Curious, Jeeves

What are the **1001** most intriguing questions asked on the Internet? **Ask!**

Jack Mingo
Erin Barrett

ASK JEEVES • EMERYVILLE, CALIFORNIA

Publisher's Note:

As far as we know, the information and descriptions of Web sites in this book were correct at the time the book was printed. If you find something that needs to be changed, please let us know so we can fix it the next time we go to press. We'd also love to hear what you think of the book. Send comments and corrections to Books@askjeeves.com.

ISBN: 1-930108-01-X

Library of Congress Catalog Number: 00-133567

Design and Composition by Seventeenth Street Studios

Distributed in the United States by
Publishers Group West

Distributed in Canada by Raincoast Book

Printed in the United States of America

10 9 8 7 6 5 4 3 2 1

Developed and Managed by Melissa Schwarz

Special Thanks

WE WOULD LIKE to express our appreciation to the people who have contributed their time and talents to this book.

Melissa Schwarz
Penny Finnie
Ted Briscoe
David Hellier
Sharilyn Hovind
Virginia Croft
Elizabeth Walker
Jacquie Harrison
Naomi Schiff
Bob Giles
Wallis Hendon
Karen Cross
Elise Cannon
Marcos Sorensen
Gregg Loew
Georgia Hamner
Jackson Hamner

Elana Mingo
John Javna
The folks at California
   Canoe & Kayak
Vera Mingo
Jerry & Lynn Barrett
Powell Hamner
Gloria McCracken
Kristen Mingo-Williams
Mark Hardin
Eric Eales
Simcha Shtull
Paul Stanley
Lonny Kirk
Ron Schoepel
Nancy Adamietz

And all the Ask Jeeves users whose intriguing questions gave us the idea in the first place.

Contents

A Note from the Authors

AS THE WEB'S MOST FAMOUS FACE, Jeeves is, of course, frequently approached by literary agents and publishing people brandishing book proposals and contracts. He's been invited to pen his autobiography, he's been haunted by ghost writers, and he's even been asked by a television network to play himself in the docudrama of his life. But with characteristic reserve, Jeeves has resisted the siren call of the spotlight, choosing instead to concentrate on his mission to humanize the Internet by providing relevant answers to almost any imaginable query.

It took a very special project to change Jeeves' mind. The book you're holding represents not the story of the world's first Internet butler but the story of his work. *Just Curious, Jeeves* is the fruit of one of the most ambitious undertakings in history—an attempt to satisfy curiosity on a scale never before seen.

When you think about it, each of us faces a daily obstacle course of questions—from "Where did I leave my shoes?" in the morning to "What's the meaning of my dream?" at night. Ask Jeeves was created not only to help people access the information they need but also to satisfy their curiosity. By creating the first natural-language question answering service, Ask Jeeves allowed users to pose questions in the same way they speak, without hunting for keywords or mastering computer language strings.

You're probably wondering, "What kind of technology makes Ask Jeeves run?" Actually, Ask Jeeves is one of the most sophisticated navigation systems on the Internet, combining a natural-language engine with a knowledge base compiled by resident human editors. More recently, Ask Jeeves has grown to include popularity search technology as well. Taken together, this mechanism responds to conversational language, processes meaning and grammar, and links the questioner directly to relevant, high-quality answers. Most interesting of all, the entire system is designed to learn from each interaction, thus expanding its knowledge base with each question asked and each answer delivered. Or, in the plain English that Jeeves prefers, the technology is intelligent enough to figure out what people are asking and learn from the experience.

This unique approach has made Ask Jeeves at Ask.com one of the most highly visited sites on the Internet. Jeeves receives nearly 3,300 questions a minute, 24 hours a day, 7 days a week—or 55 questions a second. In other words, each day Jeeves delivers over 4 million answers!

Even more interesting and gratifying, though, is the fact that people turn to Jeeves with all kinds of questions. They're not just looking for practical information, such as "How can I file my taxes?" Every day, people ask Jeeves questions like "What is the meaning of life?" or "Who invented time?" or "What does the 'J' in Homer J. Simpson stand for?" And all of these questions become part of the knowledge base with appropriate answers.

This book draws its impetus and energy from the spontaneity, creativity, and sheer zaniness that people express when they're invited to ask whatever's on their minds. And that's where we came in. We were asked to choose 1,001 (count them!) of the more intriguing questions that come streaming into Ask.com and then track down the answers. We instinctively knew we were the right people for the job because we love this stuff and have worked at being know-it-alls for years. We've also managed to accumulate scads of information in mouldering boxes, overstuffed computer files, rapidly depleting brain cells, and a library of books and articles (some of which we've written ourselves over the years, many of which have our own refutations and corrections scrawled into their margins).

The first step, of course, was to come up with some intriguing questions. We spent more than a week watching questions whiz by on the Ask Jeeves at Ask.com "peek box" (the place where you can see the questions that users are currently typing in) and printing out reams and reams of paper. Then we winnowed down tens of thousands of questions to the ones you'll find in this book.

How did we decide which ones to include? Although the questions we chose are not the most frequently asked questions, we did try to reflect the range of what people ask every day. (Food was such a popular topic, for example, that it warranted two chapters.) Above all, each question had to meet certain requirements. For example, questions from homework assignments were excluded. So were questions that fall into the category commonly called "adult content." We kept only those that were slightly off the beaten path or that we suspected would have a pretty darned interesting answer. Of course, what's intriguing to one person may not be to another, and we couldn't cover everything. But we're betting there's something here for just about everyone.

In compiling the book, we did depart from our source in some important ways. For example, we edited questions for grammar, spelling, and sometimes clarity. Also, as you know if you've ever visited the site, Jeeves responds to questions there with suggestions for other Web sites to access. In *Just Curious, Jeeves,* we answered your questions directly. However, we also included Web sources where you can find more information and questions for you to ask Jeeves yourself.

The experience of writing this book has been exhilarating, at times infuriating, but always enlightening. More than anything else, we've tried to remain faithful to the spirit of Jeeves by celebrating curiosity of all kinds. And in the process, we hope we've piqued yours.

Art & Artists

"**THE ARTISTIC TEMPERAMENT IS A** disease," rote G. K. Chesterton, and there are plenty of examples to prove him right. On the other hand, we tolerate artists because without them—without their art *and* their temperament—the world would be a drab place indeed.

ART CAN BE SO DEEP . . . AND SO WIDE

What was the world's widest painting?

THE WIDEST would have to be *Panorama of the Mississippi,* John Banvard's minutely detailed mural depicting scenes from 1,200 miles of the shore along the Mississippi River. Although billed as being "3 miles long!" it was painted on a 1,200-foot-long canvas and was the result of a year-long journey Banvard took by raft and boat, sketchbook in hand. The painting was a huge commercial success: Banvard displayed it to ticket-buyers around the world. Unfortunately, after his death in 1891 it was cut up and the canvas used as theatrical backdrops; there's no evidence that any of it has survived to the present.

LEND ME AN EAR, VINCENT

Why did Vincent van Gogh cut off his ear?

FOR A REASON that has brought out the best and worst in men throughout history: He was trying to impress a girl. Despite popular legend, he didn't cut off his entire ear, just the earlobe. The bloody act, accomplished with a razor, took place in Arles, France, the day before Christmas, 1888. The artist then wrapped the lobe in paper and presented it to "Rachel," a favorite prostitute at the brothel that he frequented, telling her, "Guard this object carefully." When she unwrapped it, she fell over in a faint.

The police were summoned and found van Gogh wounded and catatonic, lying in the fetal position in his bed. It was his first of a sequence of attacks of madness that came with alarming frequency until his suicide a year and a half later. Still, it was a productive time for him—of his 850 known paintings, two-thirds were created in the last two years of his life. In one of his cycles of lucidity, he wrote to his brother about Rachel's reaction: "Yesterday I went to see the girl I had gone to when I was out of my wits. They told me there that in this country things like that are not out of the ordinary. She had been upset by it and had fainted but had recovered her calm."

How many paintings did van Gogh sell in his lifetime?

ONLY TWO, both sales arranged by his brother Theo. In 1890 (the year he died), van Gogh began seeing some success. He got a highly favorable review in an influential art journal and at about the same time learned that *The Red Vineyard* had sold in an auction to painter Anna Boch. The prospect of success unhinged him, bringing on another wave of madness and a plea that the art journal not write about him again. The other painting that sold was a self-portrait sold to Sulley & Lori, art dealers in London.

What painting had van Gogh just finished when he pulled out a pistol and shot himself?

LEGEND HAS IT that he shot himself immediately after he finished the last brushstrokes on *Wheatfield with Crows.* Scholars, however, disagree. While his last painting was *Wheatfield,* on the day he died, van Gogh was out standing in the fields, without easel or paints. It was during one of his apparently lucid periods, yet at some point he pulled out a gun and shot himself in the abdomen. Surprised to find himself still alive, he staggered back to his room.

When the doctor told him he might live, van Gogh replied, "Then I will have to do it all over again." He died two days later. "Do not cry," he told his brother. "I did it for the good of everybody."

PAINT AND SUFFERING

Were any famous painters poisoned by the toxins in their paints?

SOME PATHOLOGISTS and historians think that most of them were, to some degree. Many artists ground and mixed their own pigments of lead, cadmium, mercury, and other deadly materials and may have suffered the cumulative effects of absorption through breathing, touching, and accidentally ingesting them. It has been suggested that it's no accident that Vincent van Gogh's insanity flared up during his most prolific two-year period.

The case of Francisco Goya is perhaps the most curious. Some say he was an artist whose paint poisoning actually helped his career. Through age 46, Goya was a court painter, eminently competent but tame in his choice of subject matter. In that year (1792), however, he became deathly ill with a coma, partial paralysis, impaired vision and hearing, dizziness, paranoia, and hallucinations—all symptoms of lead poisoning. Goya was a particularly good candidate for this, since he ground and mixed his own pigments, covered his canvas with an undercoat of lead white, and painted in a furiously fast and messy way with brush, trowel, rag, mop, sponge, and hands, continuously splattering himself and everything nearby with his lead whites, cadmium yellows, and mercury reds. He recovered, but over the next 36 years suffered at least five bouts of the same mysterious illness. Each time he'd have to stop painting, which allowed the lead in his body to drop below toxic levels.

> **How many of his self-portraits show Van Gogh with his ear bandaged?**
> Two.

The really interesting part is the effect this had on his art. His work suddenly went from sweet and sentimental to eerie and grotesque—from peaceful country scenes to hellish nightmares, and from safe little vignettes to devastating satires of the excesses of nobles and the Church. His frank depictions of mutilation, castration, strangulation, witchcraft, and sexual acts revolutionized his work and made his reputation in art history.

Why did the British government ban the paint called Indian yellow in 1908? Was it dangerous?

CURIOUSLY ENOUGH, the British government of the time didn't ban any of the paints made with dangerous metal pigments, but they did ban Indian yellow, which was made with natural organic ingredients and was not a hazard to artists. The paint had been developed in the 1750s and became a staple of many palettes for its rich yellow hue. To get the deep color, the manufacturers fed mangoes to cows, collected their urine, evaporated it into a concentrate, and extracted its calcium and magnesium salts. Officials decided that it was inhumane to feed large quantities of mangoes to cows, and so banned Indian yellow. It wasn't until more than a half century later that paints safer for humans began replacing the more dangerous pigments. Cynics can find in this timeline the relative value of an artist to a cow, as held by the British government more than a century ago.

> **What did Roy Liechtenstein use to paint the rows of dots that make his pop art look like a comic?**
> A toothbrush and a metal screen.

MY FAVORITE SUBJECT IS . . . ME!

Which artist painted the most self-portraits?

OF THE WORLD'S famous painters, Rembrandt comes first in the self-absorption competition, with 62 self-portraits. Vincent van Gogh is number two, with 40. He had a good excuse, though—while institutionalized for madness, he didn't have models or landscape views available. One of his portraits is *Self-Portrait with Bandaged Ear,* painted in the mental institution not long after the notorious incident in which he cut off his earlobe.

PABLO ACCRUES

Was Picasso multitalented, like all-around Renaissance men Leonardo da Vinci and Michelangelo?

PABLO PICASSO was an amazing and prolific painter. However, unlike Michelangelo, who was also an accomplished poet, or Leonardo, who dabbled brilliantly in the fields of science, math, philosophy, and music, Picasso's genius in painting did not overlap into other fields. For example, when he tried his hand at writing plays, he took just four days to create a self-conscious, surrealistic bomb called *Desire Caught by the Tail,* which contains such lines as "We sprinkle the rice powder of angels on soiled bedsheets.... Turn the mattresses through blackberry bushes!...With all power the pigeon flocks dash into the rifle bullets!" At the end of the play, all of the characters die from the fumes emitted from frying potatoes.

Luckily, Picasso quickly abandoned his literary pretensions and went back to what he did best. As a result, although the dilettante Renaissance boys frittered away their time with sonnets and impossible-to-build submarines and ornithopters, Picasso slaved in his studio to create a record number of artistic works—more than 20,000 in his 91 years. In quantity, at least, Leonardo and Michelangelo were mere dabblers.

Did Picasso smoke?

YES, AND HE credited cigar smoke with saving his life. The story that he told was that he had been born grey and wasn't breathing. The midwife thought he was dead, but luckily an uncle, who was a doctor, decided to try something desperate— he blew cigar smoke into the infant's nose. The newborn genius started coughing, crying, and then breathing on his own.

MAMA'S BOY

How many pieces of American art are in the Louvre in Paris?

ONLY ONE, the painting commonly called Whistler's Mother by Massachusetts-born James Abbott McNeill Whistler. The painting's real name, by the way, is *Arrangement in Grey and Black No. 1: The Artist's Mother.* It was painted in 1871.

Did James Whistler paint other pictures of his mother besides Whistler's Mother?

NO. THIS PAINTING has given people the impression that he was a sentimental Norman Rockwell sort of fellow, but *Whistler's Mother* wasn't his normal style. Most of Whistler's paintings were more abstract. On this occasion, he painted his reluctant mom in a straight-backed wooden chair only because his scheduled model hadn't shown up. Despite this one painting, Whistler loved seeing himself as a shocking rebel against the art establishment and presented himself and his work in ways to keep that image alive.

In one of his public melodramas, he sued English art critic John Ruskin for libel after Ruskin wrote a scathing review of his artwork. After a long and bombastic trial, the jury agreed that Whistler had been libeled...and awarded him damages of one farthing (about a quarter of a cent). For his "victory," Whistler was bankrupted by legal fees and lost his house and furniture. Ironically, he was also forced into backtracking away from his confrontational style and into more commercial, conventional etchings. Ruskin, for his part, was so outraged by the verdict against him that he stopped writing reviews, resigned from Oxford University, and became a bitter, antisocial recluse.

WOMEN COME AND GO, TALKING OF MICHELANGELO

Who designed the uniforms of the Vatican Guard?

MICHELANGELO. The assignment was one in a series he reluctantly took on by order of three consecutive popes. But

Michelangelo considered himself a poet and a sculptor, not an architect, painter, or clothing designer. In fact, he pointedly

Where can I read Michelangelo's poetry?

demanded that his painting assignment for the Sistine Chapel be made out to "Michelangelo *the sculptor.*"

Michelangelo was alternately pleased and exasperated that he was constantly being called back to Rome. The pope even made Michelangelo an honorary Roman citizen and when he died arranged for him to have an elaborate burial in Rome. A few days before his death, however, Michelangelo had told his nephew that he wished to be buried in his native city of Florence. Knowing the pope was not intending to honor that request, the nephew managed to steal the body, pack it in an unmarked shipping crate, and spirit it back to Florence, where it remains.

NOT VERY WELL HUNG

Which painting was displayed upside down in the Museum of Modern Art in New York?

FOR 47 DAYS, a painting by Henri Matisse hung upside down in New York's MoMA. One can understand how that could occur with an abstract piece, but this was a clearly identifiable painting of a sailboat. How did it happen? Well, to be fair, Matisse also painted the sailboat's reflection on the water. The exhibit's curator thought that the reflection was the boat and vice versa.

That sculpture of the naked guy who's sitting and thinking—who is it and what's he supposed to be doing?

THE "NAKED GUY" is supposed to be Dante Alighieri, the fellow who wrote *The Divine Comedy.* Its sculptor, Auguste Rodin, originally meant it to be part of a much larger piece called *The Gates of Hell,* but this was never finished. Instead, its design led to five great individual sculptures: *The Thinker, The Kiss, Ugolino, Adam,* and *Eve.*

IS YOUR ART UNTRUE?

Are there many counterfeit paintings circulating in the world?

IT IS HARD to say, but a number of works have been found to be either deliberately counterfeited or misattributed. For example, of the 600 paintings called "Rembrandts," experts believe that as many as half are counterfeit. Pablo Picasso was surprisingly practical about the fact that there were "original Picassos" available for sale that he had never seen. Said he: "If I like it, I say it's genuine. If I don't like it, I say it's a fake."

Why don't we see many of Leonardo da Vinci's paintings in museums?

THERE'S ONE very good reason—there aren't that many. In fact, there are only 17 paintings attributed to Leonardo, and there's significant dispute about half of those. Still, despite his low output, you have to admire how many of them were "hits." Of those that scholars are absolutely sure Leonardo painted, two are *The Last Supper* and *Mona Lisa,* two of the most famous paintings of all time.

Is the Mona Lisa in the Louvre a forgery?

SOME PEOPLE think it could be. Leonardo da Vinci's painting was stolen in 1911 and wasn't returned for two years. There were those who claimed it looked a little different when it got back. Most experts don't give much credence to the theory, though, and it has been weakened by X-ray results. Leonardo painted the *Mona Lisa* over four years on a piece of wood less than two feet square. Under the surface paint, there are two other portraits of the same woman. A forger in the early 1900s probably wouldn't have known about Leonardo's two failed attempts below the surface or bothered trying to re-create them.

Was the Mona Lisa ever stolen?
Yes. It was stolen in 1911 and returned in 1913.

PLUCKY GAL

Why doesn't the Mona Lisa have eyebrows?

IN THE EARLY 1500s, it was the style of women in Florence to completely pluck their eyebrows, so Lisa del Giocondo was right in fashion. This painting was Leonardo da Vinci's favorite, by the way—he even carried it with him on his travels. The rest of the world apparently feels the same way: the *Mona Lisa* is the most-viewed painting of all in the Louvre. A few years ago, the museum moved it into its own separate room to better accommodate the crowds who jostle each other to get a better view of it day after day.

> **Where can I see the entire Sistine Chapel ceiling online?**

ART MEETS SCIENCE

Was Samuel Finley Breese Morse, the painter, related to Samuel B. Morse, the inventor?

VERY CLOSELY related, yes. Samuel Breese Morse, the painter, and Samuel B. Morse, the inventor, are one and the same. Morse had a celebrated career as a portraitist and sculptor and was an art professor at New York University. In 1825 he helped found the National Academy of Design in New York City. About the same time, approaching 40, he began dabbling outside his field, experimenting with chemistry and electricity. In 1836, he filed a preliminary patent on the telegraph and invented the Morse code, the dot-and-dash language that made all that clicking and buzzing make sense on the other end. In 1843, the artist/inventor convinced the Congress to pony up $30,000 for a telegraph line between Washington, D.C., and Baltimore and on May 24, 1844, Morse sent the first long-distance message: "What hath God wrought!"

BE KIND TO YOUR FINE FETTERED FRIENDS

How did Audubon make his paintings of birds so lifelike?

JOHN JAMES AUDUBON added a birder's interest to an artist's perfectionism and created bird guides and prints that made viewers feel as if they were seeing the subjects right in nature. But his love of birds was like that of a person who "loves humanity" but is indifferent to individual suffering. In creating his sketches and paintings, Audubon refused to use stuffed models because he maintained that dead birds lose their coloring quickly. Instead, he used real birds that had been freshly killed and wired into natural-looking poses. To keep his models fresh, he shot new birds by the dozen per painting—as many as a hundred per day.

Driving Passions

IN THE LAST 100 YEARS, CARS HAVE gone from a noisy futuristic curiosity to a seeming necessity. Not just a method of transportation, the automobile is also a status symbol, a mating display, a marker of teen independence, and a pop culture icon, all at once.

WOULDN'T YOU REALLY RATHER HAVE A BATHTUB?

Who or what was the Buick car named after?

DAVID BUICK. He had the bad luck and poor business sense to found two successful companies and sell them both before reaping the rewards. By the end of his life, he couldn't even afford a telephone in his home, much less one of the cars that bears his name.

When he was a young apprentice at a foundry, Buick invented a breakthrough process to bond porcelain to iron, a method still in use for bathtubs, sinks, and other household fixtures. In 1899, just as his business began taking off, Buick sold out to Standard Sanitary for $100,000.

He used the money to hire a French engineer, who invented the valve-in-head engine design still used in cars today, and started an auto company. Perpetually strapped for cash, Buick made some unfortunate partnership deals, owning less of his own company with each of them. In 1908, he was forced out of a management position in the company by its new owner, William C. Durant.

Buick sold his remaining shares for $100,000—shares that would have been worth $115 million if he had waited another year—and invested it in some bad oil and land deals. He lost it all. In the last years of his life, Buick worked at a low-paying job as an information clerk at the Detroit School of Trades. He died at age 75 in 1929. (Louis Chevrolet had a similar sad story but managed to live long enough to became a public-relations problem. In 1934, General Motors, embarrassed at the poverty of its bestselling automobile's namesake, put Mr. Chevrolet back on its payroll.)

MISS JONES, WOULD YOU LIKE A WHIRL IN MY OLEO LOCOMOTIVE?

How long ago was the word "automobile" created?

AUTOMOBILE, meaning "self-moving," was coined in France in 1876. It was just one of a number of attempts to give a name to the new horseless carriages, but it's the one that finally stuck. Other names invented by manufacturers: automaton, oleo locomotive, motorig, motor fly, and electric bat.

$1,000 DOWN AND $100 A MONTH FOR 5,000 YEARS . . . .

What's the highest price ever paid for a used car?

YOU'D THINK the highest price for a used car might've been for a historic one belonging to a president or a gangster. But no. So far, the record has been $11 million, paid in 1989 for a 1963 Ferrari in pristine condition. Ferrari, despite its famous name, didn't produce many cars over the years. In fact, the company built only about 50,000 cars from its founding by Enzo Ferrari in 1946 until his death 42 years later. Some limited-edition models were produced in numbers of only a few hundred. Other, even *more* exclusive models (like the one sold in 1989) were produced in numbers of fewer than a dozen.

GENDER BENDERS, FENDER BENDERS— LET'S CALL THE WHOLE THING OFF

Who has more accidents, men or women?

WITH THIS question, Jeeves has that disquieting sense that he's tiptoeing into a minefield in the battle of the sexes. If you count merely the number of accidents, men have more because they drive more. If you count how many accidents people have per mile they've driven, women have more. Some people say that makes men the better drivers.

> **In what key do most car horns honk?**
> F major.

THE ORIGINS OF THE RACE

When was the first auto race?

THE FIRST organized race on record took place on July 22, 1894, in Paris. Inventors from all over Europe brought their horseless carriages to what was then the largest-ever gathering of the newfangled contraptions. Of the 21 vehicles that putted their way up to the starting line, 13 were gasoline powered and 8 were propelled by steam.

The first race in the United States took place a year and a half later, from Chicago to Waukegan, Illinois, on November 28, 1895. It was snowing that day, so of the 80 cars that had entered the race, only 6 actually started. Of these 6, only 2 finished the course, which ran more than 20 miles. James Duryea was the winner, driving a car designed by his brother Charles. His average speed was a screaming 7.5 miles per hour.

How fast did the earliest cars go?

MOST COULD barely beat a man on foot. But the Stanley Steamer, invented by daredevil twin brothers Francis and Freelan Stanley, could go quite a bit faster. In fact, the two men risked their lives regularly by partaking in knuckle-whitening speed trials. At a time when gas-powered cars were rasping and backfiring at crawl speed, the two set a land-speed record of 128 miles per hour on the hard-packed sands of Ormond Beach, Florida, in their steam-powered vehicle.

They finally gave up speed trials for good when, on the next try, they attained 197 miles per hour and the car became airborne, flying for about 100 feet before touching down again on solid earth. This was in 1906, just three years after the Wright brothers flew a comparable distance on purpose. Miraculously, the car remained upright and the driver kept driving.

ACCIDENTS WILL HAPPEN

When was the first car accident?

AS FAR AS anybody knows, the first car accident took place late in 1885, when Carl Benz was working on his prototype for the gasoline-powered automobile. Nobody had yet built anything resembling an automobile, and he was still working out the details—like how many wheels it should have, how it would be steered, how it would be stopped, and so on. While tooling around the public courtyard one night in his hometown of Mannheim, Germany, he drove his 550-pound vehicle into a brick wall. Despite this mishap, he continued experimenting and in 1886 received the first patent for a gasoline-powered velocipede. Not long after, Benz founded the company that (with a later merger) became Mercedes-Benz.

Which month has the highest number of traffic accidents?
July.

The first pedestrian ever killed by an automobile was Henry H. Bliss, on September 13, 1899. The 68-year-old real-estate broker was hit and killed by a taxi while helping a woman off a trolley at Central Park West and 74th Street in New York City. Since then, automobiles have killed more than 700,000 other pedestrians. Every September 13, street safety groups remember poor Mr. Bliss.

If I ride a million miles in cars during my life, how many accidents am I likely to be in?

ON AVERAGE, you'll be in one accident every 110,000 miles—roughly one every eight or nine years' worth of car travel. This statistic includes time driving and time spent as a passenger. In 1997, there were about 6.8 million crashes reported to police, injuring 3.4 million people and killing 41,967. So be careful out there, and wear your seatbelt.

When was the first car insurance issued?

THE VERY FIRST car insurance policy was issued by Travelers Insurance on February 1, 1898. It specifically covered liability costs if you collided with a horse or horse-drawn vehicle.

> **How much time in U.S. courts is directly related to cars?**
> More than half.

YOU MAY ALREADY BE A WIENER

How do I get to drive the Oscar Mayer Wienermobile?

TO GET A one-year assignment as a "hotdogger," you have to be a recent college graduate, preferably in the field of communications, journalism, advertising, or public relations. Be aware, though, that competition is stiff. The company gets about 1,000 applicants a year. For the 1999–2000 year, they hired 21 hotdoggers, 15 of them women. If chosen, you'll be sent to Hot Dog High in Madison, Wisconsin, for two weeks, then sent out on the road.

There are six Wienermobiles, and they each cover a region of the country. They rack up about 40,000 miles apiece, traveling 330 grueling days a year to store openings, conventions, parades, charity events, publicity stunts, and the like. If you think you have what it takes to become a hotdogger, here's where to send your résumé:

Oscar Mayer
Wienermobile Department
P.O. Box 7188
Madison, WI 53707

Good luck!

For more information about the Wienermobile, including a Quicktime virtual tour, go to www.kraftfoods.com/oscar-mayer/wmobile/ virtualt.htm

BEETLEMANIA

Is it true that the Volkswagen Beetle was designed by Hitler?

NO, BUT IT WAS financed by his government. Hitler was a car buff and he wanted industrious German workers riding around in automobiles, like the Americans. German automakers were not interested, so when Ferdinand Porsche approached him with his idea of a small "people's car," Hitler agreed to finance the project. Thus began *Gezuvor-Gesellschaft zur Vorbereitung de Deutschen Volkswagen BmbH* (Society for the Development of the German People's Car).

In 1938, Hitler presided at laying the cornerstone of the new *Volskwagenwerk* factory and announced that the car would henceforth be known as the *Kraft-durch-Freude Wagen* (Strength-Through-Joy Car). Luckily, the name didn't stick. The plant built only 210 Beetles before converting to a slave-labor camp that produced Jeep-like *Kübelwagens* and amphibious *Schwimmkübels*. It wasn't until several years after World War II that VWs started rolling off the line again.

Is it true that the Ford Company was offered the Volkswagen plant for free after World War II, but turned it down?

YES. THE occupying British army offered the Volkswagen factory and car model first to British firms and then to the Ford Motor Company. They all turned it down. Company president Henry Ford II wanted to make big, shiny sedans and took the advice of his CEO, Ernest Breech, who told him, "Mr. Ford, I don't think what we are being offered here is worth a damn."

What is the bestselling car of all time?

THE ORIGINAL Volkswagen Beetle. The second bestselling is the Model T. However, if you are asking about total market penetration, Ford's old "Tin Lizzy" wins, hands down. By 1927, Model Ts made up 68% of the world's cars—15 million total rolling. The Model T was much more than a vehicle for transportation for many people. It was also a dependable engine that could be used to run almost anything on a farm that might not even

Where can I see classic VW beetle ads?

yet have electricity. In its 1920s heyday, the Sears Roebuck catalog featured 5,000 items that could be added to or run by the Model T, including plows, harvesters, butter churns, flour grinders, generators, and even centrifuges for extracting honey from bee combs.

Twenty years later, VW used the same strategy as Ford had: build a good, no-frills car that's easy to fix, price it cheaply enough for almost anybody to afford, and don't mess with a new design every year. In fact, VW designer Ferdinand Porsche traveled to America in the 1930s to meet Henry Ford, and told him his dream of creating an inexpensive yet reliable "people's car." Ford's reaction? "If somebody can build a car better or cheaper than I can, it serves me right."

PAINT IT BLACK

How many colors did the Model T come in?

ONLY ONE. "You can buy a Model T in any color you want, as long as it's black," Henry Ford was quoted as saying. He wasn't much for unnecessary add-ons (such as speedometers) and didn't want to mess around with giving consumers options, for fear of crashing the assembly line system that kept the car's price so low.

ON THE ROAD AGAIN

How many miles does an average driver drive in a year?

IN THE UNITED STATES, the average licensed driver drives about 12,500 miles a year. This varies from person to person, of course, but it also fluctuates dramatically from state to state—from a high of 19,400 in Wyoming to a low of 8,950 in Alaska.

By its size and the amount of space between towns, you might think that, like Wyoming, Alaska would also have a higher rate of driving. The fact is, though, you can't get too far in a car in Alaska—most cities have roads in their immediate area, but they don't connect to one another. For example, you can travel all the roads in Juneau, the state capital, and you still won't get more than eight miles from downtown. If you want to go farther, you have to use a boat or plane.

What U.S. organization has the most members?
The American Automobile Association.

YEAH, THAT'S THE TICKET

By law, if you see a sign ahead dropping the speed limit to 35 miles per hour, where exactly do you need to be going the new speed—at the point you see the sign, as you pass the sign, or as quickly as possible after the sign?

IT'S NICE WHEN there is a Reduced Speed Ahead warning sign posted first, but these aren't required by law. The truth is that the sign is posted at the exact point where the new speed limit is supposed to kick in. How you get your speed down to that point before passing the sign is up to you, but when you see the sign, decelerate as quickly as is safely possible. If you're planning on coasting through a grace interval of gradual deceleration, meet Officer Toughlove, constable of Speedtrapville, who will be happy to disabuse you of that idea.

Does the Autobahn in Germany still not have any legal speed limit?

ALAS, NOT EVEN freedom-loving Germany is a haven for ticket-free driving anymore. The days of a no-limit drive through the Black Forest are over. Some of the more accident-prone stretches of the Autobahn now bear speed-limit signs for a turtlelike 130 kilometers per hour (81 mph).

SAFETY FIRST

In a lightning storm, will rubber tires insulate a car from being hit by lightning?

NO, LIGHTNING is strong enough to travel through or around the rubber. According to the Boston Museum of Science, your tires would have to be solid rubber a mile thick to actually insulate you from a lightning bolt. Does that mean, then, that you should avoid your car in a thunderstorm? No, the good news is that your car is the safest place to be if you're outside during a storm—the lightning will most likely travel around the metal shell of your car and not do any damage to it or you. That is, if you have a metal car and don't park under a tree or touch the metal. The bad news is that if you have a convertible or plastic car, or if you touch the metal skin of your automobile when lightning strikes, you may be in for a profoundly shocking experience.

Is using a cell phone in a car dangerous?

YES. ANY DISTRACTING gadget is dangerous in a moving car. One study, in the *New England Journal of Medicine,* concluded that talking on a phone while driving made you four times more likely to get into an accident—comparable to the increased risk of accident if driving while legally drunk. It doesn't seem to make a difference whether the phone is hands-free or not—simply talking on the phone creates the risk. Does this mean that talking to a passenger might be equally dangerous? Not necessarily. Most passengers suspend conversation if they become aware that the driver is distracted, driving badly, or in the middle of difficult traffic conditions. Passengers even add an extra set of eyes and can help prevent accidents by giving helpful warnings to the driver.

> **Is it illegal anywhere to talk on a cell phone while driving?** *Ask!*

***I keep hearing that 75% of all fatal auto
accidents occur within 25 miles of home.
Why is that? Do people become more
careless on familiar ground?***

THIS STATISTIC is rather alarming. It does make it sound like
there's a bubble of danger around your own home—or that
you'll be safe if only you're willing to stay more than 25 miles
from your house. The truth behind the statistic, though, is that
most people do the bulk of their driving within 25 miles of their
homes, so of course the preponderance of accidents will happen
there. You're actually safer on familiar territory than not.

What's the safest color for a car?

TWO DIFFERENT studies indicate that bright yellow and bright
blue are the most visible colors. The University of California
found that of the two colors, yellow
shows up best at night, blue in
fog and daylight. A test
by Mercedes-Benz
came up with the
same conclusion, but
suggested that white
might be even better than blue and yellow except in snow and
white sand. The worst colors for visibility, day or night, are
grey and dark green.

*What's the most popular car
in the U.S.?*
White. Then silver, then green.

COMES WITH OLFACTORY AIR

What exactly is that "new car smell"?

THERE'S NOTHING quite like it, and all attempts to reproduce
it artificially for colognes and air fresheners have been disap-
pointing. It is a combination of scents from things one would-
n't normally smell voluntarily, condensed in intensity by the
size of the relatively airtight passenger compartment. The odor
components that go into it include fresh primer and paint, plastic, leather, vinyl, rubber, glues, sealers, and carpeting. The
smell fades with time, as residual solvents leach away from
exposure to light, heat, and air.

TRANSPORTATION FOR THE NUCLEAR FAMILY

Has anybody ever designed a nuclear-powered car?

YES, THE Ford Motor Company, for one. In the nuclear-happy 1950s, Ford engineers began drawing up preliminary designs for a car they called the Ford Nucleon. The car was to be propelled by a small atomic reactor in the rear of the car and would need to be driven into a nuclear station now and again to be recharged with nuclear fuel. The car was never built.

FREEDOM, NOT LICENSE

Where can I find license plates for my collection?

THERE ARE seven clubs for license collectors. The biggest ones are the Automobile License Plate Collectors Association (ALPCA), found on the Internet at *www.alpca.org,* the Numberplate Collectors Club (NPCC), and the European Registration Plate Association (ERPA).

To see an amazing collection of plates from Abu Dhabi to Zimbabwe, see http://danshiki.oit.gatech.edu/~iadt3mk/

Landmarks Around the World

"SEE THE PYRAMIDS ALONG THE Nile . . . . " There are certain landmarks that are immediately recognizable—that have become a visual shorthand to identify an entire region or country. Yet, as familiar as they are, there is always more to be learned about them.

BIG GREEN PARIS SITE

What color is the Eiffel Tower?

IT'S PAINTED reddish green, a color the city of Paris believes goes best with the blue sky and green landscape. The tower is beloved now, but when it was built in 1884, it was nicknamed "the tragic lamppost" and nearly universally hated as a blot on the Parisian landscape. One clever novelist ate lunch in a restaurant on the tower every day because, he said, "it is the only way I can be sure I won't have to see the damned tower."

> **Where can I see the view from the top of the Eiffel Tower online?**

Why was the Eiffel Tower built? Does it have a practical purpose?

WITH ITS MASSIVE concentration of steel perfectly aligned to the four points of the compass, the tower makes a very good tourist magnet. It was built as a temporary building for the 1884 Paris World's Fair, which commemorated the 100th anniversary of the French Revolution. At the end of the exhibition, the city considered selling the Eiffel Tower for scrap metal, but decided the design wasn't so bad after all, and the tourists seemed to like it. So they kept it.

Most people who haven't actually been to the tower don't realize that there are shops and restaurants on several levels. In fact, it is one of the few French public projects that began making a profit within a few months of its completion. Gustave Eiffel, its designer and builder, fashioned the tower with another purpose in mind as well: He reserved the rooms at the very top for his own personal use, as a trysting place. One can imagine how the trip up four elevators to the top of Paris would be a successful seduction technique.

I LEFT MY HEART . . .

How many people have committed suicide by jumping off the Golden Gate Bridge?

NOBODY KNOWS for sure, because it's a sure bet that many people have leapt to their deaths without their bodies being recovered. What we do know is that more than 1,200 have jumped since the San Francisco landmark opened in 1937. Although primarily a motorway, the bridge is open to pedestrians and is a popular tourist attraction. The record suicide year to date is 1995, with 45 known suicides (most years average less than half that), plus 68 people who were stopped from jumping. Of those who have taken the 250-foot drop, only 23 are known to have survived. Although people might imagine that this is a peaceful way to go—being swallowed by the soothing waters—in fact it is more like hitting pavement. When jumpers crash against the water at 75 to 80 mph, their ribs are usually broken into shards that puncture their vital organs as they drown.

Why doesn't San Francisco put up fences to stop suicides on the Golden Gate Bridge?

THE CITY has experimented with a number of deterrents, including anti-suicide squads, suicide prevention phones on the bridge, and a spider's web of thin wire barriers. The most obvious solution—high fences—would not only ruin the aesthetics of the world-famous bridge but would also endanger the entire structure due to the increased resistance to strong Pacific winds.

MY FAIR LADY

When did the London Bridge fall down?

IT DIDN'T FALL; it was pushed. Or to be technical, it was *pulled,* back when the Danes controlled London in the year 1014. Their enemies, the Saxons and the Norwegians, rowed their warships up the Thames to the then-wooden bridge, hitched cables around its pilings, and rowed away at full speed, pulling the bridge down.

What do the people in London do, now that Arizona has their bridge?

THERE ARE several bridges over the Thames, which flows through London. In fact, the bridge in question is only one of several bridges that have been named London Bridge through history. After the wooden London Bridge was torn down by the Danes in 1014, city leaders were determined that the next London Bridge would be a little more durable. In 1176, the city built the first stone London Bridge, a drawbridge that lasted 600 years. This was the most famous London Bridge, the one where heads of executed criminals—from common thieves to Oliver Cromwell—were displayed on poles in groups of up to 30 at a time.

Where can I see a livecam of the London Bridge?

But all good things must come to an end. In 1823, the city tore down the aged structure. The old bridge was recycled into building projects and was replaced with a granite bridge called the *New* London Bridge. It didn't last as long as its predecessor, though—not even 150 years. In 1962, it was replaced and sold to an American developer for a little under $2.5 million. He had it dismantled block by block and shipped to the New World, where he rebuilt it over an artificial lake in Arizona. (Rumors at the time had it that he thought he'd bought the picturesque *Tower* Bridge instead of the relatively ordinary-looking bridge he got.) The London Bridge that replaced the "New" London Bridge continues to stand.

CAPITOL PUNISHMENT

How many steps does the Capitol Building in Washington, D.C., have?

IT HAS 365 STEPS, one representing every day of the year. If you're patient, you can count as you climb to find the step that represents your birthday. Unless, of course, you were born on February 29—sorry!

SIZE *DOES* MATTER

What is the topmost point of the Washington Monument made of?

IN THE 1800s, when the monument was built, aluminum was a rare and valuable semiprecious metal, so a pyramid was made of it and placed on top. The reasons for having a metal tip are good: for one thing, it's lighter and safer than stone, and for another, it acts as a lightning rod. Considering how many thunderstorms Washington, D.C., gets and that by law the Washington Monument is the highest thing in the city, a metal tip was a pretty wise choice.

What are the measurements of the Washington Monument?

THE WASHINGTON MONUMENT is 55 feet across on each of the four sides at the base and 555 feet high. Why all the fives in the measurements? Some sort of secret Masonic thing? Nobody knows for sure.

TAKING LIBERTIES

Where can I find the sculpture Liberty Enlightening the World?

LOOK IN NEW YORK harbor for a big green lady holding a torch. Although we've come to know her as the "Statue of

Liberty," sculptor Frédéric-Auguste Bartholdi of France gave his creation a more elaborate name because he intended the sculpture to represent a woman escaping the chains of tyranny.

How many times larger than life size is the Statue of Liberty?

20.

Why is the Statue of Liberty green?

SHE'S MADE OF thin copper sheets that are about the same thickness as a penny. They were hammered into the correct shapes in France, transported by ship to America, and riveted to an iron framework created by French engineer Gustave Eiffel (who later built the Eiffel Tower in Paris). When copper rusts, it turns a bluish green.

Who was the Statue of Liberty modeled after?

SCULPTOR Frédéric-Auguste Bartholdi of France used his mother as the model for Liberty's face and his girlfriend as the model for her body. Dr. Freud will see you now, Monsieur Bartholdi.

THAT OLD-TIME RELIGION

When was Stonehenge built?

THE MYSTERIOUS STONE monoliths set in four circles were built in several different stages separated by hundreds or even thousands of years. A circular outer bank, a ditch, and 56 pits were apparently dug about 3100 to 2300 B.C. in the late Stone Age or early Bronze Age. The main monoliths were put up later in the late Bronze or Iron Age (2100 to 2000 B.C.) And bluish monoliths and smaller blue stones were brought in from the north flank of the Preselly Mountains in Wales about 2000 to 1500 B.C. and 1500 to 1100 B.C.

Despite now-popular misconception, Stonehenge was not built by the Druids, but by a flourishing community that had extensive trading contacts throughout Britain and Europe. Sometime between 55 B.C. and A.D. 410, the site was desecrated by the Romans, who tore down some of the upright stones. Gravity, weather, or vandals brought down a total of five of the uprights and lintels in 1797 and 1900. In 1958, those five fallen stones were raised to their original positions, but those knocked down by Roman hands were left where they were.

IS IT LOVE . . . OR OBSESSION?

Is the beautiful love story behind the Taj Mahal true? Or was it manufactured by India's tourist department?

IT MUST BE hard to grow up in such an age of cynicism, when even the most lyrical love stories are assumed to be mere marketing. The answer to your question is, the love story is true, but certain facts are generally left out. Here's the oft-told romantic tale: Indian mogul Shah Jahan was deeply in love with his one of his four wives, whom he called Mumtaz Mahal ("Ornament of the Palace.") In 1631, Mumtaz, on her death bed, asked Shah Jahan to take care of her children and build her a suitably lavish monument. Shah Jahan was grief-stricken. He moaned and refused to eat for eight days. Finally he emerged from his quarters and began work on a "monument of perfect proportions." Day and night for 22 years, 20,000 jewelers, masons, and calligraphers worked to create the wondrous white mausoleum still regarded as one of the most remarkable structures ever built.

Here's the part most guidebooks don't tell you: While Shah Jahan was reputedly a fairly benevolent ruler for his time and place, Mumtaz was a ruthless Islamic fanatic who demanded that her husband crush all other religions. At one time, for example, she goaded him into destroying a Christian settlement on India's northeast coast. The city of Hooghly was razed and its people forced into a 1,200-mile death march to Agra, where Mumtaz had the priests trampled to death by elephants and the rest of the Christians sold into slavery. In fact, until the British took over India, guards were posted at the Taj Mahal with a warning that any non-Moslem who tried to enter would be put to death.

One account has it that Shah Jahan beheaded his architect and chopped off the hands of his craftsmen so they could never duplicate their work. This is probably an exaggeration. He likely needed at least some of them, because as soon as the Taj Mahal was finished, Shah Jahan began work on a second mausoleum, this one in black marble, for himself.

Shah Jahan's extravagance for his wife, however endearing, eventually led to his downfall. Before his second building could be completed, he was deposed by his own son and imprisoned in a cell overlooking the Taj Mahal. The romantic story has it that every day for eight years he sat gazing across the river, pining for Mumtaz Mahal. Well, maybe not every day—he did have his entire harem with him, and he reportedly died from an overdose of aphrodisiacs at age 74.

IF IT WERE A WOMAN, WE'D CALL HER EILEEN

Why does the Leaning Tower of Pisa lean?

SPONGY SAND and waterlogged clay make for a lousy foundation. The building began to lean pretty much from the beginning in 1155, listing slightly north by the time the second floor was finished. Rather than start over, the builders adjusted the third floor, lengthening the north walls and shortening the south so that the top was level.

> **What would the Leaning Tower of Pisa look like if it fell down?**

Political unrest in Pisa stopped construction at that point, leaving a pretty, though crooked, little building for about 90 years. Between 1270 and 1278, Pisa added six more stories. But the added weight made the building lean in the other direction, toward the south, the direction it leans today. Again, construction stopped for political reasons, until finally, in 1360, Pisa added the belfry, this time making the southern walls taller than the north, trying again to level the roof, and leaving the tower slightly S-shaped.

Over the years, the tower continued to lean until it was in grave danger of tipping over. There have been many stabilization attempts. Reports have it that current work is actually doing some good, reversing the tilt a little for the first time in 600 years. Of course, the tilt is too valuable to the tourist trade—roughly $300 million annually—for Pisa to even consider straightening the tower completely.

> **Has anyone ever fallen off the leaning Tower of Pisa?**
> About 250 people.

ROCK OF AGES
What kind of rock is the Rock of Gibraltar?

THE ROCK that acts as the northern gateway of the Mediterranean Sea is mostly grey limestone, with some dark shale on parts of its western slope. Though the rock is not particularly solid (as proven by the more than 180 caves discovered in the area), in contrast to the flat but shifting-sand terrain that surrounds it, it is quite dependable—thus the origin of the phrase "solid as the Rock of Gibraltar." Historically, the Rock has been a great object of conquest for various European countries, as it's ideal for monitoring movement into and out of the Mediterranean Sea.

PYRAMID SCHEME
What building had the status of being the tallest in the world for the most years?

AT 481 FEET, the Great Pyramid was the world's tallest structure for more than 4,000 years. It wasn't surpassed in height until the Eiffel Tower (measuring 984 feet without its modern broadcasting tower) was built in 1886. The base of the pyramid covers 13 acres, roughly the size of 10 football fields or seven city blocks in New York City.

How many pyramids did the Egyptians build?

THERE ARE remains of at least 70 still standing in Egypt and Sudan, and archaeologists know of about 88 more that no longer exist. The pyramids were made to last more or less forever. In actuality, they've done a pretty good job of holding up, considering that they were built between 2700 and 1000 B.C. However, the pyramids' designers didn't account for one human foible in their bid for monumental immortality: that if something is lying around not being watched, someone's going to try to take it. Whenever later Egyptians needed chunks of rock for construction, they'd pry pieces off the local pyramid. This apparently went on for centuries, leaving many of the pyramids mere shadows of what they once were. The pyramids at Giza, to give a notable example, have lost all but a few blocks of the polished limestone that once made them shine bright white in the sunlight. The Great Pyramid even lost 31 feet off its height. The most complete, best-preserved, least-vandalized pyramid? It stands at Saqqara, near Cairo. Make your reservations before it disappears.

EGYPT LOSES FACE

Who knocked the Sphinx's nose off?

THE SPHINX is the giant statue of a lion with the face of the pharoah Khafre that guards the pyramids. You may have heard a story of what happened to the Sphinx's nose: that somebody or other shot it off. But this is just an old legend—and with each telling the culprit changes. Some say Napoleon's troops shot it off with a cannon for doltish fun. According to Louis Farrakhan's speech at the 1995 Million Man March in Washington, D.C., the French did it because the nose revealed that the Sphinx was a black man. In other stories, the Germans or British did it during the 1800s or during one of the world wars.

None of these things really happened. In fact, the nose has been gone so long that Arab conquerors were accused in 693 of knocking it off. That probably didn't happen, either. Although there's a chance that somebody along the line really did try to spite the Sphinx's face by cutting off its nose, there's a much better chance that it was merely worn away by thousands of years of wind, rain, and blowing sand. It's carved out of sandstone, after all. Pieces of the Sphinx have been wearing away for centuries, so it's not surprising that the thinnest part would show the most dramatic wear.

To see a plastic surgeon's digital reconstruction of the Sphinx with its nose back (based on a more complete statue of Khafre), check out this Web page: www.plasticsurgery4u.com/procedure_folder/ nasal_deformity_sphinx3.html

TAKING HEROES FOR GRANITE

Was "Rushmore" the guy who carved the mountain?

NOT QUITE. After gold was discovered in South Dakota in 1874, the Sioux tribes that lived there were forced out, and prospectors and a smattering of tourists and curiosity-seekers moved in. In 1885, a New York attorney named Charles Rushmore was riding through the area on a guided horseback tour and asked the name of the mountain. His guide teased the city slicker: "Hell, it never had a name, but from now on we'll call the thing Rushmore." Strangely enough, the name stuck. The lawyer Rushmore, by the way, never abandoned his rocky namesake—he was one of the first to donate a large sum of money toward carving the mountainside.

How did they decide on the faces for Mount Rushmore?

IN 1923, South Dakota's tourism board got the idea to carve western heroes Kit Carson, Jim Bridger, and John Colter into a mountain to attract out-of-state tourists. They approached John Gutzon Borglum, who had just accepted a commission to carve Robert E. Lee on the side of Georgia's Stone Mountain. Borglum hated the idea of the Western heroes. "Why not four presidents instead?" he said. He suggested "Father of the Nation" George Washington, "The Expansionist" Thomas

Jefferson, "Preserver of the Union" Abraham Lincoln, and "Protector of the Working Man" Theodore Roosevelt.

Borglum intended to carve the presidents from the waist up, but chronic budget problems and faults in the mountain's granite forced him to scale back the project. Even scaled back, carving took 14 years and had to be finished by his son because Borglum died a few months before the project was completed.

Where can I see pictures of Mount Rushmore online?

What did they use to carve Mount Rushmore?

NOT A HAMMER and chisel, let me assure you. Dynamite to get the rock into rough shape, then a lot of strong men equipped with jackhammers and other industrial power tools to add the artistic contours. Imagine the artist standing at a distance with a walkie-talkie to give guidance: "A little more off the left cheek . . . more, more, now taper it down into the chin. Taper more, taper more . . . Violà! A masterpiece!"

FACE OFF

Which has the biggest face—the Sphinx, the Statue of Liberty, or the presidents on Mount Rushmore?

ABE, GEORGE, Teddy, and Tom win by a nose. The boys on Mount Rushmore each have faces about 60 feet tall. The Sphinx's face is about half that size, and Liberty's is only about two-thirds the size of the Sphinx's face.

EDIFICE REX

What wrecked the Parthenon?

FIRST SOME BACKGROUND: Built in the fifth century B.C. on the Acropolis hill in Athens, Greece, the Parthenon was a temple dedicated to the virgin goddess of wisdom, Athena Parthenos. Even after being pretty thoroughly wrecked, the building still gives a clear picture of ancient Greek ideals of harmony and balance in architecture.

So what left the Parthenon in such bad shape? Several things. One of them is time, of course. Natural degradation from 25 centuries of weather and unnatural degradation from a century of air pollution have both taken a toll. However, the most devastating single thing occurred when the Turkish army got the bright idea that the Parthenon would make a great place to store its gunpowder as it battled the Venetians for control of the city in 1687. A Venetian bombardment ignited the powder magazine, blowing the Parthenon's roof off and destroying much of its center.

> **How long is the Great Wall of China?**
> The main part of the wall is about 1,400 miles long.

The Turks kept control of the city and added more injury to injury in 1806 by selling sculptures from the building's frieze to a British aristocrat, Lord Elgin. Lord Elgin claimed he was merely trying to save the sculptures from being pulverized for building materials, but immediately sold them to the British Museum, which, despite repeated pleas from Greece, holds them to this day.

Further damage occurred, ironically, during bungled restorations. In 1844, hundreds of loose blocks were randomly cemented into the walls. In the British Museum, the Elgin sculptures were likewise marred by good intentions in 1938, when restoration there also went awry. Finally, yet again *more* damage to the Parthenon took place during an earthquake in 1981.

At this writing, the Parthenon is going through another attempt to undo some of the damage of the past, including putting back some long-fallen pieces and putting right the misplaced blocks from 1844.

LOOK, BLIXNAR, THE GREAT WALL

Is it true that the Great Wall of China is the only human-made thing visible from the moon?

"CECIL ADAMS" (Ed Gotti), author of the Straight Dope columns and books, claims that everyone believes this "wall seen from the moon" myth because it was reported in Trivial Pursuit once. But it was presented as fact before Sputnik even went into space. No, the Great Wall cannot be seen from the moon, and neither can any other object constructed by humans. If you don't believe it, look at pictures. All that's possibly visible from the moon are clouds, water, and land masses, and even the land is not always clear. The astronauts who've walked on the surface of the moon have also confirmed that nothing human-made is visible.

SUGAR, SALT, FAT, CARBOHYDRATES, and additives—these are the five major food groups of snack foods. Here are some of Jeeves's favorite questions about empty calories.

A SALT ON A KERNEL

How does popcorn pop?

POPCORN HAS a higher moisture content than other varieties of corn. Each kernel of corn consists of a soft starch inside and a hard shell outside. As the kernel is heated, the moisture inside the kernel expands, the soft starch is cooked, and it bursts the outer shell with a "pop!" The kernels must contain at least 13.5% water in order to explode.

For more popcorn facts from the Encyclopedia Popcornica, check out The Popcorn Board's Web site at www.popcorn.org/mpindex.htm

Was Orville Redenbacher a real person or an advertising gimmick?

ORVILLE REDENBACHER was as real as you and I. Redenbacher was born in 1907 on a farm in Indiana. He spent his spare time growing and selling popping corn before going to college. After earning his degree in agromony (crop production) at Purdue, he and his partner, Charlie Bowman, developed their revolutionary new popcorn hybrid. A better popcorn was the result, and a bow-tied pop-culture icon was born. Although the company Redenbacher started was eventually bought out by Hunt-Wesson in 1976, he stayed on as their spokesperson for the popcorn brand that bore his name. He passed away in 1995 at 88 years old.

To find out more about the man and how he revolutionized the popcorn industry, look up an article published in the Detroit News *two months after his death in September 1995 at* www.detnews.com/menu/stories/26078.htm

Is it the popcorn or the peanut that's the "Jack" in Cracker Jack?

NEITHER. F. W. Rueckheim was a German immigrant who'd made a name for himself in Chicago as a popcorn vendor. His little shop on Federal Street dealt in popcorn, taffy, marshmallows, peanuts, caramels, and other treats. When he decided to mix various popular ingredients together and sell them, he was on to something good. Cracker Jacks were officially born in 1893 at the Columbian Exposition, at the F. W. Rueckheim and Brother booth. The name for the sweet snack came from popular slang, "That's a crackerjack!," meaning "that's excellent." The boy and dog on the package are in honor of Rueckheim's eight-year-old grandson, Robert, who had a dog named Bingo. (The boy is now known as "Jack.")

Unfortunately, that's not the happy ending: Robert died of pneumonia not long after the characters appeared on the box. In his honor, Rueckheim had the sailor boy and his dog carved onto Robert's tombstone. It can be seen in St. Henry's Cemetery in Chicago.

Why are Cracker Jack toys so boring?

THEY HAVEN'T always been. Early on, kids could find metal whistles, miniature American flags, working tops, baseball cards, and other captivating playthings. However, the toys that the Borden company now puts into the box must meet certain criteria. First, they must be easily playable. Early on, when Borden first acquired Cracker Jacks, they filled the boxes with complex puzzles, and sales dropped off suddenly because children found them too difficult. Second, the toys must meet approval by a rotating panel of kids. If a toy doesn't meet with child approval, it doesn't go in. Third, the toys must be cheap. And fourth, they must be a standard shape and size for quick insertion by high-speed machinery. That now means paper "toys" only—tattoos, stickers, riddles, and such.

Collecting the little toys from Cracker Jack boxes has become the passion of many. Some of the earlier toys and cards are valued at hundreds and even thousands of dollars. A full lineup baseball card set from 1914, at last word, is valued at over $17,000.

> **Which came first, Oreo or Hydrox cookies?**

For more information on Cracker Jacks, check out the Cracker Jack Collectors Association at www.collectoronline.com/CJCA/index.html *or the official Cracker Jack Web site:* www.crackerjack.com/index-nf.html

DYE! DYE! DYE!

Why is there red stuff on the outside of some pistachios?

IT WAS A CLEVER marketing tactic by nut importers in the 1930s. Around this time, America was being introduced to the vending machine, and taking their place in the newfangled contraption were nuts. Mostly, nuts were light colored, and among the many different varieties, pistachios blended in like a brown chameleon on a tree branch. However, one nut-seller discovered that if a little colored vegetable dye was put on pistachios, they sold like hotcakes. Every little boy and girl wanted the bright red nuts instead of those plain old other nuts.

Coloring the nuts also offered a solution to bruises and scratches that were easily seen on the shell of the pistachio nut. When pistachios were later offered in unblemished ivory-white shells, they flopped. People had grown so accustomed to the dyed color, the industry went back to adding the red.

Today, with awareness of the dark side of food coloring, au naturel pistachios have surged in popularity.

WHEN THE CHIPS ARE DOWN

What is the story behind the potato chip?

THE POTATO CHIP came from the "chip," or French fry. It all happened in 1853 because of a picky patron in the Moon Lake Lodge in Saratoga Springs, New York. Commodore Cornelius Vanderbilt kept complaining that his fried potatoes were too thick. The restaurant's chef, George Crum, finally sliced them extremely thin as a joke against the Commodore. He was shocked at the positive reaction from Vanderbilt and the other customers at his table. Crum took his newfangled delicacy and opened a specialty shop dealing only in potato chips—and an American snack industry was born.

> **What does "Frito" mean in Spanish?**
> Fried.

Which sells more: corn chips or potato chips?

DESPITE THE RISE in popularity of corn or tortilla chips and salsa, plain potato chips are still bought and consumed more than any other chip variety. The Lay's potato chip company gauges its production schedules based on the fact that Americans are consuming about seven million pounds of potatoes in the form of their chips, every single day.

How many banana chips would you have to eat to equal the fat content of one potato chip?

YOU'D THINK banana chips would be healthy, like raisins or dried apricots, but they have a lot of fat in them. There's a quarter gram of total fat in a banana chip, and twice that much in a potato chip. However, remember how much smaller a banana chip is than a potato chip: they are usually only one-quarter the size. Now let's compare saturated fat, the fat that causes problems. In one banana chip, there's .23 grams of saturated fat, yet in a potato chip, we find only .15 grams. The potato chip wins!

If processors would leave bananas alone, this wouldn't be the case. Natural bananas are low in fat and high in carbohydrates, potassium, and other vital nutrients. But oils, flavorings, coloring, and sugar are added to them when they are dried.

How do they make Pringles all the exact same size and shape?

PROCTOR & GAMBLE, the manufacturer, uses dried potato flakes blended with sugar, oil, salt, and water to form a dough. The dough is then squeezed out of an extruder and stamped into discs before being fried on a curved screen. In other words, they're not real slices of potato and they're all completely formed and shaped exactly the same way by machines. Because of this, they stack well.

> **How are gourmet jelly beans flavored?**

Pringles hold an important chapter in the annals of potato chip history, although the debate still rages over whether a Pringle is a real "potato chip" at all. Potato chips were once a regional product because they broke easily in shipping and their shelf life was limited. Pringles, on the other hand, packed in a vacuum-sealed tennis ball canister, could be shipped to the four corners of the earth with less destruction and greater longevity and could be included in Proctor & Gamble shipments alongside their laundry detergent and other assorted goods.

Calling themselves potato chips, Pringles took a bite out of the market, making the other potato chip companies good and angry. Several sued P&G in an effort to force them to put the word "imitation" on their potato chip label. The FDA, however, ruled in favor of P&G. Proctor & Gamble could continue calling their potato paste product a "chip" as long as they had the words "made from dried potatoes" on the package somewhere. In recent years, offered in a wide choice of flavors, Pringles have been in the top five most-popular salty snacks in the United States.

KID-A-PEEL
Can I make fruit roll-ups myself?

OH MY, YES! Here's the recipe: Puree your fruit of choice. Many people use plain applesauce, but you can use a number of different fruits and/or berries as long as they are pureed and strained. Pour the mixture onto a cookie sheet that has been covered in plastic wrap. Set your oven to "low" and leave overnight to dry. In the morning, remove, cool to room temperature, and you're ready to peel. Violà! Food fit for a kindergartner!

For other dried fruit information, see the message boards at www.30daygourmet.com

NO, NOT STYROFOAM
What's the orange stuff on Chee-tos?

IT'S A COMBINATION of various dyes and seasonings, and it's the only part of Chee-tos that has any cheese whatsoever in it. Like similar products, the main part of these "cheese"-coated chip products is not cheese but a cornmeal concoction. The cornmeal, with whey and oil added, is mixed into a dough, then squeezed out into a long worm shape by an extruder. When the dough meets the cooler air, it sort of explodes or puffs, like popcorn. Blades cut it into bite-sized pieces, which are then fried.

From there, the pale white morsels are shaken in colored and flavored powder. Real cheese, Yellow No. 6, annatto, and turmeric give the pieces that cheesy effect. A little more salt and vegetable oil are added for sticking power and flavor. Despite rumors, the powder coating is not toxic, but because it's brightly colored and relatively loose, it can be lethal to furniture and clothes.

THAT, AND JERRY LEWIS
Do they have French fries in France?

THEY HAVE *pommes frites* (pronounced "pum fritt") in France, which are in essence what yanks call "French fries." The

American term reportedly came, it is believed, from Thomas Jefferson. He brought a recipe for fried potato sticks back to the colonies and referred to them as "Potatoes, fried in the French manner." The phrase stuck and was shortened over time. *Pommes frites* literally means "apples fried." Apples? The word "potato" in French is *pomme de terre*, literally "apple of the earth," but *pomme de terre frites* was too much of a mouthful, so the name was informally shortened with use.

Where can I find French fry recipies from different cultures?

Most of the world refers to French fries as "chips" or some variation of *pommes frites.* In actuality, they are made a little differently in each country. The British chip is slightly larger than the American French fry and is traditionally served with deep-fried haddock (fish and chips). *Pommes frites* in Belgium are larger and fried twice in very hot oil and for just a short time. As a result, they are not usually as greasy as the American French fry or the English chip. In other countries, French fries are often eaten with a mayonnaise sauce instead of ketchup.

AIN'T IT OFFAL?

What's a chitlin?

CHITTERLINGS, or "chitlins," are pig intestines. Seen in Southern stores alongside pig snouts and pig feet, either pickled in jars or fresh at the butcher counter, this homey ingredient has recently made its way onto the menus of upscale restaurants in Europe and New York. Like so many soul food dishes, it's become quite trendy and popular over the last couple of decades.

Fried chitlins are first boiled with spices, then fried. Often, they are made with the maw (stomach) cooked at the same time as part of the same dish.

For more on soul food and chitlin recipes, see The Soul Food site at www.chitterlings.com/. And while your pot is boiling, you can play the game "All My Chitlins" on www.y'all.com—*an Atlanta, Georgia–based site about the South. Point your browser toward* www.accessatlanta.com/global/local/yall/games/

How do they make pork rinds?

Pork rinds, or pork cracklin's, are made from pig skin left over from processing pork. They are dropped into a deep fat fryer until they are crispy and crackling. Come and get 'em!

For more information on pork rinds, try the Online Pork Rind Resource at www.porkrind.com/porkrind.html

SQUARE PEG, ROUND HOLE

Why do they put pimientos in olives?

PIMIENTOS are only one of several stuffings commonly used in green olives; others include onions, garlic, and sardines. Pimientos, sweet red peppers, are the most colorful. Today, many olives are stuffed with pimiento paste rather than actual pimientos because it's easier to handle and can be cut into small, stuffable pieces that fit each olive hole perfectly.

To find olives stuffed with real pimientos, look in gourmet food stores, or try searching for "olives" at www.webvan.com/

GOING CRACKERS

Is "graham" the type of grain in graham crackers?

GRAHAM FLOUR is whole-wheat flour, which is simply flour without the bran removed. But it got its name from a health food fanatic and minister named Dr. Sylvester Graham. In the early 1800s, Graham preached that it was a sin to alter natural foods, that God intended food to be consumed exactly the way it was given to us. He believed that meat and altered foods roused desire and anger in people, and that foods made naturally—like crackers using unaltered flour—suppressed those tendencies. One of Graham's followers invented the flour and named it after his spiritual leader. As a result, generations of preschoolers have worshiped at his altar.

Did the Ritz cracker get its name from being "ritzy"?

THAT WAS WHAT the National Biscuit Company had in mind back in 1934 when this cracker was invented. The company took a regular cracker recipe, took out the yeast, and added more shortening. When the cracker was finished baking, it was slathered with coconut oil and dashed with salt. Because it looked shinier and richer, they named it the "Ritz." Like everything else dubbed "ritzy," the name is taken from the opulent Ritz hotels.

> **How do you make a mock apple pie (no apples) with Ritz crackers?**

TWINKIE, TWINKIE, LITTLE STAR

What food was dubbed "white man's soul food"?

TWINKIES. The description came from Archie Bunker on the television show "All in the Family."

Is it true that Twinkies last forever?

TWINKIES DON'T last forever. Yes, their low water content and airtight packaging make them longer-lasting than most baked goods, but the Hostess company allows Twinkies to stay on shelves for just a few weeks.

What's the "creme" inside Twinkies?

IT WAS BANANA CREAM until the 1940s, when Hostess replaced it with vanilla. When asked about specific ingredients, the company has simply responded, "We make these cakes out of the same ingredients that you'd find in a typical kitchen. It's a fun food. That's our position." But you can get a pretty good idea from reading the ingredients panel on the package.

How many colors does a Hostess Sno Ball come in?

SNO BALLS, those spongy half-domes of cake and marshmallow, traditionally come in white and pink. But the Hostess company isn't beyond surprising consumers with special colors on holidays or for special events. For example, when the Broncos made the NFL play-offs, the Hostess bakery in Denver filled each package with one orange and one blue Sno Ball. For Christmas, Sno Balls come in red or green. For St. Patrick's Day, they're all green. Some of the regional Hostess bakeries will color them for Halloween (orange), July 4th (red, white, and blue), and Easter (yellow and lavender). Final word: Colors look nice, but think twice about eating a yellow Sno Ball.

What inspired the name of Hostess Twinkies?
A sign that said "Twinkle Toe Shoes."

What is the Twinkies Project?

IT'S A SERIES of tests on Twinkies done by Rice University students during finals week in the 1995 school year. What kind of tests? Subjecting Twinkies to the forces of gravity, radiation, heat, flame, and so on. The T.W.I.N.K.I.E.S. Project, which stands for Tests With Inorganic Noxious Kakes In Extreme Situations, has a Web site with details on the experiments that walks budding scientists through Twinkies experiments of their own: *www.twinkiesproject.com/*

ICE, ICE BABY

Why are they called "Popsicles" when they don't pop?

THE MAN WHO created them, Frank Epperson, originally called them "Epsicles," a cross between his name and "icicle." His kids playfully called them "Pop's cycles." Eventually Epperson decided it made a better name.

Why are there two sticks in some Popsicles?

THE DOUBLE STICK was introduced during the Depression so that a Popsicle could be shared. Deliberately breaking a double down the middle produces two single Popsicles. Although there aren't too many Americans who can't spring for their own Popsicle these days, the idea of sharing this icy treat is still appealing.

DAYS OF WINE AND WEINERS

Aren't there some really silly holidays we don't hear much about?

YES, THERE ARE. In an effort to glean support from government officials and money from consumers, all sorts of commercial boards and associations have set up "official holidays" or honorary months for their products. The Snack Food Association, for one, celebrates National Snack Food Month in February. The goal of the holiday, according to the association, is to make consumers aware of how healthy snack foods can be. Potato Day is August 19. National Pickled Pepper Celebration runs from October 1 to 31. National Pizza with the Works Except Anchovies Day? That's on November 12.

For a calendar of food celebrations, see http://portia.advanced.org/2886/foo.htm

Have a Beverage and a Smile

SOFT DRINKS HAVE GONE FROM being the target of prohibitionists to being a fixture on the breakfast table, while Welch's has filled the Sunday pews on Communion Day and coffee has made its way out of the kitchen and into midday business breaks. Through it all, Gatorade never left the field. Here are some of the more interesting facts about nonalchoholic drinks, their origins, and their contents.

POP CULTURE

What was the first soda drink?

SODA WATER. Back in the early 1800s, there was a drink that consisted of plain carbonated water, called Impregnated Water. Bottled and sent to cooks and pharmacists all over the United States, it was mixed with herbs, roots, and berries and became the basis from which our first sweet, bubbly sodas came.

What's the history behind soft drinks?

MANY SOFT drinks were created to be medicinal. From the tingling bubbles to the mysterious herbs used to flavor them, it was believed they held some healing and soothing powers. Dyspepsia, or indigestion, is one of the ailments that many soft drinks claimed to cure. Until recently, soda fountains could be found in almost any drugstore or pharmacy in North America. And before those pesky truth-in-advertising laws, the drinks' ad campaigns touted healing properties above and beyond what the companies thought they really *could* do. For instance, here's an early Hires Root Beer ad: "Soothing to the nerves, vitalizing to the blood, refreshing to the brain, beneficial in every way."

That was mild in comparison to others. How about this 7-Up blurb: "For Home & Hospital Use." Or an early Moxie ad, which claimed to cure "nervousness, exhaustion, loss of manhood, imbecility, helplessness, paralysis, softening of the brain, locomotor ataxia, insanity (when caused by nervous exhaustion). It gives a durable solid strength, makes you eat voraciously, removes fatigue from physical and mental overwork, will not interfere with the action of vegetable medicines."

Where did the term pop come from for soft drinks?

BECAUSE THE carbonated water in them caused pressure in glass bottles, they had a tendency to explode or, at the least, blow the cork. When the cork came out—whether by accident or design—the noise it made naturally led to the name "pop." With the introduction of the crown cap and the improved quality of glass, the sound virtually disappeared, but the name stuck.

COLA MY WORLD

If you drop a tooth into a glass of Coke, how long does it take for the sugar and carbonation to dissolve it?

AS LONG as it would take a glass of water to do the same thing. Although it's one of the more widespread and believed myths—that Coke dissolves teeth—it just isn't so.

Which has more caffeine: Coke or Pepsi?

COKE. It has 46 milligrams of caffeine for every 12 ounces, whereas Pepsi has 38. They aren't the most caffeinated soft drinks, though: Jolt cola has 72 milligrams and Mountain Dew has 54. To put this in perspective, a cup of coffee has anywhere between 50 and 200 milligrams of caffeine.

Where did the name Pepsi come from?

FROM ONE of its main ingredients, pepsin, a substance used to relieve indigestion. When pharmacist Caleb Bradham concocted the kola nut, pepsin, sugar, and vanilla mixture in 1893, he called it Brad's Drink. When it became popular, he changed the name and began the PepsiCola company.

Wasn't Coca-Cola originally made with cocaine?

BAGS OF white processed cocaine weren't dumped into the liquid, if that's what you're asking. However, coca leaves were deliberately added to the recipe to give Coke that natural little cocaine punch. Coke today even registers traces of cocaine, because it still contains coca leaves for flavoring. The cocaine is removed and given to pharmaceutical companies for making anesthetics. But back in the good ol' days, Coca-Cola was a real party drink. Originally, it not only had cocaine in it; it was also made with wine. But because teetotalers wouldn't tolerate the wine, Coke's creator, John Pemberton, replaced it with kola nuts, which gave the drink a caffeine kick instead.

> **How much was a bottled six-pack of Pepsi when they first hit the market?**
> A quarter a pack, back in the 1930s.

NEVER HAD IT, NEVER WILL

Did other soft drinks besides Coca-Cola originally contain hard drugs?

7-UP, for one. Originally named Bib-Label Lithiated Lemon-Lime Soda, it was aimed at mothers with young children (hence the Bib-Label) and contained the drug lithium, a strong antidepressant. It was billed as a cure for "grouchiness," "hangovers," and upset stomachs.

Does 7-Up have seven different ingredients?

PROBABLY, BUT that's not why it's called 7-Up. When the Depression was over, creator C. L. Grigg decided his lemon-lime lithium drink needed a name change. He bought the 7-Up name from a Minnesota chocolate company that sold candy bars with seven different fillings. There's no other connection. He just liked the name.

GETTING BACK TO ITS ROOTS

Which root is root beer made from?

SARSAPARILLA. But other flavors also dominate. Wintergreen root is the primary flavoring used in most commercial brands today, mixed with vanilla for smoothness. Many brands also include anise for a licorice taste. Unlike most other sodas, root beer is often still made with a mix of roots and herbs.

Sassafras root, a common ingredient in days of old, is no longer included. Sassafras contains a substance called *safrole*, which has caused cancer in lab animals. As a result, it was banned by the FDA. Sassafras extract is still used in some brands of root beer, but with the safrole removed.

What makes root beer foamier than other kinds of soft drinks?

IT'S THE extract from the yucca plant. Not all commercial root beer companies add this, though. Some are downright ornery when it comes to the subject of froth. Barq's, for instance, decided to focus more heavily on carbonation instead of worrying about frothiness. Rick Hill, a Barq's executive, actually told the *Chicago Tribune* in 1994, "Foam is for shaving and birth control."

IS THERE A DOCTOR IN THE HOUSE?

Is there really celery in Dr. Brown's Cel-Ray soda?

IT HAS EXTRACT of celery seed in it. Not much, but enough to clearly give it that clean celery taste. The ingredients list? Carbonated water, high-fructose corn syrup, citric acid, extract of celery seed with other natural flavors, sodium benzoate (preservative), and caramel color. Believe it or not, Dr. Brown's celery tonic used to have competitors. Celro-Zola, Celery-Cola, and others offered celery-flavored drinks as well, but the original outlasted them all. Dr. Brown's other original hit was cream soda, which spawned many competitors still around today.

Is Dr. Pepper made out of prune juice?

THAT'S BEEN a rumor since the 1930s, but it's not true. Prune juice has never been in Dr. Pepper. So what is the flavor? According to inside sources, the original soda jerk who concocted the brew was looking to duplicate the sweet smells of a soda shop in his drink. He mixed his favorite flavors together—23 in all—and the result was Dr. Pepper. In other words, mind your own business, the flavor's a secret. So much for inside sources.

> **Is Dr. Brown's Black Cherry Soda kosher?**
> Only when bearing a "K".

Who was Dr. Pepper?

UNLIKE Dr. Brown, Dr. Pepper was very much a real person— Dr. Kenneth Pepper of Rural Retreat, Virginia. The story goes that the founder and creator of the Dr. Pepper Company, Wade Morrison, got his first job at Pepper's pharmacy in the 1880s. Morrison eventually left and settled in Waco, Texas, where he opened his own pharmacy. His soda-fountain man and pharmacist, Charles Alderton, concocted the drink, and Morrison probably decided to name it after his former boss as a tribute for giving him his first job and a head start in the business.

That's the whole story, but there's a much-circulated version that bears mentioning, if for no other reason than to refute it. It goes something like this: Wade Morrison fell in love with his boss's daughter. But Dr. Pepper refused to give his approval to the young Morrison until he had gone out adventuring a little to gain life experience. Morrison went west and eventually settled in Waco. He named his new drink after his boss in order to win Pepper's daughter's hand in marriage. It's a nice story, but untrue. Pepper's daughter was only about eight years old when Morrison left Virginia.

STRIKING A NERVE WITH MOXIE

What product can boast the first recorded singing commercial ever?

MOXIE NERVE Food Soda, a sweet-then-bitter concoction, made the first singing commercial jingle and released it on record in 1921. With the voice of a popular singer, Irving Kaufman, the recording made a huge splash. Moxie can also claim to be the first mass-marketed soft drink, dating back to 1884.

What makes Moxie so bitter?

GENTIAN ROOT. The soft drink has a shockingly bitter after-taste, credited with leading to the noun *moxie*, meaning "spunk"—as in "you've got moxie." Some describe the taste as being "like Dr. Pepper with a wicked afterbite."

Moxie Soda, as well as other specialty sodas, can be ordered online at http://soda-pop.site.yahoo.net/

ADDITIVES AND SUBTRACTIVES

What do coffee makers do with all that caffeine they remove when making decaffeinated coffee?

MOSTLY IT GETS put into caffeinated soft drinks, aspirin, and over-the-counter stimulants. Only 5% of the caffeine in a cola drink, for example, actually comes from kola nuts. The rest is added artificially.

What are those suspended colored balls in the trendy soft drink Orbit?

ACCORDING TO the label, they're made from gellan gum and xanthan gum. This gives them their floating ability, which leads to the name Orbit and the slogan "Defy Gravity!"

How much sweeter is Nutra-Sweet than sugar?

MUCH, MUCH sweeter. Aspartame (the generic name for Nutra-Sweet) is about 200 times sweeter than pure cane sugar. But wait, there's more: saccharin is a whopping 500 times sweeter than plain sugar.

MADE WITH GENUINE, NATURAL, 100% GATORS

Why does Gatorade taste like sweat?

BECAUSE THAT'S exactly what was studied to produce the sports drink. Kidney researcher James Robert Cade took sweat samples from University of Florida football players to analyze exactly what vitamins, minerals, and other important things were being lost during play through sweating. He discovered that potassium and sodium, as well as water, were the main things athletes lost, so he created a liquid with a similar composition to sweat and added lime flavoring. The name came from the team that Cade did all these experiments for—the Florida Gators.

TO JUICE OR NOT TO JUICE

Was Welch's grape juice originally a wine?

HEAVENS, NO. Welch's grape juice was originally made to be an *alternative* to wine. Creator Thomas B. Welch was upset that wine was served during Communion at his Methodist church. So, with careful pasteurization to help prevent fermentation, he made grape juice as a wine substitute. He never was able to get his own church to switch from wine to his grape juice, but he was successful with others. Like other beverage products of the time, Welch's grape juice was initially promoted as a cure for all sorts of ailments. Along with the claims,

> How many varieties are used to make cider?
> Usually three to five per batch.

ads bore a picture of a pretty young woman and the slogan "The lips that touch Welch's are all that touch mine."

Why is it called Kool-Aid instead of Kool-Ade?

YOU THINK Fruit Smack would've been better? That's what creator Edwin E. Perkins's original concentrated-liquid version was called. But Perkins wanted to do what Jell-O had done, so he kept concocting until he came up with a powdered concentrate for his fruit-flavored drink. He named it Kool-Ade, but had to change the name when the FDA decided that "ade" legally had to mean "a drink made from . . ." Perkins then changed it to Kool-Aid. It gave the drink a double meaning, too: it aids your thirst.

COFFEE, TEA, OR BROWN, MUSHY BRAN?

I've heard the name, but what is Revolutionary tea, exactly?

IT'S HERBAL TEA. During the Boston Tea Party era in colonial America, no imported black tea could be consumed, because the colonists were boycotting British tea. So tea drinkers took to brewing and consuming herbal teas, which they dubbed "Revolutionary teas."

> **How many cases of tea were thrown into Boston Harbor?**
> 342.

What's the history of Lloyd's of London insurance group?

BEFORE INSURING things like Bruce Springsteen's voice and Betty Grable's legs, the company was just a java dive where insurers and bettors hung out.

Several hundred years ago, Lloyd's was one of the first coffee houses in London. It opened its doors in response to the new beverage fad, and soon ship brokers gathered there to buy and sell stock in a ship's cargo (thus insuring a vessel's voyage) while drinking steaming cups of java. From ships to other things, Lloyd's of London continues to push the insurance policy envelope.

Why is the coffee brand called Chock Full o' Nuts?

YOU'D THINK it would be Chock Full o' Beans, wouldn't you? Chock Full o' Nuts coffee got its name from the fact that the company used to be a nut business. William Black sold nuts from a street pushcart in the mid-1920s, but sales slowed to the point where he needed to diversify. He baked his nuts into delicious breads and served them with his own house blend of hot coffee. The pastries and nuts eventually fell by the wayside, but his coffee blend lives on with the odd-sounding name.

What is Postum?

IT'S A DRINK made of bran and molasses that was originally concocted as a substitute for coffee and a digestive aid. C. W. Post created it, then had to convince people to buy and consume Postum instead of coffee. So he did what every desperate businessman would do: scared the bejeebers out of people by embarking on an all-out anti-coffee campaign, followed by praise for switching. The whole campaign was a lesson in why truth-in-advertising laws are an absolute necessity.

Where can I see descriptions of the different teas?

Post began by introducing two coffee maladies, "coffee heart" and "coffee nerves," which he claimed were real conditions. Then his ads started suggesting that coffee was wearing away consumers' stomachs, drip by drip. He told of a man who lost his eyesight from drinking coffee and others who went sleepless from drinking too much of the black stuff. Then he went in for the kill, claiming that coffee contained "poisonous alkaloids" and that it was the cause of rheumatism and worse. Postum blamed every ill, from work-related stress to bad parenting, on coffee.

He knocked the public off balance by placing just enough fear out there that people began to question whether coffee was really hurting them. Many consumers did switch to Postum as a result, and he rewarded them in his ads, showing Postum drinkers as healthy, happy people. In every package of Postum, Post included a brochure that hyped the product and healthy living, called "The Road to Wellville."

Today Postum continues to be advertised as a coffee substitute. There's even a coffee-flavored alternative to the original to encourage consumers to give it a go.

Our Animal Friends

CUTE, CUDDLY, AND PLAYFUL— that's how people usually think of traditional pets like cats, dogs, rabbits, and birds. Today, though, animals on the pet list also include decidedly uncuddly pythons, striped geckos, eels, and desert scorpions. Our taste in pets may have changed, but our penchant to make them part of our family hasn't.

THE AGE OF AQUARIUMS

What's a "twit"?

BESIDES being a rude term for someone who's not very bright, *twit* is the technical name for a pregnant goldfish.

Do fish sleep?

GENERALLY, NO. Although fish have periods when they are relatively inactive, they don't sleep. There are exceptions to this rule, however. Some species of fish in and around coral reefs will occasionally lean against coral and take a snooze.

Why do fish float upside down when they die?

GASES—THOSE in their bodies at the time of death and those released when they start decomposing—tend to collect in their internal organs, located in the front center of their bodies. This causes a fish's body to turn over and float to the top of the water.

SPACE CADETS

How many different animals have been sent into space?

ALL KINDS of fauna have taken trips on space flights and low-altitude rocket launches: bees, wasps and hornets, spiders, roundworms, earthworms, fish, jellyfish, snails, toads, newts, mice, rats, guinea pigs, rabbits, tortoises, quail eggs, monkeys, and dogs. Oh, and people, too.

The animal that is glaringly missing from this lineup is the cat. Scientists apparently learned something from an early-19th-century launch of a low-altitude black-powder rocket, which contained a cat and a squirrel to see if they could survive the trip. The launch and recovery by a man named Claude Ruggiere were surprisingly successful—considering that it was one and a half centuries before the major space programs were in existence—with one exception: after the rocket landed, the squirrel was nowhere to be found. It was concluded that its copilot must have gotten hungry on the short journey.

ALL THE PRESIDENTS' PETS

How many pets have lived at the White House?

AROUND 400, not counting horses used for transportation before cars. Besides many dogs and cats, there were pet horses, mules, cows (Taft was the last president to keep a cow at the White House), birds of all sorts, reptiles, silkworms (belonging to Louisa Adams), an alligator, tiger cubs, a lion, a wallaby, a pigmy hippopotamus, a hyena, bears, a zebra, owls, raccoons, coyotes, hamsters, rabbits, goats, mice, turkeys, a badger, and several snakes.

Teddy Roosevelt and his children ran a small zoo that included Emily Spinach the snake, Jack the turkey, and guinea pigs named Dewey Senior, Dewey Junior, Father O'Grady, and Bishop Doan. However, Roosevelt's bull terrier, Pete, takes the cake for causing the most political stink. He tore the pants off the French ambassador and was thereafter banished from the White House.

PEANUT GALLERY

Who are Snoopy's brothers and sisters?

HERE IS THE order in which they were introduced in Charles Schulz's *Peanuts* comic strip: Spike, Belle, Marbles, Olaf, and Andy. Once, Snoopy's father received a Father's Day card from "all eight" of his kids, so there are two more whose names we don't know.

EVERY DOG HAS ITS DAY

Have St. Bernards ever really carried brandy casks?

YES, THEY DID, indeed, tote brandy on collars around their necks. The fellow who gave the St. Bernard dog its name was an Italian churchman, also

> **Where can I see pictures of the hairless Xoloitzcuintli dog?**

named Bernard, who founded a hospice in the Alps. He bred the dogs to work as rescue dogs in the Valle d'Aosta in northwest Italy.

Another St. Bernard, a French monk from Clairvaux, was recorded as saying "love me, love my dog" in 1150 or so. He wasn't the first to express unconditional affection for his dog. Variations of the phrase have been found in earlier cultures, but he is remembered for it.

Why do we say "a little hair of the dog" will cure a hangover?

THIS PHRASE describes an old remedy for imbibing too much alcohol, which consists of getting a taste of the drink that made you feel ill in the first place. The origin of the phrase, however, comes from an even older remedy. It was once believed that if someone was bitten by a dog, a hair from the attacking dog should be burned and then placed on the wound to prevent the victim from contracting rabies. So drinking a little "hair of the dog" is the same—albeit equally ineffective—principle.

IT'S A DOG'S LIFE

Is one "people year" really the equivalent of seven "dog years"?

NOT EXACTLY. The first year for a dog is devoted to growth—physical, sexual, and everything else. During that first year, a dog goes through the equivalent of babyhood, early childhood, adolescence, puberty, and the late teens. When it begins its second year, the dog is already a young adult. You can count a dog's first year as being the equivalent of 20 human years, then figure that every additional year equals about 4 human years.

Do dogs see in black and white?
Yes—and in color, too.

Why do dogs' hind legs move when they are petted in certain spots?

FOR THE SAME reason some people get shivers when someone touches their back or shudder when fingernails are scraped down a chalkboard. It's a reflex. Some experts say it's a method that dogs' wild ancestors once used to scare away predatory animals looking for a dog-sized lunch. Others say it's there to keep a dog from drowning.

Why do people clip dogs' ears and tails?

CROPPING IS the practice of surgically clipping a dog's ears, followed by stringent taping so that they stand upright. The whole point is to make them look "better" to humans: the procedure makes the ears triangular and pointed up, whereas left natural, the ears are more floppy. Two breeds well-known for their cropped ears are Dobermans and Boxers. These breeds and some sporting breeds, like Weimaraners and German Shorthairs, also undergo tail docking, so that only a nub or very short tail remains. At this same time, the dewclaw—the fifth claw, up higher on the leg—is snipped off as well. These procedures are usually performed without anesthesia within a few days of birth, but on older animals, anesthesia is used.

How did the Jack Russell Terrier get its name?

IT WAS NAMED for English clergyman John Russell (1795–1883), who was curate for Swimbridge village in southern England. He was also an avid dog breeder and developed a fox terrier with distinctive tan, black, and white coloring, drooping ears, and short legs.

What's the real name of the dog from "Fraiser"?

HIS NAME IS Moose, and no, he's not the same Jack Russell Terrier that plays Wishbone on the PBS series (that Jack Russell's name is Soccer). But Moose does have a body double. His son fills in for him on days where he's not feeling up to taping. Moose's credits are impressive, with several appearances in print and television commercials. He's been on the covers of *Life* magazine, *TV Guide*, and *Entertainment Weekly* and has his own calendar, according to his publicity people at *www.thepoop.com/dogsonfilm/frasier/*

What does "Dachshund" mean?

IN GERMAN, *Dachs* means "badger," and *Hund* means "hound." When hunting badgers was a common sport, Dachshunds were used to ferret them out of holes: the dogs are small and low to the ground, with a strong digging ability. The Dachshund, by the way, is one of the oldest dog breeds around. Records indicate the ancient Egyptians favored them for their hunting ability and loyalty.

What's the origin of the Bulldog?

BULLDOGS were bred during the Middle Ages, when a sport known as "bullbaiting" was in its heyday in merrie olde England. Bullbaiting consisted of setting vicious dogs loose on a tied or chained-up bull and watching them tear it to pieces. Some sport, eh? Over time, the Bulldog was bred to be particularly vicious and fearless. In a similar sport called "bearbaiting," a bear replaced the bull. Sometimes the dogs were left at home, and men and women alike taunted the bull or bear with loud, shrill noises, then chased it down and beat it to death.

In 1835, all of these blood sports were finally banned in England. At that point, breeders began eliminating the viciousness from the Bulldog breed so that the dogs would make better house pets.

FANCY FELINES

Why do cats hate water?

THEY DON'T really hate water. Cats actually are known fishers, and in the wild can sometimes be found cooling in pools of water. What cats are is incessantly neat. When water gets on a normal housecat, the cat responds to the droplets just as it would food or dirt particles—as something that needs to be cleaned off with a good tongue bath. This can be tiring, so cats tend to shy away from situations that might make them have to bathe themselves, including, ironically, baths.

> **Chocolate is poisonous to dogs, but is it bad for cats?** Yes, very bad.

There are many miniature dogs, but how come there aren't any miniature cats?

THERE ARE, and they're right under your nose if you're a cat owner. Little Snowball and Sox are miniaturized versions of the big felines: lions, tigers, and cheetahs, oh my!

How can I tell what gender my cat is?

THINK PUNCTUATION. When you raise the tail of a cat, a male's genitals will resemble a colon (:) and a female's will look like an inverted semicolon (⁏). Keep in mind, like many punctuation rules, these, too, are sometimes difficult to see or make sense of.

Does a cat's purr mean it is happy?

NOT NECESSARILY, say most experts, because cats purr when they are hurt and sick, too. A cat's purr probably means it is open to being approached socially.

How can I encourage my cat to become a vegetarian like me?

YOU CAN BEST help your cat by understanding that you and it are not the same species with the same needs. If you try to force a cat to eat only vegetable matter, it will eventually die. Cats are not made to be vegetarians—they are carnivores. (Humans, on the other hand, are omnivores, which means we can survive on animal and/or plant matter.) A cat's teeth and body are designed for meat and the vital nutrients it supplies; the same nutrients are not found in meat substitutes like soy. Without those essential nutrients, a cat's organs will fail. If you really want a vegetarian pet, consider a rabbit.

KERMIT & FRIENDS

Do frogs and toads cause warts?

NO. NEITHER frogs nor toads cause warts; a human virus causes warts. Toads secrete a slimy substance out of glands in the back of the head that can cause an allergic reaction in some people. Its primary function is to make a toad taste horrible to anything looking for amphibious cuisine.

If I kiss a frog, will I get a prince?

NO, BUT YOU might get very sick from salmonella. Even if you just hold hands, there's a chance you could pick up the bacteria. Granted, you have a greater chance of picking it up while working with raw chicken in the kitchen, but you should be aware that salmonella may be present when you handle and care for an amphibian or reptile. Always use a disinfectant soap after touching them, and if you have them as pets, make sure their habitat is cleaned regularly and have a veterinarian check them for salmonella.

A word on kissing your frog: Reptiles and amphibians aren't made to be cuddled and they don't like it. Many of these pets can cause damage with their teeth if you put your lips to them, so a frog (or toad or newt or iguana) must never be kissed! Alas, you must find your prince elsewhere.

THE VIVARIUM

Where does the Tokay gecko get its name?

THE NAME comes from the noise the Tokay makes, a very distinctive cry that sounds like "TO-kay! TO-kay!" Since it's nocturnal, its call is clearly heard on calm evenings.

Tokay geckos, indigenous to southeast Asia, are blue to grey in color and have red spots. They look a bit like lizard-shaped dyed Easter eggs. They have feet that allow them to climb vertical surfaces, although their toes are not sticky suction cups, as commonly thought. The pads of their toes have a series of strips on them that can pull away from one another and squeeze together, forming individual suction areas and gripping tiny imperfections on a surface.

Is there really a legless lizard? Isn't it just a snake?

ACTUALLY, THERE are several, including the California legless lizard, the European legless lizard, and the Eastern glass snake (so named from the lizard's ability to break off its tail as a form of self-preservation). Why aren't these lizards classified as snakes? They

What should I know before getting a big snake to keep as a pet?

have a couple of very distinctive physical characteristics that snakes don't have—namely, external ears and movable eyelids.

The question that then begs to be asked: If there are legless lizards, are there any legged snakes? Only if you count the boa. It has little legs on the sides of its body that it uses only during mating, to stimulate its partner. Little snake ticklers, as it were. Oh boa, behave!

I don't like feeding live things to other animals. Is there a vegetarian snake I can get?

NO. THERE are no vegetarian snakes. Some merely eat worms or insects, but none survive without meat. Don't be discouraged; you can still own a snake without having to handle live food. It's strongly encouraged by many snake experts that you train your snake to eat dead mice or small rats instead of live ones, anyway. This is primarily because countless snake injuries and even deaths have been caused by live food being introduced into a snake cage—scared mice can do a lot of damage with tiny, puncturing teeth.

"IT ALL STARTED THE DAY I WAS BORN"

What is pet therapy?

ALTHOUGH you can find pet psychologists, *pet therapy* is actually for people. It's used in nursing homes, schools, prisons, and other places where people are at high risk of stress, depression, and loneliness. Pets are brought in to help reduce the effects from these problems. Research has shown significantly improved mood, blood pressure, and heart rate in people who are entrusted with the care of a cat or dog. It's a win-win situation: positive changes are also seen in the animals that are cared for or adopted.

Music Hath Charms

IF MUSIC BE THE FOOD OF LOVE, play on!" cheered Shakespeare. Music is likely the oldest art and an intrinsic part of every culture on Earth. In some cultures, it is so ingrained in everyday communication that there is no separate word to differentiate it from talking. So without further ado, a look at music . . .

PRECOCIOUS CHILDREN

Who wrote the piano song "Chopsticks"?

IN 1877, A 16-year-old English girl euphoniously named Euphonia Allen wrote "Chopsticks" and published it under the name Arthur de Lulli. Despite Euphonia's promising beginning, it was the only song she ever wrote. The name had nothing to do with Asian eating utensils, she explained: the original sheet music instructions told the pianist to "play with both hands turned sideways, the little fingers lowest, so that the movement of the hands imitates the chopping from which this waltz gets its name." Piano owners everywhere are no doubt grateful for Miss Allen's effort.

> **How old was Michael Jackson when he got his first gold record?**
> Eleven.

At what age did Mozart write his first pieces?

THE FIRST TO BE published were five short piano pieces the young Amadeus wrote at age six. They are still often performed today.

ABSENTEE BALLADS

How many songs were written about Charles Lindbergh's famous transatlantic flight?

IT USED TO BE that any major news event would spur songwriters to compose quickie commemorative ballads and then rush to get the sheet music out almost as fast as the evening papers. After Lindbergh's 1927 flight, songwriters pumped out more than 250 songs in his honor, including the most famous of the bunch, "Lucky Lindy," by Vernon Dalhart.

When I was a kid, we used to sing "Lizzie Borden took an axe . . . " How much of that tune is true?

> LIZZIE BORDEN took an axe
> Gave her mother 40 whacks
> When she saw what she had done
> She gave her father 41.

Officially, none of the song is true because after a year in jail awaiting trial, Ms. Borden was acquitted of the 1892 murders.

Although there were no other credible suspects and there were many discrepancies in her story, the verdict was based on the assumptions that a woman would be too inept and frail to wield an axe with such effectiveness and that a good unmarried Christian woman of 32 would not do such a thing to the dad and stepmom she lived with. The public didn't buy her story and most believed that Lizzie got away with murder. But even with that assumption, the song took some poetic license with the truth. Whoever wielded the axe gave only 19 blows to Mrs. Borden and 10 to Mr. Borden.

Upon release from prison, Lizzie and her sister, Emma, inherited the $500,000 family estate in Fall River, Massachusetts, where they led long and comfortable lives.

MILITARY BRASS

Who wrote the bugle call "Taps"?

"TAPS" was first played to put the troops of Brigadier General Daniel Butterfield to sleep during the U.S. Civil War. There are many stories of how this song came into being, but the most widely accepted is that Butterfield rewrote the tune of "Lights Out," a song then used

> **Where can I hear the song "Taps" online?**

to indicate the end of the day, with the help of his company's bugler. (According to his own account, he whistled his new tune for his wife, who could read music, and she transcribed it for him.)

For a more thorough look at the history of the song, visit www.westpoint.org/taps/

What are the words to "Taps"?

ALTHOUGH OFFICIALLY there are no words to "Taps", that doesn't stop people from singing to the tune. The most common verses originate from an earlier song, "Go to Sleep, Go to Sleep":

> Day is done, gone the sun,
> From the hills, from the lake,
> From the skies—
> All is well, safely rest,
> God is nigh.

Who wrote the "Marine's Hymn"?

ACCORDING to tradition, the first verse—"From the Halls of Montezuma"—was written by a Marine on duty in Mexico after the Mexican War. The origin of the rest of the verses is shrouded in mystery. The music itself was taken from Jacques Offenbach's comic opera *Genevieve de Brabant*, in which the melody (with different words, of course) is sung by two gendarmes.

What the heck is a "Yankee-Doodle"?

A 15TH-CENTURY Dutch song began with the nonsense phrase "Yankee dudel doodle down." The song spread to England, where it was first sung to children during the Elizabethan era and then (with new words) to taunt Oliver Cromwell and his Protestant forces. The Brits continued the tradition of singing it as things got tense in their North American colonies.

A British army surgeon stationed in Albany, New York, is credited with rewriting the song during the 1750s to make fun of the simpleminded American bumpkins around him; they were apparently doltish enough to adopt the song as their own and especially liked to sing it while pursuing retreating Redcoats. "I hope I shall never hear that tune again!" British General Thomas Gage was quoted as saying. Eventually the song was adopted as a patriotic American air, and the term *Yankee-Doodle* has come to mean "inhabitant of the United States"—though the song still doesn't make much sense.

MUSICAL ROYALTIES

What was Duke Ellington's real name, and how did he get his nickname?

EDWARD KENNEDY ELLINGTON, a successful big-band leader and composer of more than 2,000 musical works, got his noble nickname because he had a dignified bearing. The name may have been influenced by its similarity to "the Duke of *Wellington*," who was famous in schoolbooks for defeating Napoleon in the 1800s.

> **What bandleader always carried a chihuahua under his arm?**
> Rumba King Xavier Cugat.

Why was Arthur Sullivan knighted in the 1890s but his collaborator, William Gilbert, wasn't knighted until a decade later?

GILBERT HAD to wait until Queen Victoria died. It's true that Gilbert and Sullivan were both talented men and they equally contributed to the operettas that made them famous. However, Victoria "was not amused" at Gilbert's lyrics, especially the devastating satires of her governmental officials. She didn't hold Sullivan's music responsible for this, and was impressed by the fact that he also wrote such hymns as "Onward Christian Soldiers" and other uplifting music. So she knighted Sullivan, and after her death, her eldest son, Edward VII, knighted Gilbert.

AGITATED YET LISZTLESS

Were the beatles the first pop musicians to have girls screaming and fainting?

TWO DECADES earlier, Frank Sinatra had the same effect on girls and young women. It started because of a great publicity stunt and the power of suggestion. At one performance, Sinatra's press agent paid a handful of girls to scream, jump up and down, and pretend to faint. After they went into their schtick, the other girls in the audience didn't need cuing or payment to start acting the same way—and wide press coverage of the performance ensured that paying women for this service would never be necessary again.

However, Sinatra was not the first musician to get the treatment either. Over a hundred years earlier, a fiercely handsome pianist and composer, Hungarian Franz Liszt, left a trail of swooning female fans throughout Europe. Fortunately for music lovers, he tired of the virtuoso superstar life in 1847 and put his energies into composing and arranging.

MUZAK TO OUR EARS

Why do they play music on elevators?

ELEVATOR MUSIC is a throwback to a time when people were nervous about riding elevators and weren't sure whether they'd manage to go up a few floors or would plunge to their death. Elevators could also be noisy—grinding and rattling—and music served to cover the noise while it soothed the nerves of riders. The practice continues today in many public buildings, even though people are less nervous and elevators are much quieter. Many people find that while riding through 30 floors with strangers, even a pizzicato strings version of "Raindrops Keep Fallin' on My Head" is better than a long, awkward silence.

If nobody likes Muzak, why is it played everywhere?

FIRST OF ALL, disabuse yourself of the notion that nobody likes Muzak. Some listeners do—but more to the point, business owners like it. Muzak is not supposed to be "listened to"; it's there to alter people's mood and behavior. If you're a worker or a shopper, it's supposed to keep you relaxed but alert, ready to work or shop tirelessly without actually being distracted by the music being played. To this end, voices are never heard in true Muzak, and any other distractions that might make you actually pay attention to the music—loud drums or guitar solos, for example—are filtered out.

Muzak now has 12 different channels that a subscriber can choose from, depending on the demographics of the audience. Whatever the mix, it seems to work. Since World War II, it's been found in stores, offices, restaurants, hotels—and even in a brothel in the Netherlands.

DON'T KNOW MUCH ABOUT GEOLOGY

I've got a geology professor who claims that "country rock," "acid rock," and "hard rock" were all geologic terms before they became popular music genres. Is that true, or is he trying to throw basalt in our eyes?

IT'S TRUE, and there was also "boss rock" in geology long before Bruce Springsteen came on the scene. "Heavy metal" came from chemistry, but it was a one-hit wonder. If you're looking for a description for your band's music, geology is your best hope. Try out one of these geologic terms:

arenaceous rock
rudaceous rock

igneous rock
gangue rock
conglomerate rock
grit rock
dyke rock
ultrabasic rock
intermediate rock
pyroclastic rock
sedimentary rock
boudinage rock

SONGS FOR SALE

Where was Tin Pan Alley?

IN THE LATE 1800s, sheet music publishing became more and more centralized to New York, in particular to the area of 28th Street between Broadway and Fifth Avenue, near Union Square. In the summer, with windows open, pedestrians could hear the tinny tintinnabulation of cheap pianos up and down the street as songwriters hoping to be the next Irving Berlin or Cole Porter pounded out song after disposable song for the entertainment trade.

> **What piece has sold the most sheet music?**
> *"Yes, We Have No Bananas."*

Eventually Tin Pan Alley shifted to West 28th Street and finally to offices in and around the Brill Building, on Broadway near 50th. In the 1960s, most rock and pop performers chose to write their own songs, forcing the last crop of professional songwriters—like Carole King, Barry Mann, Neil Diamond, and Neil Sedaka—into writing TV theme songs and commercials or becoming performers in their own right.

What's the bestselling single recording of all time?

ELTON JOHN'S tribute to Princess Diana, "Candle in the Wind, 1997," which was adapted from his earlier "Candle in the

Wind," about Marilyn Monroe. It sold 31.8 million copies worldwide in the weeks after Diana's death, beating out Bing Crosby's rendition of "White Christmas," which has sold an estimated 30 million single copies since 1942.

However, this answer doesn't really tell the whole story. If you throw in *all* recordings in *all* media, Crosby's song wins, hands down. After nearly six decades, "White Christmas" continues to be released on Christmas anthology albums and has sold untold millions of copies that way as well.

Like "Candle," "White Christmas" was wildly popular from its first release. However, unlike the Elton John song, its appeal has held up over the years. Crosby even had to go back into the studio with the same band in 1947 to re-record the master because it had been worn out from stamping out millions of 78-rpm records. The song has been a centerpiece of two movies and has appeared on 78s, 45s, 33s, eight-tracks, cassettes, videos, and CDs, selling copies through the rock 'n' roll era to the present. "Candle, 1997" hasn't sold many copies since its first release.

Who sold the most records—Elvis, the Beatles, Michael Jackson, or the Rolling Stones?

ACCORDING TO the Recording Industry Association of America (RIAA), the "most successful act of the 20th century" was the Beatles, who sold more than 106 million albums. Elvis, however, released more albums and so had more gold (80) and platinum (43) albums than any other "act." The Rolling Stones had the most successful tour of anybody, with its Voodoo Lounge tour, grossing $121.3 million in 1994.

Which album sold the most copies in the 20th century?

FROM 1984 UNTIL 1999, it was *Thriller* by Michael Jackson. However, as the turn of the century loomed, the self-proclaimed King of Pop lost out to the Eagles. *The Eagles: Their Greatest Hits,* originally released in 1976, pulled ahead from second place by selling more than 26 million copies.

What exactly does a "gold" or "platinum" record represent? I thought a gold record was for a million copies and a platinum was for two million or five million or something, but my friend says I'm wrong.

YOU ONCE WERE RIGHT, but standards were loosened in the record industry in 1989, ostensibly because compact disks cost more than vinyl records and so should count more. A gold record used to take sales of a million copies, but the RIAA lowered it to a mere 500,000. A platinum record used to mean two million copies sold, but it's now a mere million.

I heard Rumours by Fleetwood Mac described as a "diamond" record. What does that mean?

DIAMOND IS A NEW category designed to add an additional superlative to the old categories of gold and platinum records. It means you've sold more than 10 million copies. In the case of *Rumours*, in excess of 18 million.

Is the soundtrack from Titanic the bestselling movie soundtrack of all time?

NO. IT'S NOT even close. As of the beginning of the year 2000, *The Bodyguard* was number one with 16 million sold; *Saturday Night Fever* number two with 15 million sold; *Purple Rain* number three at 13 million; *Dirty Dancing* comes in fourth at 11 million; and *Titanic* tied at number five with *The Lion King*, with sales of about 10 million each.

BLOW OUT THE CANDLES AND PAY THE ROYALTIES

What is the most performed song in the last 100 years?

IT MAY BE the most performed song ever. It's "Happy Birthday to You," which almost everyone hears at least once a year and sings many more times. The song is still copyrighted and won't legally enter the public domain until 2010. Until then, if you record it or perform it in a public place, you're supposed to pay royalties to the estates of Mildred and Patty Hill, the Kentuckian sisters who wrote it.

I want to surprise my mom. How do you play "Happy Birthday to You" on a the buttons of a phone?

WELL, KEEPING IN mind the penalties for unauthorized public performance (see previous question), you can get reasonably close to the melody with *1121#6, 1121#6, 11##841, ##6421.* Jeeves is certain that your mother will be impressed.

What important musical personality was born on August 31, 1945?

ACTUALLY THERE WERE two of them: Van Morrison and Itzhak Perlman. Some other coincidental musical birthdates include August 10, 1928 (Jimmy Dean and Eddie Fisher), September 5, 1946 (Loudon Wainwright III, Freddy Mercury, and Buddy Miles) and September 16, 1925 (Charlie Byrd and B. B. King).

COMPOSING AND DECOMPOSING

Which of the well-known composers cranked out the most music in his lifetime?

THE HIGHEST achievers among the famous-name composers were Franz Josef Haydn, who wrote 340 hours of music in 54 years of composing; George Handel, 303 hours in 54 years; Wolfgang Amadeus Mozart, 202 hours in 29 years; and Johann Sebastian Bach, 147 hours in 47 years.

On the other hand, the most famous low achiever was Maurice Ravel, who produced only 19 hours in 42 years, a career average of about 30 seconds of music a week.

Which great composer could write the fastest?

FRANZ SCHUBERT had the reputation of being able to write music so quickly and effortlessly that he often wouldn't recognize his own work when set before him. Mozart also could write fast yet brilliantly—he wrote his last three symphonies over a period of only three months and the entire opera *Don Giovanni* in one sitting. (It premiered the next day without rehearsal.)

Was Sousa's famous "Washington Post March" named after some military base or the newspaper of the same name?

THE NEWSPAPER. In 1889, the U.S. Marine Band played at an awards ceremony for an essay contest sponsored by the *Washington Post*. John Philip Sousa, the band's leader, dashed off a little something for the occasion. To Sousa's surprise it quickly became one of his most popular marches.

Is it true that Richard Wagner composed while dressed up in costumes?

HISTORICAL ACCOUNTS say that Wagner wrote his operas dressed in historical costumes for inspiration. But he wasn't the only composer with quirks: Christoph Gluck would write only while seated in the middle of a field. Franz Joseph Haydn believed that he couldn't write well without wearing a ring given him by Frederick the Great. And Gioacchino Rossini reportedly found inspiration by getting profoundly drunk while putting pen to paper.

Was there ever an opera featuring Eskimos?

YES. *KADDARA*, by Hakon Borrensen. It was first produced in Copenhagen in 1921 and set in Greenland. For an audio excerpt, go to: *www.mic.dk/opera/Borr/Kadd/kadd.html*

Why didn't Beethoven ever get to hear his Ninth Symphony performed?

IN THE HISTORY of music, many composers never got to hear some of their best works performed, either because they couldn't find an orchestra that would perform it, or because they died soon after finishing it. In Beethoven's case, he got to see his Ninth Symphony performed...he just didn't get to hear it. When he wrote it he was completely deaf, a remarkable accomplishment even for a veteran composer.

Wasn't there some kind of riot when Igor Stravinsky's Rite of Spring was first performed in 1913?

THE PIECE was greeted with catcalls and fistfights. *The Rite of Spring* is recognized by musicologists as a classic that ushered in 20th-century music. At the time, much of the audience thought it ridiculous and insulting.

Why was the "Wedding March" banned in some churches?

"HERE COMES THE BRIDE . . . ." One major reason was the opera it came from. Richard Wagner didn't write the piece for the wedding in *Lohengrin*, but rather for the *post*-wedding scene. So for anyone who has seen the opera, the music conjures up images of Wagner's bride and groom nervously undressing, preparing to consummate their marriage. Church officials—back when opera was popular entertainment—opposed placing the secular, sexy piece into a church ceremony on the grounds that it was vulgar and maybe even blasphemous.

HIGH NOTES AND LOW

What's the highest and lowest frequency that most people can hear?

ABOUT 30 HERTZ (sound wave cycles per second) is the lowest; 40,000 hertz is the highest.

What is the difference in frequency between a middle C and the C above middle C?

THE HIGHER NOTE is vibrating exactly twice as fast. For example, 261.625 hertz is a C and 523.25 is a C, though an octave higher, and 1046.5 hertz is a C an octave higher than that. This doubling is true of any two notes separated by a full octave.

Is there a frequency limit after which a sound will damage the human ear?
No. After a certain frequency you just won't hear it.

What percent of the population is tone-deaf?

THERE ARE VERY few people who are actually tone-deaf—that is, who have a neurological disorder that renders them unable to distinguish among musical pitches. Truly tone-deaf people even have trouble with the "music" of spoken language, for example, discerning whether a speaker's inflection is going up into a question or down into a statement. They can have trouble hearing the tiny differences in pitch that show whether a speaker is expressing anger, sadness, joy, or whimsy. If you don't have that trouble, then it isn't tone-deafness that plagues you.

So why can't some people sing? Lack of practice, training, and confidence. Teaching your voice to reach the tones you want to reach can be as hard as teaching yourself to pitch a baseball over the plate—it's naturally easier for some, but nearly anyone can do it if willing to practice.

What are the different musical scales used around the world?

WESTERN MUSIC USES the *chromatic* scale, equivalent to the white and black keys on a piano, which divides the scale into 12 equal parts. Most popular and folk music uses only 7 of them—the equivalent of do, re, mi, fa, so, la, ti. The Arab scale divides the octave into 17 steps; the Indian scale, 22. The Chinese use 5 notes, most commonly F, G, A, C, and D, which can be simulated by using only the black keys on a piano. The Japanese use the Western scale, with one exception: their fa step is sharpened up a half step. (For example, in a C scale, they'd use F-sharp instead of F.)

INSTRUMENTAL BREAKDOWN

If you straightened out a French horn, how long would it be?

THE BEAUTIFUL, circular-shaped French horn is one of the most tightly coiled of the brass instruments. (In fact, among orchestras, its players often have the same tightly coiled reputation.) If you straightened all that winding tubing, the instrument would be about 22 feet long.

When did the Scots invent the bagpipe?

THEY DIDN'T . . . and it's not clear who did. The droning instrument, originally made from reeds and an inflated pig's bladder, was apparently invented thousands of years ago in Asia. The Roman emperor Nero was reputed to be a bagpipe virtuoso, playing it for public ceremonies and athletic contests. Roman troops brought the instrument all over the world, but most countries outside Scotland rejected the musical gift.

Is it true that Ben Franklin invented the harmonica?

THE EVER-INVENTIVE Dr. Franklin came up with a lot of useful items, from the Franklin stove to lightning rods to lending libraries. And he did, in fact, invent an instrument that he called the "harmonica." As a result, there has been a great deal of confusion over the years because the harmonica he invented is not the small, rectangular wind instrument one usually thinks of. Franklin's harmonica—now usually called the *glass harmonica* to avoid confusion—is a series of tuned spinning glass disks on a spindle that are half-submerged in a pan of water. To play it, you put your fingers lightly on the wet spinning disks, and each makes an ethereal high tone like the sound of rubbing a wet finger along the rim of fine crystal glassware.

The sound is otherworldly, and several composers have written music for it. However, for some listeners, the high tones send a sonic chill down the spine, and the early novelty of the instrument eventually was overshadowed by overblown accusations about its harmful effects: that it caused nervous disorders in its players, made women faint, sent dogs into convulsions, and caused sleeping girls to wake up screaming.

What does ukulele mean in Hawaiian?

"LITTLE JUMPING FLEA." Hawaiian craftsmen copied a miniature guitar that a Portuguese sailor brought to the island. A diminutive British sailor stationed in Hawaii learned to play the tiny instrument, and his lively performances got him the "flea" nickname, which eventually stuck to the instrument itself.

Who created the first keyboard synthesizer?

ROBERT MOOG built the first Moog synthesizer in 1964. The electronic instrument was enormous and could play only one note at a time. When Walter Carlos recorded *Switched on Bach* on it, he had to laboriously build Bach's chords and counterpoint by repeatedly recording separate tracks on tape. In 1970, advances in electronic miniaturization and computers led to a portable Moog synthesizer that could play chords, leading to a synthesizer boom in studio recordings and live performances.

> **Where can I hear a bassoon online?**

SILENCE IS GOLDEN

I found an old record called "Three Minutes of Silence" in a junk shop. Sure enough, it was a three-minute record with nothing on it. What was that all about—a joke?

NOT SO MUCH A JOKE as a tribute to how ubiquitous and popular jukeboxes once were. Sometimes in a crowded bar or restaurant, you'd be willing to pay money for just a few minutes of relief from the constant music. You could choose "Three Minutes of Silence" and, for a nickel, actually get enough quiet time to think or talk to your date. Pretty smart on the part of the jukebox makers—you had to pay money if you wanted to hear music, and you had to pay money if you wanted a break from it.

SHAVE AND A HAIRCUT

Why hasn't barbershop quartet singing gone out of style?

YOU CAN THANK the Society for the Preservation and Encouragement of Barber Shop Quartet Singing in America. It was founded by a Tulsa attorney named Owen C. Cash in 1938 when it appeared that his favorite style of close-harmony singing was becoming extinct. Between the SPEBSQSA and the women's equivalent, the Sweet Adelines, barber shop harmonies are still commonly heard throughout the land.

RAPTUROUS SOUNDS

When did the first rap record come out?

A LOT OF PEOPLE don't realize how far back rap goes. In fact, it overlapped the dying days of disco in the 1970s. The genre owes a lot to earlier styles, including spoken-word calypso, reggae, the "dirty dozens" (ad hoc rhyming competitions full of bragging and insults), and groups like the Last Poets, who shouted out political poetry over music in the 1960s. (Their biggest hit, by the way, *The Revolution Will Not Be Televised,* was recycled in the 1990s as a commercial for an amusement park.)

At first, rap went through a gestation period in New York City in which turntable-spinning, rapping DJs competed against each other in city parks, their sound systems powered by hot-wired street lamps. Finally, the first rap recordings were released in 1979: "King Tim III (Personality Jock)" by the Fatback Band and "Rapper's Delight" by the Sugarhill Gang. (Unlike most rap groups of the time, the Sugarhill Gang actually hired a band instead of using prerecorded material on a turntable, replicating the basic groove of the hit song "Good Times" by the disco group Chic.) "Delight" reached number 36 on the *Billboard* charts and inspired a host of imitators.

When did the term hip-hop first appear in rap music?
In 1979, in "Rappers Delight."

When rap artists "sample" other songs for their own records, do they pay the original artist?

SAMPLING IS WHEN an another artist digitally copies a piece of a song—perhaps a short drum break, a guitar riff, or a word, phrase, or wail—and uses it to build the background of his or her own song. For a long time, that was the only way to construct a rap background, and the artists that were copied didn't get paid. James Brown, perhaps the most sampled man in show business, had no direct benefits coming back to him for years. By the early 1990s, though, a system of requesting permission and negotiating payment for sampled material became the norm. As a result, some commonly sampled artists who had long resented having their work "stolen" began welcoming young rap artists with their digital recorders and bags of money. George Clinton and some other commonly sampled artists even released CDs with dozens of sample-friendly snippets to make copying them easy.

MUSIC MISCELLANY

When did written musical notation first come into use?

THE EARLIEST KNOWN example of musical notation was carved onto a clay tablet in what's now Iraq. It dates from about 1800 B.C.

Where did the term ragtime come from?

FROM "RAGGED TIME"—that is, syncopated beats that were uneven sounding to waltz-accustomed ears back in the early 1900s.

How many encores did Elvis Presley normally give in a concert?

NONE. INSTEAD, the lights would come up and an announcer would say, "Elvis has left the building." Perhaps this is a good idea—why should audience members have to beg and applaud in order to finally hear a performer's best song?

What did Mick Jagger do before singing?

HE WENT TO the London School of Economics for two years and also worked as a physical education teacher.

In Greek mythology, who was the muse of music?

ACTUALLY THERE were three: Euterpe for lyrics, Polyhymnia for sacred song, and Terpsichore for dance and choral song. In fact, the word *music* (from the Greek *mousa*, or "muse") comes from the nine sister muses who lived on Mount Olympus with their parents: Zeus, the king of the gods, and Mnemosyne, the goddess of memory. The other muse sisters were Calliope, muse of epic poetry; Erato, love poetry; Melpomene, tragedy; Thalia, comedy; Clio, history; and Urania, astronomy.

Which countries have the shortest and the longest national anthems?

THE JAPANESE national anthem is expressed in only four lines. The Greek anthem runs 158 verses.

In the 1960s, who won the most Grammies— Bob Dylan, the Rolling Stones, Jimi Hendrix, Janis Joplin, the Who, or the Beach Boys?

NONE OF THEM won Grammies in the 1960s. Frank Sinatra, Henry Mancini, Tony Bennett, Glen Campbell, the Fifth Dimension, and Stan Getz each got more Grammies than all of these rock artists combined.

> **Who was the Gregory that the Gregorian chant was named after?**
> Pope Gregory I.

I ran across a word I couldn't find in my dictionary: "chantepleure." What does it mean?

TO SING AND WEEP at the same time. From the French words that mean, sensibly, "sing" and "cry."

Dollars & Nonsense

"**MONEY MAKES THE WORLD GO** around," goes one unsentimental song. While that is not literally true (the Earth's rotation has more to do with gravity and inertia), money is a powerful driving force. Perhaps this has been true for all time—as even the Bible says, you can get joy from the simple pleasures of the world, "but money answereth all things."

MONEY: HOT OFF THE PRESSES

How much extra money was printed up for the Y2K scare in 1999? What happened to all of it?

THE FEDERAL RESERVE printed up an extra $50 billion in small bills in anticipation of money hoarding and distributed it to banks around the country. That's $183.39 for every person in the United States. Little of it was actually withdrawn by nervous citizens, as most of the population took the 2000 turnover in stride. As to the extra bills, long-term storage posed a problem, so most of it was recycled into mulch.

Of all the bills printed by the U.S. Mint, how many are $1 bills?

NEARLY HALF. About 48% of the 38 million notes printed each day are dollar bills. The total face value of a day's printing is approximately $541 million. Regardless of the bill's denomination, the actual cost of printing it is about two cents—not a bad markup.

When was the U.S. Mint founded? In 1792.

When was paper money first used?

CHINESE EMPEROR Hien Tsung (A.D. 806–821) was the first to introduce paper money, when his country faced a shortage of copper. The Chinese at least had the benefit of early printing blocks. In Tibet, paper money was hand painted on rice paper from an ink extracted from leaves and yak dung. While coins have the advantage of a long life, bills are, of course, much cheaper to make. At least two countries—Laos and Paraguay—use no coins at all.

How much U.S. currency is circulating outside the country?

A RECENT REPORT from the Federal Reserve states that two out of three U.S. dollars in currency are circulating *outside* the borders of the United States. Here's how it breaks down: Of the $460 billion in circulation, only $153 billion is actually in the country; $307 billion of it is abroad. In addition, the agency keeps $150 billion worth of currency in its vaults as a reserve.

How many coins drop out of circulation every year?

COINS DISAPPEAR from circulation at an alarming rate, especially those worth the least. Within two years, 70% of all pennies made today will have disappeared into drawers, piggy banks, or sofas. As the value rises, the disappearance rate goes down: only 14% of nickels, 10% of dimes, and 8% of quarters drop out in the same period of time. Ironically, the lower the denomination, the higher the proportionate cost to replace them. Pennies cost about half a cent to manufacture; nickels, about two and a half cents; dimes only a penny; quarters, three cents; and fifty-cent pieces, five cents.

Why are most of the world's coins so unattractive?

YOU CAN imagine that some of it has to do with the fact that governmental functionaries are not always the best judges of aesthetics. Furthermore, leaders often come up with beauty-killing mandates—like requiring that coins depict dead heroes or (as in the case of Caesar) the leader himself. Most people barely glance at the designs on coins, and don't care about them as long as they can easily differentiate one from another. Also, the fact that making coins is relatively expensive compared to printing bills or stamps, both in materials and equipment, makes whimsical, ever-changing designs rather unlikely. In fact, officials in most countries insist that coin designers *not* make the designs too pretty. Pretty coins drop out of circulation faster—they're collected, hoarded, and even turned into ornamentation and jewelry.

GOT CHANGE FOR AN ELEPHANT TUSK?

What sorts of things have been used as money?

ALMOST ANYTHING that is relatively rare has been used as money at some point or another. Metals have been popular for their durability and relative rarity—most often gold, silver, and copper, but also iron and bronze. However, people have also used salt, shells, cheese, tea, wood, leather, velvet, silk, beads, elephant tusks, skins, livestock, bullets, playing cards, tobacco leaves, beetle legs, bat hair, and even huge stone wheels.

A PENNY SAVED IS A PENNY COMPOUNDED

Ben Franklin left money in his will for Boston and Philadelphia to divide 200 years later. What happened to it?

WHEN HE DIED in 1790, Benjamin Franklin bequeathed the two cities 2,000 pounds sterling, with two provisions: First, they must use the money to make loans to young apprentices (which he'd once been). Second, they must wait 100 years to withdraw part of the money for themselves—and another 100 years to withdraw the rest. The cities followed the terms of the will and in 1990 split what remained of his fortune, $6.5 million, which they added to their general funds.

How rich are the richest people compared to average individuals?

MUCH, MUCH RICHER. The 400 richest people in the United States, according to *Forbes* magazine, have combined assets that exceed the total bank savings of the 272 million Americans who are *not* on the list. Those 400 people could pay off the total United States debt and still have billions of dollars left over.

DOLLARS TO DOUGHNUTS

Where did the word "dollar" come from?

FROM A LITTLE Bohemian mining town called Joachimsthal. In the 16th century, the government opened its mint near a source of metal ores there, so the coins that came from it were known as *Joachimsthalers.* Over the years, wind, rain, and vernacular usage eroded the name down to *thaler* or *taler.* The English heard it as "dollar," and a new word was coined (no pun intended).

Why do some old Chinese coins have a hole in them?

THE REASON was very practical. You could string them together for carrying. It was such a good idea that early on, the U.S. Mint considered doing the same.

IT'S WHERE THE MONEY IS

How good a career option is bank robbing?

NOT SO GOOD. The average robbery takes in less than $6,500, and with video cameras, bulletproof teller stations, exploding money packs, and rapid police response, the chance of arrest is about 70%. Besides, who wants to wait in those long lines?

DIRTY COPPER

How much copper is actually in today's penny?

NOT MUCH. Just 2.5%—enough to plate it with a thin layer of the distinctive penny color. The rest is zinc. Pennies made before 1982 were about 95% copper, but the amount was changed when the copper became worth a little more than the penny itself.

COPING WITH CHANGE

When did they start putting "In God we trust" on all U.S. coins?

IN 1955. It was the middle of the worst part of the Cold War, when McCarthyism, nuclear fears, and hysteria ran rampant. The government made the slogan mandatory on all U.S. currency to show that Americans would not have anything to do with "godless communism."

Why are the tails of coins positioned upside down from the heads?

WHEN YOU FLIP a coin, the back is upside down in relation to the front. Not even the U.S. Mint seems to know why. "All U.S. coinage is produced with what is commonly called a 'coin turn,'" says their Web page. "That means that the reverse side (tails) of the coins is upside down to the obverse side (heads). While we have researched the history of this practice, we have been unable to determine the exact reasons. The Mint still produces U.S. coinage in this manner for traditional reasons and not due to any legal requirement."

For more facts about coins, as well as some money-themed screensavers, check out the U.S. Mint's Web site: www.usmint.gov/

GREENBACKS

Why is U.S. paper money green?

EVEN THE U.S. Treasury Department's Bureau of Engraving and Printing admits it doesn't quite know. However, here is the story of how it originally happened.

During the mid-1800s, the Treasury Department learned that counterfeiters were using the new medium of photography to make nearly perfect copies of currency. They added colors to thwart the counterfeiters, which worked for a while because color film did not yet exist. When green currency was photographed, it turned a telltale gray. However, the counterfeiters soon discovered ways to remove the colored inks. Then they could photograph the money and ink the colors in manually.

Abraham Lincoln's secretary of the treasury, Salmon P. Chase, contracted with the American Bank Note Company to create colored inks that would be as difficult to erase as black inks. The most successful of the early ink formulations was green ink, so Chase decided to print all new currency with green ink on the back. Some of the first recipients were Union soldiers, who promptly dubbed the new bills "greenbacks."

What started as a practical solution became a tradition. Green money is what Americans have come to expect and trust. So green money is what Americans still have a century and a half later.

MONEY MISCELLANY

How heavy is the vault door at Fort Knox?

THE DEPOSITORY of much of the world's gold is 30 miles southwest of Louisville, Kentucky. The vault door itself weighs more than 20 tons (40,000 pounds) and can be opened only after several people each dial in separate combinations that are known only to them.

Does the United States still print a $2 bill?

DESPITE PUBLIC indifference and the hostility of storekeepers—whose registers don't have a compartment for them—$2 bills are still alive . . . barely. According to the U.S. Government Bureau of Engraving and Printing, at last count there were 583,045,729 in circulation worldwide.

> **What is the fear of money called?** Chrematophobia.

For more facts and trivia about paper money, see the Bureau of Engraving and Printing's Web site: www.bep.treas.gov/

Celebrate!

WHO CAN ARGUE WITH A DAY OFF to spend with family or friends? Sure, holidays could be distributed a little better—fewer in winter, more in summer—but their traditions can strengthen bonds and brighten memories. Here are some answers to enliven your Kodak moments.

JUST ME AND MY SHADOW

How did Groundhog Day come to be? Did anybody ever really believe that groundhogs could tell when spring was coming?

WHEN FARMERS in Germany came up with this cockamamy idea in the 1500s, the prescient animal wasn't even a groundhog, but a badger. And the tradition seems to be related to an earlier pagan celebration called Imbolc, which occurred midway between the winter solstice and the spring equinox. If the sun came out on Imbolc, it meant six more weeks of wintry weather, regardless of whether a groundhog or badger was involved.

When Germans settled in Pennsylvania, they brought their badger tradition with them, but Pennsylvania had no native badgers. Luckily, the settlers were able to place their spring hopes on an earth-dwelling animal that was plentiful in those parts—the groundhog, a type of woodchuck.

How accurate has the groundhog's prediction on Groundhog Day been through history?

ONLY ABOUT 39% accurate—no better than an almanac or TV weather announcer. This figure is based on records kept since 1887, in Punxsutawney, Pennsylvania.

To see the official list of Groundhog Day predictions for the last 100 years, go to www.stormfax.com/ghogday.htm

COAX ME, DIG ME, HUG ME, KISS ME, HUBBA HUBBA!

Who thinks up the sayings on Valentine's Day candy hearts?

FOUR OUT OF FIVE candy message hearts are made by the New England Confection Company (NECCO) in Cambridge, Massachusetts, which has been making the hearts since 1902. There's a NECCO vice president who makes the final decision about which sayings to retire and which new ones will replace them, typically a half dozen of each of the 125 phrases in circulation at any given time. Retired messages include HUBBA HUBBA, GROOVY, HANG TEN, DIG ME, and U-R GAY. New ones include AWESOME, E-MAIL ME, PAGE ME, and BE MY ICON. Writing the slogans is a science, as well as an art, since there are only so many letters you can print onto one of those tiny hearts.

For which holiday do Americans buy the most candy?

YOU MIGHT think it would be Halloween, Christmas, or Valentine's Day . . . but the most candy-filled holiday is Easter.

BANG UP HOLIDAYS

Why are firecrackers used in so many Chinese celebrations?

THE CHINESE culture lights off fireworks for everything from store openings to weddings to New Year's celebrations. The idea is that the loud noises scare away bad spirits. In South

America as well, every civil or religious holiday is punctuated by the constant snapping of firecrackers.

SUCKER!

Why do people celebrate April Fools' Day?

THERE ARE several theories, but the most likely is this: The French used to celebrate New Year's Day on April 1 with the new spring. When France adopted the Gregorian calendar in 1564, King Charles IX decreed that New Year's Day would henceforth be celebrated on January 1. Not everybody got the word, and even among those who knew of the changes, not everyone wanted to go along with it. As a result, that year a number of people continued to celebrate New Year's Day on April 1 as usual, throwing parties and exchanging gifts. To make fun of the clueless and conservative, various wits marked the non-holiday by mocking those who still celebrated. They invited people to nonexistent events or gave them absurd presents, and anyone who fell for the joke was dubbed a *poisson d'Avril* ("April fish"). Even emperors were not immune to the April foolishness—centuries later, when Napoleon I got married on April 1, 1810, he was thereafter known as the "April Fish." Even after everybody got used to the new calendar, the April fooling continued every year on April 1. Over the centuries, the holiday spread to England and eventually to America.

On what religious holiday was Abraham Lincoln assassinated? Good Friday.

WITH KID YOU GET EGG ROLL

What do they actually do at the White House Egg Roll on Easter?

EVERY YEAR on the Monday after Easter, children ages three to six are invited to roll decorated hard-boiled eggs across the White House lawn. Tens of thousands of kids compete in egg races while the president looks on. Other egg games include Toss and Catch, Egg Ball, and Egg Croquet. At the end of the event, participants receive a wooden commemorative egg that was made especially for the occasion.

If you'd like to learn more about the White House Egg Roll tradition, or want to get a ticket to it for your child, go to www.whitehouse. gov/WH/glimpse/Easter/index.html

To buy a White House commemorative Easter egg (about $3 apiece), you can order from their Web site: whitehouseeasteregg.com/

TIES THAT BIND

What gift is given most often on Father's Day?

PITY THE POOR DADS. The number-one gift on Father's Day is a new tie, about $20 million worth every year.

Dads get relatively little respect in this mother-loving culture. Father's Day wasn't made an official holiday until signed into law by President Richard Nixon in 1972, 58 years after the Mother's Day's

> **What is the official Father's Day flower?**
> A rose.

designation. Only 85 million Father's Day cards are sent each year, compared to 150 million for its maternal counterpart. And while Mother's Day is the day when the most phone calls are made, Father's Day is the day when the most *collect* phone calls are made.

How many children did the originator of Mother's Day have?

NONE. Even though she'd been a model daughter, Anna Jarvis, a West Virginia schoolteacher, was filled with regret and guilt when her mother died in 1902. Over the next decade, she worked tirelessly to get a celebration of motherhood recognized, badgering cities, towns, and states into supporting Mother's Day resolutions. Finally, in 1914, seeing a mom-and-apple-pie no-brainer political decision, the U.S. Congress passed a bill making Mother's Day a national holiday. President Woodrow Wilson signed it into law. The holiday became one of the most-celebrated—who could be against motherhood?—today inspiring the sending of more than 10 million bouquets of flowers and 150 million greeting cards. Restaurants and long-distance carriers both report that it is their busiest day of the year.

However, Jarvis did not wring much happiness out of the holiday she created. Upset by the commercialization of what she had visualized as a religious holiday, she found each Mother's Day a painful mockery of her life and ideals. Heartbroken by a disastrous love affair, she remained unmarried and childless and became a recluse. Jarvis died poverty-stricken and alone at age 88 in 1948.

SEE YOU IN SEPTEMBER

What month has the highest birthrate?

SEPTEMBER. Blame it on the high spirits, and the high *consumption* of spirits, nine months earlier, during the holiday season.

PILGRIMS' PROGRESS

Can you give me the unvarnished version of the first Thanksgiving?

THE PILGRIMS left England and then Holland because they believed that modern society was a threat to their strict views of Christianity and morality. In 1620, they journeyed across the Atlantic to Massachusetts. The trip was financed by a group of English investors called the Merchant Adventurers, who agreed to pay the Pilgrims' expenses in exchange for seven years of labor. On the *Mayflower,* the 41 Pilgrims called themselves "the Saints" and dubbed the 61 other passengers and members of the crew "the Strangers."

In the New World, the first winter was devastating, killing more than than 60 of the 102 Saints and Strangers who left England. The following March, a terrifying thing happened that all had been dreading: a Native American walked into their camp.

"Welcome," he said—in English—and introduced himself as Samoset. He'd learned some of the language from fishing crews who sailed the American coast. The next day he left and returned with an Indian named Squanto, who spoke even more fluent English. It turned out that Squanto had been kidnapped as a child and taken to Spain as a slave, but had escaped to England and eventually returned to his home village in America.

What percentage of American households eat turkey on Thanksgiving?
About 90%. That's 45 million turkeys.

Squanto taught the Pilgrims how to plant corn, tap sugar maples, and identify edible, medicinal, and poisonous native plants. The Pilgrims started becoming self-sufficient and had a good harvest that year, and in gratitude invited Squanto and his tribe to a feast. That was the model for the modern Thanksgiving dinner.

Technically, the first Thanksgiving dinner came two years later. When the Pilgrims finally got some rain after a long drought, their governor, William Bradford, proclaimed it a day of thanks-giving.

After the American Revolution, a group proposed celebrating the Pilgrims' Thanksgiving, but Thomas Jefferson and others opposed the idea, saying that a tiny, starving community of ill-prepared religious fanatics was not an appropriate event to commemorate in a new and optimistic country. Finally, after a tireless 35-year crusade by a women's magazine editor named Sarah Josepha Hale, Abraham Lincoln issued a proclamation shortly after the battle of Gettysburg in 1863 setting aside the fourth Thursday in November as a national Day of Thanksgiving.

UPON A MIDNIGHT CLEAR

My birthday's on Christmas, and my uncle says that makes me a "kallikantzaroi". What does that mean?

THAT YOUR uncle is probably of Greek descent. The *kallikantzaroi* in Greek tradition are centaurs that show up in the middle of the night before Christmas to play malicious practical jokes. They aren't too clever. They'll do things like souring your cow's milk or braiding its tail, stealing your hen's eggs, or putting out your family's hearth fire by urinating on it. Part of the Greek folklore is that children born on Christmas may join the *kallikantzaroi* ranks, which is why your uncle is teasing you. Tell your uncle he can repel the pesky creatures, and perhaps you as well, by burning an old shoe and hanging a pig's jawbone on his door.

Is there anything good about being born on December 25?

TRUE, EVERYBODY forgets your birthday, but most European traditions hold that being born on Christmas makes you special. For example, it's said in parts of France that you'll have the gift of prophecy. In Russia, that you'll be witty, wise, and virtuous.

On the other hand, in parts of Poland, they believe that a child born on Christmas is likely to become either a thief or a lawyer. Be that as it may, you're in good company. Other Christmas babies include musicians Annie Lennox, Jimmy Buffett, Cab Calloway, Dean Martin, and Barbara Mandrell; actors Sissy Spacek, Charlie Chaplin, and Hattie McDaniel; Red Cross founder Clara Barton; physicist Isaac Newton; painter Joan Miró; and writer Rod Serling.

Was Jesus really born on December 25?

SOME HISTORIANS believe Jesus might have been born in the autumn. But in third-century Rome, the Christians were competing with other sects that had big winter solstice holidays. The Christians were worried that they were losing converts to the jollier sects, so they adopted as much as they could from the other groups' holidays into their Christmas celebrations: the birth of a god from the sun-king religion, Mithraism; feasts and parades from the worshippers of Saturn, god of agriculture; and lights and wreaths from the cult of Bacchus, the wine god. (Some people suggest that Bacchus inspired even more among the Christians: he was the son of a god and a mortal woman, had a halo, and his followers ate bread and wine to symbolize his body and blood—in fact, Bacchus' blood *was* wine.) By celebrating Christ's birth during other Roman holidays, the persecuted sect was less conspicuous and authorities were less alert. Eventually the pagan traditions became associated with Christmas as the other sects were persecuted to extinction when the Christians took power in Rome.

Why did the English once put holly on their beehives at Christmas?

FOR MANY centuries, Christians took pains during the Christmas holiday to honor their two-, four-, and (in this case) six-legged friends. This was based on the belief that Jesus was born surrounded by friendly animals. The English thought that if they decorated hives, the bees inside would hum Christmas carols. In Spain, Christians pampered cows on Christmas for warming the baby Jesus in the manger. In the Tyrol Alps, villagers whistled on their way home from church for the birds' benefit. And in the German Alps, people would sneak into their barns at midnight Christmas Eve in the hope of catching the animals talking.

PUTTING THE X BACK IN XMAS

How did "Xmas" come to stand for Christmas?

IT IS EASY to assume, as many evangelists have, that *Xmas* comes from the secularization of the holiday by nonbelievers, commercial interests, and humanists. In reality, though, the "X" in Xmas descends from the Greek letter *chi*. This letter has stood for "Christ" among Christians since about A.D. 1100, and words like *Xmas* and *Xianity* have been used since about A.D. 1550.

PUTTING THE $ BACK IN CHRITMA

Where can I find this year's Nieman-Marcus His-and-Hers Christmas Gift?

OH YES, the ultimate token gift for the hard-to-buy-for. Recent years have included matching his-and-her hot-air balloons ($6,850 each), camels ($4,125 each), Chinese junks ($11,500), robots ($15,000), mini-submarines ($7,500), windmills ($16,000), and, in the 1970s recession, a modern-day Noah's ark complete with international servants ($588,247). If you want to view a video of this year's gift, try the Nieman-Marcus Web site: *www.neimanmarcus.com/*

> About how many Christmas cards are sent each year in the United States? Three billion.

BAH, HUMBUG!

Did Jesus' followers celebrate his birth when he was alive?

NO. IN FACT, for 200 years after the birth of Jesus, the early Christians did not celebrate Christmas at all—the church announced that it would be sinful to celebrate his birth "as if he were a pharaoh." Railing against "the long Eating, hard Drinking, lewd Gaming and mad Mirth of Christmas," the Puritans in England and America followed the same course in 1643: they made it a crime to sing Christmas carols, possess a Christmas tree, bake mince pies, or even hold Christmas church services.

Is there any Christian group that doesn't celebrate Christmas?

YES, THE Jehovah's Witnesses, for one. They don't celebrate any holiday that isn't specifically sanctioned in the Bible. Jesus told his disciples at the Last Supper to remember his death, so the Witnesses do that only.

BLUE CHRISTMAS
Doesn't December have the highest number of suicides?

NO, THAT'S a popular misconception. It's true that many people go through a seasonal depression around the winter holidays for reasons as diverse as sad memories and shortened daylight. Still, statistics show that December and January have the *lowest* rates of suicide. In fact, studies indicate that suicides decline markedly a few days before any holiday. Although the rate goes up slightly after the holiday, it isn't enough to equal out the earlier dip.

So what month has the highest rate of suicide? April. In some years, there is also a measurable rise in suicides in late summer and early fall.

ALSO KNOWN AS "MARY CHRISTMAS" AND "CHRISTMAS CAROL"
Why "Santa" Claus? Isn't Santa Spanish for "female saint"?

BLAME THE dutch and early New Yorkers for the confusion. The Dutch called Saint Nicholas "Sint Nikolass." When they colonized what is now New York City, the hard-edged New Amsterdam accent rendered it "Sinterklass." When the Dutch were driven out by the English and high rents, the name was Anglicized to "Santa Claus."

AND TO ALL A GOOD NIGHT
Why does my copy of " 'Twas the Night Before Christmas" say it's written by "Anonymous" when the author is Clement Moore?

FOR A LONG time, the author wouldn't admit he wrote it. Here's the story: Dr. Clement Clarke Moore, a classics scholar, wrote the poem in 1822 simply for the fun of reading it to his children on Christmas Eve. A family friend—without asking for permission or crediting an author—mailed a copy of it to a newspaper, which printed it. Other newspapers picked it up, then magazines and anthologies—but no one knew who wrote it. Within a few years, nearly every child in America knew the still-anonymous poem by heart, and Moore's vision of Santa—from reindeer to jolly fat man coming down chimneys—became America's vision as well.

It wasn't until 1838 that Moore admitted having written it. Why did he hold back and forfeit years of author royalties? As a serious scholar, he feared that having written a popular child's poem might set him up for ridicule in the cutthroat academic world and damage his professional reputation.

REINDEER GAMES

Who created Rudolph the Red-Nosed Reindeer?

AN ADVERTISING writer for the Montgomery Ward department store. Store management wanted something unusual to distribute to shoppers during the 1939 Christmas season, and one of its writers, Robert May, suggested an illustrated poem for children. Everybody knew about Santa's eight fly-

> **Where can I find all the words to the song "Rudolph the Red-Nosed Reindeer"?**

ing reindeer from Clement Moore's poem (see previous question) but some wondered how Santa flew in rain and fog. To Robert May, the question suggested a ninth reindeer—one who could provide illumination with his nose on stormy nights.

In his first draft, May called him Rollo the Red-Nosed Reindeer. The Montgomery Ward people loved the poem, but not the name . . . or the next name, Reginald. So May compiled a list of names starting with R and read them to his four-year-old daughter. When he came to Rudolph, she smiled, and so did May's corporate bosses, who then distributed 2.4 million copies of the illustrated booklet to their stores around the country.

In 1947, one of May's friends with musical aspirations, Johnny Marks, put the poem to music and started shopping it around. Singer after singer turned it down. Finally Marks sent it to an over-the-hill cowboy movie star named Gene Autry, who decided he had nothing to lose in recording it. In the Christmas season of 1949, the record flew like a reindeer to the top of the charts. Since then, more than 300 different artists have recorded it in dozens of languages, selling close to 100 million copies of the song and spawning both a popular animated TV special and another element in the ever-growing Santa Claus mythology.

SEVEN CANDLES

Can you explain Kwanzaa? What religion is it?

KWANZAA was designed as a nonreligious holiday for African-Americans. It promotes coming together with others to better oneself, one's family, and one's community. For seven days, beginning on December 26, celebrants light a candle on the menorah-like *kinara* and honor one of the principles of the holiday: *Umoja* (unity), *Kujichagulia* (self-determination), *Ujima* (collective work and responsibility), *Ujamaa* (cooperative economics), *Nia* (purpose), *Kuumba* (creativity), and *Imani* (faith).

Kwanzaa was invented in 1966 by Ron Karenga while a student at the University of California, Los Angeles. He gave the holiday's ritual components Swahili names. "I could not have predicted the success of Kwanzaa," he said in an interview, "but I certainly wanted it to grow and be something beautiful." The Swahili word *kwanza* (with one "a") means "first."

To find out more about Kwanzaa, go to www.rats2u.com/ christmas/kwanzaa_index.htm

Wasn't Kwanzaa once controversial?

YES. IT HAS been controversial in large part because of its founder. In the 1960s, Ron Karenga, who now goes by the first name Maulana ("master teacher" in Swahili), was the leader of a student black nationalist group at UCLA. The group, known as US (United Slaves), was involved in a bloody rivalry with the local chapter of the Black Panthers. In 1969, US members were convicted of killing two Panthers in the UCLA cafeteria. Two years later, Karenga himself was convicted of assaulting a female US member.

Since then, Karenga has become a professor of black studies at California State University and is a promoter of an Afrocentric educational curriculum. Because of Karenga's history and Kwanzaa's origins, a number of African-Americans have mixed feelings about the holiday.

WALTZING ROUND THE BILLABONG

Does Australia Day commemorate when the country won independence from England?

NO, THE JANUARY 26 holiday celebrates the arrival of the first shipload of British convicts to Australia in 1788. When America gained its independence from England, the crown could no longer use its Virginia penal colonies, so it began shipping prisoners to Australia. From these captive men and thousands more like them, cast adrift because England didn't want to go to the expense of building more prisons, the Australian nation arose.

What do Australians do on Christmas?

SINCE IT'S the summer solstice there at that time of year, the traditions are a little different. First of all, the Christmas decorations end up on a gum tree instead of a pine. Furthermore, going surfing and eating holiday ham and turkey roasted on the backyard barbie are two traditions that don't happen on Christmas in most other places. Finally, Santa appears as the "Christmas Swag Man" in a cross-country jeep.

PAGAN LOVE CALL

Why are some Christian holiday traditions adopted from other religions?

MANY OF OUR Christmas, Easter, and Halloween/All Saints Day traditions are the result of a brilliant bit of marketing by Pope Gregory I in A.D. 601. He recognized that Christian missionaries were having trouble getting converts when they attacked the local religious traditions head-on. Gregory suggested adopting the local beliefs and customs into the Christian liturgy instead of trying to wipe

Where can I find a comprehensive list of holidays around the world?

them out. For example, if the locals worshipped trees and eggs, it was easier to bring those objects into the Christmas tradition than to convince the locals to give up their beliefs. Missionaries even made up church holidays to compete with the holidays of a local religion—for example, All Saints Day was invented by fourth-century missionaries to rival the Celtic holiday Samhain, and its mythology slyly designed to portray the rival Druid gods as devils, spirits, and witches.

EVERY DAY'S A HOLIDAY

When is National Peanut Month?

MARCH. It's also National Hamburger & Pickle Month and National Dandelion Month. Not to mention National Craft Month, Music in Our Schools Month, Women's History Month, National Foot Health Month, National Noodle Month, and Poetry Month. Don't ask us how you're supposed to celebrate.

Sports: The Play's the Thing

ENGAGING IN SPORTS IS BELIEVED by some to "build character," although no research supports that assertion. At the very least, the sports pages can attest to the fact that sports build characters, some merely eccentric, others downright scary. Still, where there are people, there will be competitive play. So, with an apology to a major television network, let's take a look at the wide world of sports. . . .

AMERICAN GLADIATORS

What sports originated in the United States?

THERE ARE at least three:

- Basketball (see page 123).

- Volleyball, invented in Holyoke, Massachusetts, by William Morgan in 1895, for sedentary businessmen who found the new sport of basketball too strenuous.

- Rodeo, first formalized as a sport in Prescott, Arizona.

What are the top three favorite sports in the United States?

THE THREE most popular sports to participate in are walking, swimming, and cycling. The top three to watch are baseball, football, and basketball.

HORSING AROUND

What sporting event lasts about two minutes, yet is watched by millions of people every year?

NO, IT ISN'T the Super Bowl minus the commercials. It's the Kentucky Derby. Limited to three-year-old horses only, the 1⅓-mile race is attended every year by 130,000 julep-sipping spectators and watched by millions on television.

In terms of actual paid attendance, what is the most popular sport in the world?

Horse racing.

What is a polo ball made of?

TRADITIONALLY the 3- to 3½-inch ball is made of willow root, but hard plastic has made significant inroads in the game. For indoor polo, players bat around an inflated leather ball 4½ inches in diameter.

NO BULL

Is bullfighting illegal in the United States?

NO . . . AS LONG as the matador does not harm or kill the bull. Detroit is one city that has featured bloodless bullfighting, bringing in some of the best Spanish and Mexican bullfighters to demonstrate their skills, speed, and courage without doing overt harm to the animals.

ON THE REBOUND

What is the sport that requires the fastest reflexes?

JAI ALAI. Thrown with a curved wicker *cesta*, the rubber-and-goatskin ball can rebound at a speed more than twice as fast as a baseball pitcher's fastball—as fast as 188 miles per hour. Getting hit by one can be fatal. Between 1920 and 1967 (when helmets were introduced) at least four players were killed by jai alai balls to the head.

Why can't left-handers play jai alai?

THEY CAN—as long as they're willing to use their right hands. The rules and traditions specifically forbid playing left-handed. The reason is that the court has only three walls—one at each end and a side wall on the left against which the ball can be rebounded. Spectators sit behind a chain-link fence on the fourth side. Because of the side wall on the left, it would be dangerous and almost impossible for players

> **Where can I find the official rules for jai alai?**

to throw and catch with their left hands. On the other hand (so to speak), if two left-handers wanted to play each other, they could probably just reverse the front and back walls. However, for the time being, lefties are banned from playing the game.

DIAMONDS ARE FOREVER

Who invented baseball?

DESPITE A MYTH invented and heartily spread by early baseball promoters, the game was not invented by Abner Doubleday one day in Cooperstown, New York. In fact, it wasn't exactly invented at all. It evolved from the British games of cricket and rounders (sometimes called "base ball" years ago in England).

By the early 1800s, a few American variations on the two games had already sprung up with nicknames like "town ball" and "one old cat—two old cat—three old cat." In 1845, Alexander Cartwright drew up some rules for his New York Knickerbocker Base Ball Club. He was the one who arbitrarily fixed the diamond size at 90 feet square and put the batter at home plate instead of at a special batters' box nearby. He also ruled out the deadly practice of "plugging" base runners—hitting them with a thrown ball to get them out. But even after Cartwright, the game had quite a bit of evolving to do before it closely resembled the game we know today.

I was watching the video of A League of Their Own and saw a player catch a fly ball with her baseball cap. Is this legal?

NO. YOU HAVE to catch a ball with only your glove or your hand. Major league rules specifically prohibit using your cap, protection pads, pocket, or any other part of your uniform in assisting a catch.

I've got a bet with a buddy: What's the highest-scoring game in professional baseball history?

26–23. In an excruciatingly long game on a hot summer day on August 25, 1922, the Chicago Cubs finally beat the Philadelphia Phillies by a mere three runs.

How many ways can a batter get on base without hitting the ball?

SIX. MOST people know about walking after being pitched four balls or being hit by a ball. But, according to the official rule book, you also get an automatic ticket to first base if the catcher drops the third strike; if the catcher interferes while you are trying to bat; if a pitched ball or one thrown in order to catch a man on base "goes into a stand or a bench, or over or through a field fence or back- stop"; or if, on what would have been either ball four or strike three, a pitch "passes the catcher and lodges in the umpire's mask or paraphernalia."

> **What's got 18 legs and catches flies?**
> That's an easy one: a baseball team.

As a dedicated sofa spud, I want to know: What was the first sports event that appeared on TV?

WHILE YOU'RE UP, could you get me some sushi and a Sapporo? The first televised sporting event was a baseball game between Ushigome and Awazi Shichiku higher elementary schools, battling it out on the Tozuka Baseball Grounds in Japan. It was September 27, 1931, a day that will live in infamy.

Who won the first World Series?

THE BOSTON PILGRIMS. After a two-year contractual dispute between the American League and the National League, resulting in no postseason play, 16,000 eager fans showed up to watch the first ball tossed in the first-ever World Series on October 1, 1903. Thirteen

> **Where can I find scores for all the World Series?**

days later, the National League's Pilgrims won a 3–0 victory over the favored Pittsburgh Pirates. Although the Pilgrims have been known under several different names—the Americans, the Puritans, even the Plymouth Rocks—we know them today as the Red Sox.

Whatever happened to Shoeless Joe Jackson after the 1919 World Series scandal?

JOE JACKSON and eight other White Sox players were accused of throwing the 1919 World Series against Cincinnati, and were thrown out of baseball forever—even though they were acquitted of criminal charges. For 10 years afterward, Jackson, one of the best baseballers ever, played semipro around the country under various assumed names. When he returned to his hometown of Greenville, South Carolina, he managed local teams for several years, occasionally pinch-hitting into his 50s. One admirer recalled seeing him—at age 56 and after the first of several heart attacks—smash a ball against a center-field fence 415 feet away. Jackson's wife, Katie, finally taught him to read, and they opened a liquor store that made them prosperous. In 1951, Jackson died, surrounded by family, shoeless no more.

Is there anything about Shoeless Joe Jackson in baseball's Hall of Fame?

IRONICALLY, Shoeless Joe's shoes are exhibited there.

I have a baseball card from the mid-1950s for a player from the "Cincinnati Redlegs." Is that the same as the Cincinnati Reds or was that a mistake by the Topps company?

THE TEAM was originally called the Red Stockings in 1869, but the name changed to the Reds not long after. However, during the anti-Communist witch hunts of the 1950s, a timid ball club decided "Reds" was a name that they didn't want to have to defend to the House Un-American Activities Committee and Joe McCarthy, so they switched to the Redlegs for a few years. As the political hysteria settled down and the country came back to its senses, the club quietly switched its name back to the Reds.

Is it true that the authors of the song "Take Me Out to the Ballgame" had never seen a baseball game?

IT'S TRUE. Vaudevillian Jack Norworth wrote the words in 1908 after seeing a sign on a bus advertising BASEBALL TODAY—POLO GROUNDS. His friend Albert von Tilzer wrote the music. It wasn't until the song became a big sing-along hit that either of them bothered going to "root root root for the home team." Incidentally, while almost everybody knows the chorus, almost nobody knows the verses. Here's the first one to get you started:

> Katie Casey was baseball mad
> Had the fever and had it bad.
> Just to root for the hometown crew,
> Every sou, Katie blew,
> On a Saturday her young beau
> Called to see if she'd like to go
> To see a show but Miss Kate said, "No
> I'll tell you what you can do—
> Take me out to the ball game. . . . "

Who pitched a no-hitter while tripping on LSD?

THIS IS ONE of the stranger stories of the 1960s psychedelic culture. Pittsburgh Pirate pitcher Dock Ellis thought he had a few days off and decided to take LSD. (In that era, this sort of thing was not a completely uncommon occurrence.) Unfortunately, a few hours after taking the mind-altering drug, he got a call informing him that he was pitching that night in a doubleheader against the San Diego Padres. With trepidation, he got himself to the ball park and started warming up.

> **What are *all* the words to "Take Me Out to the Ball Game"?**

Not surprisingly, a strange thing happened. He believed the ball was talking to him, telling him what pitches to throw. "I can only remember bits and pieces of the game," he admitted years later. "I had a feeling of euphoria. I was psyched." Afterward, he didn't dare admit what he'd done, and he never pitched on LSD again. Years later, after his 11-year pitching career was over, he was treated for drug dependency and became the head of an anti-drug program in Los Angeles.

RUGBY, FOOTBALL'S TOUGHER OLDER BROTHER

Does the game of rugby have anything to do with the town of Rugby, North Dakota?

EVEN THOUGH Rugby, North Dakota, is the geographic center of the United States, and therefore (you'd think) the world, it has absolutely nothing to do with the English game of rugby.

What's a scrummage? Is it the same as a scrimmage?

SCRUMMAGE isn't exactly the same thing as scrimmage from American football—in fact, you could call it the father of scrimmage. The two—scrummage and scrimmage—are similar in that they take place at the start of a play, but that is where the similarity ends.

In football, each side lines up face-to-face on either side of the line of scrimmage, while rugby's scrummage requires a circle: the eight forwards of both teams pack together in a tight knot with their arms across one another's shoulders and their heads down. Meanwhile, the rest of the players on both teams line up behind their forwards. When an official throws the rugby ball into the center of the circle, the linked players try to push forward and hook the ball backward with their feet, passing it to their team members behind them. For this reason, they're called "hookers in the scrum" (and you in the back there, wipe that silly smirk off your face). Those players can then kick, run, or pass the ball with the hope of eventually getting it over the other team's goal line.

Is a loosehead prop a type of single-engine plane?
No, it's a rugby position.

Rugby is a chaotic game with no substitutions, and there is a great amount of injury involved. However, it's also a game in which good sportsmanship is highly valued—opposing teams often retire arm-in-arm to a pub afterward, but not before giving a heartfelt, "Hip, hip, hooray!" to the officiating referees. Both are customs that American sports teams might do well to emulate.

How did the game of rugby start?

ACCORDING TO the most likely story, it originated with the actions of a renegade schoolboy playing football (soccer) at Rugby School in Warwickshire, England, in 1823. To the dumbfounded amazement of onlookers, a frustrated student on a badly losing team picked up the ball and ran for the goal. Of course, he was heavily penalized on the field and forced to write a letter of apology afterward. However, the idea of a game in which players kick or run with the ball was inspired by this simple act of defiance, and "Rugby-style football" eventually became just "rugby."

A historical marker at Rugby School reads:

This stone commemorates the exploit of William Webb Ellis, who, with a fine disregard for the rules of football, as played in his time, first took the ball in his arms and ran with it, thus originating the distinctive feature of the rugby game.

DAY IN COURT

Why are tennis balls fuzzy?

THE FUZZ is to slow the balls down. Tennis balls are made to exacting standards so players have a relatively decent chance of hitting them. The fuzz makes the ball softer and less bouncy and increases wind resistance. In addition, the fuzz adds to a player's racket control because the strings hold onto the surface of the ball longer.

What's the fuzz made of? Felt cut into two shapes that look like peanuts or figure-eights. When glued together, they cover the hollow rubber core of the ball completely and give it that distinctive look.

Why is the game called "badminton" and not "goodminton"?

BADMINTON was invented in the 1860s by the daughters of the Duke of Beaufort, based loosely on an ancient game called "battledore and shuttlecock" and using the same equipment. It was named after their dad's summer mansion, Badminton House in Gloucestershire, England, where they first played it. The dimensions of the modern official badminton court, 44 feet long and 17 feet wide, reportedly match those of the room where the young women developed the game.

Does anybody actually play badminton seriously—like for money?

YES, ALTHOUGH badminton, from its founding, had the reputation of being a sport for members of the upper class who didn't want to work too strenuously. The feathery shuttlecock and net height were designed to encourage lobs and make slams nearly impossible. The first American badminton club, formed in New York City in 1878, specifically limited play to "men and good-looking single women." However, the International Badminton Federation—based not far from the game's birthplace in Gloucestershire (see previous question)—is doing its best to change that foppy image.

Formed in 1934, the IBF sponsors high-stakes championships for women, men, mixed couples, and children. The image upgrade seems to be working: badminton is now Malaysia's national sport and since 1992 has been a part of Olympic competition. According to the organization's Web site, the only thing the sport needs now is more and better media coverage: "In these days of mass communications, the importance of television to a world sport is self-evident. Television brings the action, the excitement, the explosive power of badminton into homes around the world." Jeeves couldn't have said it better himself.

Check out the IBF's Web page: www.intbadfed.org/

LAWN ORDER

What was croquet named after?

CROCHET, French for "hook." The French thought the game's wickets looked like the crochet hooks used for making laces and other items with string or yarn.

WORTH THEIR WEIGHT IN GOLD

Who was the biggest sumo wrestler of all time?

IF YOU'RE talking about *success,* it would be one of these three: Tameemon "Raiden" Torokichi, who had a 254–10 win-loss record in the 21 years from 1794 to 1815; Sadji "Futahayama" Akiyoshi, who had 69 consecutive wins in the 1930s; or Koki "Taiho" Naya, who won the Emperor's Cup 32 times before retiring in 1971.

However, if you're talking about *physical size,* then the hands-down winner would be Hawaiian-born Chad "Akebono" Rowan. The first non-Japanese to be promoted to the rank of *yokozuna* ("grand champion"), Rowan is 6'8" tall and 501 pounds—head, shoulders, and belly above his competitors.

Where can I see sumo matches online?

Why are sumo wrestlers so fat?

THE WRESTLERS typically weigh between 280 and 450 pounds. They work hard to achieve their heft and look over many years, by stuffing themselves with massive quantities of food and practicing a form of abdominal development called *haragei*, which distributes their bulk into an exceptional roundness. The idea is to have a great deal of weight and a low center of gravity. Why? Because there are only two ways to lose a sumo match: (1) have some body part other than your feet touch ground, or (2) be pushed out of the *dohyo*, a 12-foot ring on an earth-covered floor. As you can imagine, a bulky body will make it fairly hard for your opponent to move you while making it easier to throw your own weight around.

What are the weight classes for sumo wrestlers?

THERE ARE no weight classes. A light *sumotori* may end up wrestling another who is twice his weight. In that case, he has to hope his speed, skill, and reactions are enough to even out the weight advantage on the other side.

What is all that stuff that goes on before a sumo match?

EACH SUMO match is preceded by an elaborate ceremony based on Shintoist traditions. The judges file into the ring with attendants and sword bearers. Each official is supplied with a small ceremonial dagger, originally provided so that he could disembowel himself if he gave a miscall. They perform a short ritual and then sit in their places. Next come two groups of wrestlers whose near-nakedness is covered by richly embroidered aprons. Each group forms a circle, claps their hands, removes their aprons down to their thongs, and moves out of the way for the matches to begin.

What are the origins of sumo wrestling?
It was part of a religious service.

The matches themselves require yet more ceremony: The two opposing wrestlers flex their muscles and scatter handfuls of salt onto the earth-covered ring before crouching, pounding the floor with their fists, and engaging in a long staring contest, called *shikiri-naoshi,* which is meant to break the other's concentration. This lasts four minutes and includes stomping and ceremonial water drinking. Finally, the wrestlers charge against each other, flesh against flesh, each trying to knock the other to the ground or out of the ring by pushing, tripping, slapping, yanking, lifting, and grabbing. The actual wrestling takes much less time than the ceremonial preparations: anywhere from a few seconds to a few minutes. In the old days (about 2,000 years ago), a contest would often go on until one of the competitors killed the other.

CLASH OF THE TIGHT ENDS

What was the worst shut-out in football history?

IN 1916, Georgia Tech's football team edged out Cumberland University, 222–0. The Cumberland coach vowed, "Wait'll next year!"

Which competitive sport has the highest rate of injuries?

AMERICAN FOOTBALL. It has 12 times the injury rate of the next most injurious sport, basketball. The most common injuries in both sports are knee-related. Because of all the sudden stops and starts in high-friction shoes, two-thirds of all basketball injuries are to the knees. In football, knees are involved in one-third of the injuries.

Is it true that football was once nearly outlawed in the United States?

YES, IN 1909. Twenty-seven players died that year and hundreds more were permanently injured. Even gunfighter-turned-sportswriter Bat Masterson, no stranger to mayhem, was appalled. "Football is not a sport in any sense," he wrote. "It is a brutal and savage slugging match between two reckless opposing crowds. The rougher it is and the more killed and crippled, the more delighted are the spectators, who howl their heads off at the sight of a player stretched prone and unconscious on the hard and frozen ground."

An intercollegiate football rules committee was set up by Woodrow Wilson, then president of Princeton University. After five months, the committee issued its recommendations, prohibiting some of the most dangerous practices: diving tackles, blocking with linked arms, picking up and carrying ball carriers, and interfering with pass receivers. The death and injury rate dropped and most people supported the new changes—although some hardcore fans complained that the changes ruined the game forever.

> **Who invented the tackle dummy?**
> A divinity student at Yale.

What pro scored the most points ever in a single football season?

PAUL HORNUNG, with 176 points in 1960. This was largely because he was not only the Green Bay Packers' star halfback, but also kicked their field goals and extra points.

HOOPS AND DREAMS

There aren't any baskets, so why is it called "basket" ball?

DON'T COMPLAIN, it could have easily been called "box ball" or even "trash can ball." In 1891, when James Naismith was inventing the game for bored, snowbound students at a YMCA in Springfield, Massachusetts, he intended to use wooden boxes for his targets. But when he asked the custodian for boxes, there were none in any of the club's back rooms, so he ended up with two old peach baskets. Naismith nailed them on the balconies at either end of the gym, which happened to be 10 feet off the floor—which is why the game was first called "basket ball" and why 10 feet is the regulation height for baskets. When it became clear that the thin wood baskets weren't going to hold up for long, Naismith substituted wire trash cans, and then eventually the hoop and netting combination used today.

Where are the lakes that are referred to in the team name Los Angeles Lakers?

IN MINNESOTA. Los Angeles has a notable shortage of lakes compared to other cities—it's in a desert, after all. When the team was formed in 1948, it was in Minneapolis, in the "land of a thousand lakes." When the team got relocated to Los Angeles in 1960, the new owners didn't bother changing its name. As a result, generations of basketball fans have labored under the misimpression that Los Angeles has lakes. No wonder school kids have trouble with geography.

WHERE SAND TRAPS POSE NO THREAT

How many golf balls are on the moon?

TWO. Alan Shepard hit them both but he neither played them where they lay nor picked them up afterward.

What are the rules for "ice golf"?

IT REALLY depends on the golf course and the people you're playing with. Playing in snowdrifts and subzero temperatures usually requires a certain flexibility when applying the rules. In Greenland's World Ice Championship, for example, the rules are the same as for regular golf, with a few exceptions:

1. Players are allowed to sweep their putting lines clean with a broom on the "whites" (there are no greens in winter golf).

2. Balls on the fairway can be played off rubber tees, while balls in the rough can be moved a few inches without penalty if otherwise unplayable.

3. The holes are twice the size of a standard golf cup.

4. Although not mandatory, purple or yellow optic balls are encouraged.

5. Finally, the starting tee is moved a third of the way up the fairway for winter golf, because subzero temperatures freeze the balls solid and thus make any golf shot 30% shorter than it would be in shirtsleeve weather.

Where's a good place to play "ice golf"?

ONE OF THE best locations—with rustic cabins, a nine-hole course in the Arctic Circle, and reindeer pulling sleds as caddies—is the Arvidsjaur Wintergolf Course in northern Sweden, open annually from February to April. According to its English-language literature:

> The 9-hole course is partly located on a lake. It's prepared with a mobile pist machine to make the ice more frictional. The result will be a surface with similar qualities as grass. This unique method, developed by the local organizers, in combination with the Lapland climate and thick lake ice, has created the best ice golf course in the world.

Maybe so, but Jeeves suggests watching out for that "mobile pist machine."

For more information and pictures of the reindeer caddies, check out the Web site www.northerner.com/icegolf.html

RIGHT UP YOUR ALLEY

Why does bowling now have 10 pins when it used to have 9?

BOWLING historians swear that it's because of anti-bowling laws in colonial America. An 18th-century Connecticut ordinance forbade "bowling at nine-pins." To avoid being put in jail or the stocks, players added an extra pin to the game and called

| What is "vertical moves" in bowling? | |

it . . . ten-pins. The strategy seemed to have had the desired effect, because it's ten-pins we still play today.

I GET A KICK OUT OF YOU

Who has scored the most goals in soccer?

THE LEGENDARY player Pelé. Born Edson Arantes do Nascimento, the native Brazilian scored 1,281 goals in 1,363 games in a 21-year career. He retired from the Brazilian team in 1974. Then, in 1975, the New York Cosmos lured him out of retirement with a $4.5 million contract, making him at the time the highest paid athlete ever. He retired a second and last time in 1977.

GOALIES AND THEIR PUCKISH HUMOR

Did Canadians invent ice hockey?

SORT OF. Similar stick-and-ball games, with balls and without ice, were played by ancient Egyptians, Greeks, Arabs, Romans, and Persians. A precursor called hurley was developed by the Irish more than 2,000 years ago, and native South Americans had a similar game when Columbus arrived in 1492. However, the dubious idea of playing the game while hurtling wildly about on ice skates took a special kind of crackpot genius you'd expect to find only among extremely bored soldiers in a wintry clime.

And so it was: British soldiers stationed in Canada in the mid-1850s came up with the basics of ice hockey, and the rules were refined and set down by students at McGill University in Quebec in 1879. The name comes from the old French word for a shepherd's crook, *hoquet*. By the beginning of the 20th century, the sport had spread to the United States and Europe. In 1917, professional players formed the National Hockey League.

Where was the first professional hockey league formed?
In the U.S.

Who is this Stanley that the Stanley Cup is named for?

HE WAS Frederick Arthur, who had the title Lord Stanley of Preston in England. Arthur was Queen Victoria's governor-general of Canada when the country was still a British colony. His son played hockey and the lord was a fan. As the governor-general finished his term in 1893, he presented the trophy to Canada for its amateur hockey champions. In 1910, the trophy became the property of the National Hockey Association. When the NHA became the NHL, the Stanley Cup went pro too.

What are the mascots for the Sydney Olympic games?

OLYMPIC DREAMS

For how many centuries have the Olympic Games been held?

IN THEIR latest incarnation, only a little more than one century. They were started in 1896 by a French educator and sportsman, Pierre de Coubertin, who was inspired by the games held in ancient Greece. In their original heyday, from about 776 B.C. until A.D. 393, the Olympics drew athletes from more than 100 Greek cities. The games were abolished by the Roman emperor Theodosius I. A Christian, he apparently objected to them because of their pagan origins and ceremonies.

What were the original Olympic sports in Greece?

AT THE VERY first Olympics, in 776 B.C., there was only one event: a one-kilometer foot race down the center of the Olympia stadium. From there, the one-day, one-event spectacular expanded to a seven-day extravaganza with more foot races, the discus throw, the javelin throw, the long jump, boxing, wrestling, the pentathlon, chariot races, and more. All athletes competed naked, and women were not allowed to compete or attend. For applause, spectators showed their approval by snorting and smacking their lips.

What famous people have competed in the Olympics, beyond the usual athletes?

GEORGE PATTON competed in the 1912 pentathlon. He didn't win anything. Baby doctor Benjamin Spock competed in the 1924 rowing competitions. He didn't win anything, either. Alfred C. Gilbert, inventor of Erector Sets, co-won the 1908 gold medal in pole vaulting. In A.D. 66, Emperor Nero competed in the chariot races. Since he had unlimited power and a nasty temper, the other contestants wisely let him win. Princess Anne of England was not as lucky when she competed in horse events in 1976: she lost the competition. However, she was the only female athlete that year who was not forced to take a gender test.

Which of our modern Olympic traditions came from the ancient Olympics?

VERY FEW. The five rings and the Olympic torch, for example, were the brainchildren of the spectacle-loving Nazi regime that sponsored the 1936 Olympics in Berlin.

The French baron who started the modern games in 1896, Pierre de Coubertin, hoped that the games would promote peace and that the world would follow a legendary and perhaps mythical tradition of the ancient games: battles would stop to allow the games to go on. Instead, the half-century after the founding of the games was the bloodiest ever, and during both world wars, the Olympics were canceled instead of the wars. The only nonathletic tradition carried over from the ancient games is the spectacle of commercial gain by winning athletes and their sponsors. Then, as now, they were lionized and often made rich.

Under the Big Top

LADIES AND GENTLEMEN! Children of all ages! Step right up and learn about the fascinating world of the circus.

THERE'S A SUCKER BORN EVERY MINUTE

What were P. T. Barnum's most famous exhibits?

HIS TOP four exhibits were General Tom Thumb, a midget, whose real name was Charles Sherwood Stratton; Jumbo, an extremely large elephant bought from the London Zoo; the FeeJee Mermaid, a female orangutan sewed to the body of a salmon; and the famous Siamese twins, Chang and Eng, who were joined at the chest.

For an online look at the P. T. Barnum Museum in Bridgeport, Connecticut, point your browser to www.barnum-museum.org/

Who said, "There's a sucker born every minute"?

IT IS POPULARLY attributed to showman P. T. Barnum, but there is no evidence that he ever said it. On the other hand, Barnum *is* responsible for coining many other well-known phrases and terms. "Jumbo" was the name of the huge elephant in his sideshow act, and the name came to represent anything oversized. "Grandstand" referred to the more prominent seats in the

> **Where can I find out about sideshow exhibits?**

stands and is now used as a verb meaning to attempt to impress an audience. Other Barnum phrases include "Siamese twins," "let's get the show on the road," and "rain or shine."

FEW BROTHERS ARE THIS CLOSE

What was life like for Siamese twins Chang and Eng?

CHANG AND ENG (their names mean "left" and "right" in Thai) were three-quarters Chinese and one-quarter Thai. Born conjoined at the chest, they grew up just outside Bangkok with their mother and their father, a Chinese fisherman. A British merchant "bought" them from their mother to show to the Western medical community. When that didn't bring in the desired revenue, the twins were shown to sideshow audiences in Europe and the United States. They were marketed as "Siamese twins" because they were from Siam, now known as Thailand. Thanks to P. T. Barnum, this name became synonymous with "conjoined twins."

Is Monty Python's Flying Circus online?
Yes. See www.pythonline.com/

The twins made enough money in the sideshow circuit to buy a tobacco farm in North Carolina, and like most other southern farmers in the mid-1800s, they owned slaves. Not long after they bought their farm, they married twin sisters and caused a big uproar in the press with speculations about their bedroom lives—especially when they quickly began the process of siring 21 children, 10 by Chang and his wife, Adelaide, and 11 by Eng and his wife, Sarah. When money got tight, they'd return to touring under the name Chang and Eng Bunker.

How did Chang and Eng die?

CHANG AND ENG were joined together by a thick ligament that looked like a third arm. Their heartbeats were different;

when one drank, the other remained sober; when one fell ill, the other often did not. Still, at that time, the doctors couldn't be sure how many (if any) internal organs they shared, so there was simply no guarantee that they would survive if they were separated. When Chang

Where can I see different types of clowns?

had a stroke in the 1870s and lost the use of the side closest to his brother, Eng had to lie beside him during recovery.

Chang, always the weaker of the twins, came down with bronchitis in 1874 and passed away while they were sleeping. Eng was terrified upon waking, saying, "Then I am going!" After suffering through shakes and pains, Eng, too, died. An autopsy revealed that Eng didn't die because of the disease that killed Chang. Tragically, he died of fright from thinking there was no way to survive the death of his brother.

CLASS CLOWN

How do I get a job as a clown in the circus?

MOST ENTERTAINERS—clowns and contortionists alike—start out in circus families: they learn their skills early and well and are graduated into performing. Still, it's not impossible to break into the business even if your rearing was less than ideal. The first thing you need to do is acquire the necessary skills, and a good place to start is a school for the circus arts. Today the Ringling Bros. and Barnum & Bailey Clown College offers two-month summer sessions teaching basic acrobatics, juggling, face painting, and theatrics. Competition is tight, though, and you have to agree to work for Ringling Bros. in low-pay servitude for a while if they want you. (They usually take only one in ten potential clowns, but your name is on their call list for several years.)

Where can I learn circus arts like juggling and trapeze?

THE FOLLOWING site lists courses that are available to people wanting to learn juggling, theater, and other circus skills:

www.juggling.org/help/circus-arts/courses/us.html. Or check out the well-known San Francisco School of Circus Arts, which teaches skills to all kinds of circus performers: *www.sfcircus.org/*

Is a hobo-type circus character also considered a "clown" or is it called something different?

A CIRCUS HOBO is also a clown, although clowns are classified into three categories. The first—and highest up in the social hierchy—is the White Face clown; the painted clown like Bozo. Second is the Auguste clown—flesh tones are used to paint the face; this clown is usually the fall-guy clown who escapes at the last moment. Last comes the Character clown—distinguished by a black painted-on beard. Tramps and hobos fall in the last category. Other Character clowns can include policemen, women, and sometimes babies, all with heavy five o'clock shadows.

> **What size shoe does Bozo the Clown wear?**
> 83AAA

Is it true that clowns register their faces so nobody else can copy the design?

TO PROTECT against theft of idea and business, any clown can register their face with the National Clown and Character Registry (cost: about $20), sort of a trademark locale for clowns. A clown sends photos of his or her made-up face and a replica is painted onto a goose egg for archive purposes. Registration forms and instructions can be found online at *www.webclowns.com/tomeboy/national.htm*

A LEOTARD CAN'T CHANGE ITS SPOTS

Why is a leotard called a leotard?

THE TERM comes from the inventor of the flying trapeze, Jules Leotard. He wore a peculiar costume in the mid-1800s to perform his aerial stunts. His tight, one-piece outfit made it easier for him to accomplish dazzling, death-defying flips and jumps. When other performers adopted the costume, it was so associated with Leotard that the name stuck.

THE SHOW MUST GO ON

How dangerous is it to be shot out of a cannon?

QUITE DANGEROUS. A lot of people have been killed performing this circus act. The danger doesn't come from an explosion, though. Like so many acts, there is more to it than meets the eye. Compressed air is what really catapults the performer out of the cannon and into the air. The explosion that you hear is a large firecracker being set off simultaneously for effect. Most injuries occur because the person misses the safety net. This can happen when there is a misfire or because the jolt of the launch knocks the performer unconscious.

How do trainers tame lions?

IN THE 1960S, while earlier lion tamers could get big cats to do tricks, David Hoover of the Clyde Beatty Circus, was the first to train the "Total Lion." Hoover brought a philosophy to lion taming that gave credence to an individual lion's set of fears and motivations. Sound complicated and a little too touchy-feely? Simply put: Each lion responds to different stimuli in different ways. If one lion shows a distaste for the sound of spoons clinking together, the trainer should use that to continuously break up that lion's concentration. If pointy kitchen chairs do the trick

Where can I see circus posters online?

with another lion, then the trainer has his instrument of choice for that particular lion. The sound of a whip is a useful tool for many big cats, which is why it is a common sight within the lions' cage at the circus. Why do they want to break concentration? Because a thinking lion is a dangerous lion, in that most cats' thought process goes something like: "A moving thing! Food! Ready? Pounce! Tear! Eat!"

Primarily, Hoover believes, a trainer must never let a lion know how powerful it is. If that happens, no amount of training will work. Hoover says that the well-trained cat *believes* that it can't hurt its trainer, so that even if a trainer is hurt while handling the lion, he or she should not leave the cage quickly—this would let on to the lion that it holds power over the trainer. If that happens, "you can't handle that animal anymore," claimed Hoover.

How do sword swallowers make it look like they're swallowing swords?

BY ACTUALLY swallowing them. There's no illusion to this favorite sideshow. The swallower must learn to relax the throat muscles long enough to get the sword down—no easy feat.

The swords they use are very dull, but the tips must be allowed for—not only is there some risk to hitting the bottom of the stomach, but nicking the sides of the throat, esophagus, or stomach is also a possibility. This is not a safe pastime. It takes a lot of skill, and even the pros get hurt doing it.

What is a doniker?
It's circus talk for "toilet."

What were those organ things in circus parades?

CALLIOPES. A calliope is a sort of steam-powered organ that sounds like a set of tuned teapots. The boiler inside the machine generates steam, and the pressure makes the shrill whistle sound. But steam-operated devices sometimes blow up and calliopes were no exception. To reduce injury as much as possible, they were placed at the end of the circus parade.

To see pictures of calliopes or listen to calliope music, try these Web pages: www.calliopes.com/; www.mybonbon.com/bandorgan.htm; www.carousels.com/muscat.htm

CIRCUS PERFORMER BITES DOG, DETAILS AT 11:00

What are flea circuses, exactly? A joke?

WELL, A JOKE maybe, but not a hoax. Flea circuses really do exist. By using the insects' natural response to certain stimuli, people are able to "train," or condition, them to move in certain directions or to jump. Add a few props and a lot of stage talk, and you have an entire show. Admittedly, it is hard for fleas to hold anyone's

Where can I find a glossary of circus slang?

attention for very long, and because they are so tiny, only a few people can really watch at once. In the flea circus heyday—from the 1830s to the 1930s—owners would host up to six short street shows an hour.

Flea circuses are still alive and well today. For details, see www.trainedfleas.com/

AND NOW FOR SOMETHING COMPLETELY DIFFERENT

What other names were considered for "Monty Python's Flying Circus"?

OTHER NAMES considered for the popular BBC program included "Owl-Stretching Time"; "A Horse, a Spoon, and a Basin"; "Bunn, Wackett, Buzzard, Stubble and Boot"; "The Toad Elevating Moment"; and "Gwen Dibley's Flying Circus" (named after Michael Palin's boyhood piano teacher).

This Land Is Your Land

EARTHQUAKES, MOUNTAINS, LAKES, and streams; islands, tourist traps, and dreams. Some of the most intriguing questions asked Jeeves regard the great blue ball we call Earth.

MERRIE OLDE ENGLAND

What does "started at pudding and ended at pie" mean?

IT'S A BRITISH saying that has come to mean anything all-encompassing or far-reaching; figuratively, from one end of town to the other. The origin of the phrase dates back to the Great Fire of London on September 2, 1666, which started in the royal baker's house on Pudding Lane. Over the next few days, the fire spread all the way across town to Pie Corner, burning down four-fifths of the city.

You may recognize the "pudding" and "pie" part of the phrase from the children's nursery rhyme "Georgie Porgie." King George IV was known for his amoral behavior all around town, hence the reference: "Georgie Porgie, Pudding and Pie / Kissed the girls and made them cry."

Where is Sandwich, and is it the origin of the lunchbox favorite?

SANDWICH is in the southeast of Kent, which in turn is in the southeast of England. The fourth Earl of Sandwich, John Montagu (1718–1792), was a renowned gambler and, tired of getting food on the playing cards and having both hands tied up for eating, popularized the sandwich by insisting it be the food served while he and his cohorts gambled.

WHERE IN THE WORLD?

Was the city of Troy in Greece?

NO, TROY was in what is now Turkey, around the mouth of the Dardanelles Strait, at Hissarlik. Destroyed in 1200 B.C., it was excavated in 1871 by Heinrich Schliemann.

Where did the country Turkey get its name?

NOT BECAUSE the country is supposedly shaped like a bird, despite what you may have heard. The Turks got their name from the Chinese. By A.D. 500, Chinese records clearly call these early ancestors of the Huns *Tu-Kue*.

What does "Iran" mean?

"LAND OF THE ARYANS." Iranians have always called their country Iran, even when the rest of the world referred to it as Persia. The name Persia comes from a southern region of the country, Parsa, and has been used by outsiders to refer to the entire country since about the sixth-century B.C. Iran finally requested in 1935 that the world officially recognize "Iran" as the country's name.

Do Pago Pago, Bora Bora, and Walla Walla really exist?
Yes. Yes.

What is the smallest country in the world?

VATICAN CITY has held that honor since it became independent in 1929. It measures .16 of a square mile and has about 750 full-time residents. Not surprisingly (since most residents are priests and nuns), it also has the lowest birth rate in the world.

How long a way IS it to Tipperary?

TIPPERARY, or *Conae Tiobraid Arann*, as the locals call it, is a county located in the Munster Province of Ireland between the

Suir and Shannon rivers. The famous WWI song "It's a Long Way to Tipperary" is about an Irish soldier who is homesick. Whether in London or on the battlefields of France, he was a long way from home.

POOF! THEY'RE GONE

Besides the USSR and the two Germanys, what other countries no longer exist?

FAR TOO MANY to list in this book. But here are a few that you many have been familiar with before their changes. As of this writing:

- *Tibet* was invaded by China in 1950 and is now officially known by the Chinese as *Xizang Autonomous Region of China.*

- *East Pakistan* became *Bangladesh* in 1971.

- *Rhodesia* has been *Zimbabwe* since 1980.

- *Burma* has called itself *Myanmar* since 1989 (it is still known as Burma by many countries that refuse to recognize the change).

- *Czechoslovakia* split in two in 1993: the *Czech Republic* and *Slovakia.*

- *Zaire* is now the *Democratic Republic of the Congo,* as of 1997.

DOWN IN THE COLD, COLD GROUND

Who owns Antarctica?

SEVEN DIFFERENT countries have laid claim to parts of Antarctica, the world's fifth largest continent. Those claims, however, have been put aside since the 1961 Antarctic Treaty, which stated that since international scientific cooperation on the continent is a priority, no one should be recognized as owning any of it.

> **Where can I see a Web livecam in Antarctica?**

You may be surprised to learn that neither Russia nor the United States was one of the seven countries who tried to claim territory. The countries that did are Great Britain, Chile, Norway, Australia, Argentina, France, and New Zealand.

Where is most of the fresh water on Earth?

IN ANTARCTICA. It holds a whopping 90% of the world's fresh water.

How much ice is in Antarctica?

ANTARCTICA'S ice sheet, for the most part, is 6,500 feet deep. It covers almost the entire continent.

OL'FACTORY DELIGHT

My friend says the whole island of Madagascar smells like dessert. What's she talking about?

AT LEAST HALF of the world's vanilla is grown on Madagascar, and as a result the whole island has that very distinctive, sweet smell. Many people say it smells like vanilla ice cream.

THE U.S. OF A.

Where can I find the Corn Palace?

IN MITCHELL, South Dakota. Or check it out online at *www.roadsideamerica.com/attract/SDMITcorn.html*

What is the Rubber Capital of the World?

ACCORDING TO Ohio, it's Akron. "Cement City" is in Allentown, Pennsylvania, and Kalamazoo, Michigan, holds the honor of being "Celery City." If it's pretzels you're looking for, Reading, Pennsylvania, is the city to visit.

What's the lowest point in the U.S.?

Death Valley, at 282 feet below sea level.

Which American state gets the most tourists?

FLORIDA USUALLY has the highest rate of tourism, but in some years California edges it out. The beaches, steady weather, and Disney attractions can all be counted as reasons why over five million tourists a year visit either state. The next most visited states are Hawaii and New York.

Where is the Silicon Valley?

IT'S THE AREA between San Jose and San Francisco, about a 55-mile stretch of California.

Where does Wall Street get its name?

THERE USED to be a wall there, in the city that was called New Amsterdam. Dutch settlers in the 1600s erected the wall to protect against natives, wild animals, and those pesky British fleets that wanted to land. Alongside the wall ran a dirt road, aptly named Wall Street.

> **What's the northern-most state in the U.S. besides Alaska?**

Of course, a wall made of wood didn't hold out the British for long. They tore down the wall, used it for firewood, and renamed the city New York. Under British rule, the road became a major thoroughfare, and the name stuck.

What does "Bronx" mean, as in the Bronx in New York?

IT'S THE POSSESSIVE form of "Bronk." In 1639, Jonas Bronk (or Bronck) moved into the area and laid claim to the place, naming a river, burgs, and streets after himself. The Dutch made "Bronk's" easier to write by using their possessive "x" and spelling it "Bronx."

What's the most popular street name in America?

AT LATEST count, "Second Street" came in first. But stay tuned, these things change.

Where is the windiest city in the United States?

ALTHOUGH CHICAGO is called the Windy City, truth be told, it's a wimp in comparison to the big boys. It comes in 21st in a top 68 list of windiest cities. Cheyenne, Wyoming, is the windiest. The average speed of Cheyenne's wind is about 12.9 miles per hour, while Chicago's is only 10.3 miles per hour.

Where does the state name Louisiana come from?

IT COMES FROM French king Louis XIV. The French settled the area in the early 18th century. Over the next 100 years, several wars were fought and secret treaties forged over this territory, among Spain, France, Great Britain, and the United States. Finally, in 1803, the portion of what is now Louisiana west of the Mississippi River and including New Orleans was purchased by the United States. Along with Louisiana, this $15 million deal included the territories that now make up portions of Montana, Wyoming, Nebraska, North and South Dakota, Arkansas, Missouri, Oklahoma, Kansas, Iowa, Minnesota west of the Mississippi River, and Colorado east of the Rocky Mountains. It was the largest land acquisition the United States ever made at one time.

Has any state undergone a name change?

THERE WAS once the state of Franklin. It became Tennessee in 1796.

Which U.S. states have no straight-line boundaries?

JUST HAWAII. All the other states have at least one.

SHAKE, RATTLE, AND ROLL

Can weather be a predictor of an earthquake?

NO, WEATHER doesn't play a role in shifting the Earth's plates. Although heat or water can seep into concrete and help contribute to the wear and cracking of asphalt, the Earth's crust is equipped to handle both. What it doesn't handle is pressure over long stretches of time, but those are huge pressures—far more than those exerted by climatic conditions.

What did the 1906 San Francisco earthquake measure on the Richter scale?

IT MEASURED 8.3, killed over 700 people, and caused over $500 million worth of damage. The northern California earthquake in 1989, in comparison, measured 7.1, killed 67 people, and caused billions of dollars in damage.

What are "Moodus' Noises"?

Noisy seismic activity below Moodus Connecticut.

Was the San Francisco earthquake in 1906 the largest in U.S. history?

NO. THE strongest earthquakes recorded in U.S. history took place in a series from December 1811 to March 1812. Occurring in the New Madrid faults in the middle of the country, the quakes changed the course of the Mississippi River, created new lakes in several states, shook two-thirds of the entire country, and were felt all the way into Canada. Because the area was relatively uninhabited, there were no known deaths associated with these quakes. But earthquake experts warn it will likely happen again.

STRAIGHT TO THE TOP

How tall does a hill have to be to be considered a mountain?

MOST SOURCES agree that a *hill* is smaller than a *mountain* and is usually a gentle rise in the Earth's surface. A mountain is a natural elevation that rises more abruptly to a peak and is larger than a hill. In an effort to be more exact, some experts claim height requirements for each.

What is the largest volcanic mountain in the U.S.?

Some say 1,000 feet is the dividing line between the two; some say 2,000 feet. Of course, both divisions are wrought with problems because there are always exceptions. For instance, many of the Ozark Mountains don't attain an elevation of

2,000 feet. So most geographers say that if a rise occurs abruptly from the Earth's surface, it constitutes a mountain and that a land formation that rises slowly from the earth is a hill.

THE SEVERAL SEAS

What's the largest lake in the world?

THE CASPIAN SEA is the largest saltwater lake. It borders Iran, Kazakhstan, and Russia. It runs 750 miles from north to south and about 200 miles from east to west, with a total area of about 143,250 square miles. The largest freshwater lake in the world is Lake Superior, the deepest of the Great Lakes. Its borders are Canada and the United States. It's about 350 miles long and covers approximately 31,700 square miles.

What is the lowest point on Earth?

THE MARIANA Trench, between the Mariana Islands and Guam, is believed to be the lowest point on the Earth's surface. It is about 36,000 feet below sea level. The lowest point bounded by land is the Dead Sea, between Jordon and Israel. It lies about 1,300 feet below sea level.

Why is it called the Dead Sea?

THE WATER in the Dead Sea has no outflow, so anything that comes in can't leave. As water evaporates, minerals are left behind, forming a salinity rate of 25% and rising. Nothing can survive salt levels that high; therefore "Dead" Sea is a pretty good name for it.

How far out to sea does a country's territory extend? Usually, 12 nautical miles.

Is there anywhere you can see the sun rise above the Pacific Ocean and set over the Atlantic Ocean?

YES. BECAUSE of the curve of the isthmus, people in part of Panama can watch the sun rise over the Pacific and set over the Atlantic.

> **Where can I buy a submarine?**

Where is the Bay of Fundy?

IT'S LOCATED in Canada, between New Brunswick and Nova Scotia. The bay is famous for its high tides and reversing water flow. The tide differences are extreme, as much as 60 feet. High tide is often marked at 5 feet above either of the arms of the bay itself. When this happens, the tide actually pushes water back up the river and up its waterfalls. This rushing tide is referred to as a *bore*, but despite the name it's fascinating to watch.

The Wonderful World of Disney

DISNEY HAS BECOME SUCH A HUGE part of popular culture worldwide, it would be impossible to skip over the hundreds of questions Jeeves receives about the rides, the rumors, the movies, the mouse, and the man behind the mouse. As Walt Disney himself put it, "Remember, this all started with a mouse." So here we go . . .

THE MOUSE THAT ROARED

What's Mickey Mouse's original name?

MICKEY WAS born Mortimer Mouse and remained so until Walt Disney's wife, Lillian, talked Walt into changing the name. Mortimer/Mickey, however, wasn't Walt's first cartoon character. That honor belongs to Oswald the Rabbit, contractually owned by Universal Studios. When Oswald became popular, Disney, who did not share in the profits from his creation, was displeased. He left with these words for his distributor: "Here, you can have the little bastard! He's all yours." From the ashes of a bunny named Oswald rose Mickey and the Disney empire. (Mortimer Mouse wasn't dead forever, as it turned out. In later episodes of Mickey Mouse comics and cartoons, a mouse with an elongated, sinister face named Mortimer appeared as a brutish rival of Mickey's out to win Minnie's love.)

> **How many spots are painted on cartoon dogs in 101 Dalmatians?**
> According to Disney, 6,469,952.

What's Mickey Mouse's name in other countries?

IN ICELANDIC, it's Mikki Mús. In Farsi, the language spoken in Iran, it's Mickey Moosh. Italians call him Topolino. Sweden? Musse Pigg.

For a more thorough rundown of Mickey's name around the world, visit http://home.att.net/~mickeymousemania/language.htm

What day is recognized as Mickey Mouse's birthday?

ACCORDING TO the Disney corporation, Mickey's birthday is celebrated on November 18, the day in 1928 when the classic Disney short film "Steamboat Willie" was introduced. Mickey had appeared in at least two other short silent films, but went relatively unnoticed until the "Steamboat Willie" release.

My daughter has a letter for Mickey Mouse. Does he have an address?

CHANCES LOOK grim from the Disney Web site. Disney gives its visitors the chance to e-mail specific departments, but provides no direct mail addresses for their characters and no mailing address at all. Like most stars, though, letters usually get to them through the agencies they work for. We're not guaranteeing a reply, but her best bet is the publications division.

Address the envelope to:
Mickey Mouse
c/o Walt Disney Publications
500 South Buena Vista
Burbank, California 91521
USA

Good luck!

Who does Mickey Mouse's voice?

ORIGINALLY Walt Disney himself did the high-pitched, squeaky voice of Mickey Mouse, followed by several others over the years. Most recently, Wayne Allwine has lent his vocal cords to the cartoon character.

ALL HE'S QUACKED UP TO BE

Who does Donald Duck's voice?

CLARENCE "DUCKY" NASH gave his voice to Donald Duck in 1933. Nash began his long career as a mandolin picker in vaudeville who incorporated bird and animal noises into his act. When Disney heard Nash on the radio doing a goat voice, he hired Nash to give voice to his newest creation, Donald, and the rest is history. Nash's vocals were synonymous with the cartoon duck for more than 50 years, until his death in 1985, when Tony Anselmo took over the role.

> **Does Donald Duck have a middle name?**
> Yes, Fauntleroy.

Where did the triplets Huey, Dewey, and Louie come from?

DONALD DUCK'S nephews arrived on the animation scene in 1938 in the film "Donald's Nephews." They were sent by Donald's sister, Dumbella, with a note describing them as "angels," but it didn't take long for Donald to realize he'd been tricked or, at the very least, misled. The origins of the three pranksters' names are stories in and of themselves. Contemporary political figures Huey P. Long of Louisiana and Thomas E. Dewey of New York were the inspiration for two of the boys; a friend of Walt Disney's, Louie Schmidt, was the third. Later, writers of the comic created a new variation—that their names were short for Huebert, Deuteronomy, and Louis.

What was Goofy's original name?

GOOFY MADE his debut in *Mickey's Review* in 1932 under the stage name Dippy Dawg. His name changed slowly over several years—first to just Dippy, then Dippy the Goof, and then to Goofy by 1939. Suffering a slight identity crisis, he appeared as Mr. Geef for a while in the 1940s, but this name was short-lived and he finally settled down for the rest of his career as just plain Goofy.

DISNEY ON ICE

Wasn't Walt Disney frozen when he died so he could be brought back to life?

DESPITE THE widely spread story, Disneyland's master is buried in the cold, cold ground. At some point, the major cryogenics companies started declining to answer this question—even though the answer is "no"—for reasons of client privacy. Their discretion only served to fuel rumors about Disney's remains and where they might be stashed. For many years, legend had it that Disney was frozen and his body stored in Cinderella's Castle in Disneyland. No doubt thousands walked past a little slower (or quicker!) than normal, just in case he thawed and decided to step out and say, "Hello!"

You can visit Walt Disney's gravesite at 1712 S. Glendale Avenue, Glendale, in the San Fernando Valley area of Los Angeles.

GRIMM, YET HAPPY

How much does Disney change an original story when it makes a movie?

LET'S TAKE A LOOK at a few tales Disney has adapted and compare them to their originals. In the Brothers' Grimm tale of *Cinderella,* her stepsisters lop off their feet to fit into the slippers. What about Jiminy Cricket? In the original *Pinocchio* tale, the unnamed cricket gets squashed with a mallet by puppet Pinocchio early in the story. In the Grimm version of *Snow White,* the wicked Queen asks the hunter to bring her Snow White's lungs and liver, not her heart. He brings her a boar's organs instead, and she boils and eats them. At Snow White's wedding, the bride and groom force her into red hot shoes and make her dance until she's dead. Better to leave alone the original versions of *Winnie the Pooh, Pocahontas, The Hunchback of Notre Dame. . . .*

Was the Disney film **The Little Mermaid** original?

OH MY, NO. That story comes from none other than the great story master himself, Hans Christian Andersen. Like most of the Disney adaptations, however, *The Little Mermaid* ends a little differently than the original version. Andersen's *Little Mermaid* ends with the leading lady getting turned into sea foam. The Disney corporation added just a bit more pizzazz: They allowed her to morph into a human and live happily ever after. Who wouldn't like the Disney version better?

PUT YOUR MONEY WHERE THE MOUSE IS

How many days has Disney World been closed since it opened in 1971?

ONLY ONE—September 15, 1999. Although Disney World has shut down early or opened late for many reasons over the years, Hurricane Floyd in September 1995 has been the only event compelling enough to close down Disney's Florida amusement park for an entire day.

Did Disney deliberately build a theme park in Orange County, Florida, so that it would be a match with Disneyland in Orange County, California?

IT WOULD APPEAR that way on the surface, but in fact the names of the counties where both Disney theme parks reside is a simple coincidence. Both places were named "Orange" because they are the heart of orange production in both states. Walt Disney snatched up land in Orange County, Florida, only because it was mostly farm and swamp land selling cheaply and he wanted lots of it.

What are E tickets?

"E TICKET" may sound like an Internet firm, but in the old days, an E ticket was a

> **Where can I read Disney urban legends?**

pass to the best rides at Disneyland. Unlike the current system, in which you pay one price and then stand in line for rides, guests originally paid to be admitted to the park and then paid for individual rides. This caused traffic jams at the more popular rides like the Matterhorn, Space Mountain, and the Haunted Mansion. To solve the problem, Disney created A tickets for the smaller, less impressive rides, B tickets for the rides just up from that, and so on, all the way up to E tickets. Tickets were sold as a complete set at the admission stands. Most patrons were inclined to use up their books to get their money's worth, spreading traffic over all the rides. As a result of this system, in Southern California the term "E ticket" came to represent anything that's the best.

Does EPCOT stand for anything?

EXPERIMENTAL PROTOTYPE Community of Tomorrow. Disney designed EPCOT to be an enclosed part of Disney World, within a dome, so that everything would be totally controlled. He wanted it to be a regulated community where people lived, worked, and played and where there was no crime—no societal negatives at all. Instead, opening in 1982, EPCOT became a kiosk of corporate-sponsored technological exhibits. All the same, it's one of the most visited attractions at the park.

What is an Imagineer?

THAT'S THE NAME Disney used for his architectural engineers. It's not the only unusual job title. His employees at Disney theme parks are called "cast members" to remind them that they are always "in character," even when sweeping a street. You, as a customer, are called a "guest."

SLIP 'EM A MICKEY

Where do I learn more about Hidden Mickeys?

HIDDEN MICKEYS are silhouettes of Mickey Mouse hidden around Disney theme parks. Usually they're the familiar three circles of Mickey's face and ears, but they come in other shapes as well. Disney officially claims there are no Hidden Mickeys, but the Disney Channel has reported on them, and Disney Web sites and cast members have indirectly admitted they exist.

If you would like to search for them, here are a few tips: Hidden Mickeys are supposed to be hidden, and many are in shadows and other camouflaging spots. If the silhouette is blatantly visible, it's probably not a Hidden Mickey. If the proportions seem a bit off, count it out. Hidden Mickeys, although hidden, are deliberate. Finally, Hidden Mickeys are only on things that are Disney owned and created. If you see a shape in the Tower of London that reminds you of Mickey Mouse, it doesn't count. Not yet, anyway. The Tower is still, to the best of our knowledge, owned by England.

Here are some of the more notable places that Hidden Mickeys have been discovered: In EPCOT in the *Body Wars* mural, there is a Broccoli Hidden Mickey. There's one in the eyes of the Goofy hats for sale at the Disney parks. The Disney "recycle" logos contain an H.M., and there's one on the Disney vacation brochures, in the sky. It's been suggested by Disney

> **Where can I see posters made for the rides at Disneyland?**

employees that there may be Hidden Mickeys on every Disney ride. However, there may be another phenomenon at work here instead—the same one that allows some people to see Jesus on the side of a rusty water tank.

There are several Web sites on Hidden Mickeys, the foremost being www.hiddenmickeys.org/

"I WANNA BE LIKE YOU-OO-OO"

Is it true that Disney employees have to follow a stringent dress and conduct code?

THAT DEPENDS ON your definition of "stringent." Decide for yourself—here are excerpts from "The Disney Look," a guide for employees created in the 1960s, but still used at Disney theme parks:

- As a condition of employment with Walt Disney Attractions, you are responsible for maintaining an appropriate weight and size.

- Men's hair should be neatly cut and tapered so it does not cover any part of your ears. (Putting your hair behind your ears is not acceptable.)

- Women are required to wear appropriate undergarments.

- Neither men nor women are allowed to expose any tattoos.

- A single earring, no more than three-quarters of an inch in diameter, in each ear is acceptable (for women only).

- Fingernails should not extend over one-quarter of an inch beyond the fingertip (for women only).

- Mustaches and beards are not permitted.

That's right, no mustaches. Walt Disney himself would have been turned down for a job at his own theme park. He never claimed his rules were fair; they were just right . . . for the park image he wanted to present.

Death & Other Grave Matters

"O DEATH, WHERE IS THY VICTORY?
O death where is thy sting?" wrote
St. Paul. Death is a topic that intrigues
us all. It is something that everyone must
face, and no one truly knows what lies beyond.
It is universal yet unknown, and therefore
enthralling. For traditions (old and new), folklore, fact, and rumor, read on if you dare . . .

WHAT GOES UP . . .

Is it true that NASA sent someone's cremated body into space?

IN 1998, some of the ashes of space guru Dr. Eugene Shoemaker (discoverer of the comet Shoemaker-Levy 9 in 1994) were carried by NASA's *Lunar Prospector* as it went to map the moon. When the *Prospector* was done, it crashed on the moon on July 31, 1999, leaving the scientist's ashes there—and making him the first person to be sent to his final rest on the moon.

A couple of other space programs have also put cremated remains in space. The creator of "Star Trek," Gene Rodden-berry, for example, was one of many space enthusiasts who paid to have his remains sent into orbit on Spain's *Pegasus* rocket in 1997. If you can find a service—and there are a few out there—it will cost you approximately $5,000 to send a lip-stick-sized vial of your ashes inscribed with your name and a message into orbit. One drawback: They will stay in orbit for only 10 years at most. After that, your remains will plummet back to Earth, burning up a little of the ozone layer as they reenter the atmosphere. That is, if they don't collide with a satellite or another piece of space junk first.

IN CHICAGO IT HAPPENS ALL THE TIME

What happens when someone votes by absentee ballot, then dies?

IT DEPENDS. If the voter didn't mail the ballot before dying, it doesn't count. (Someone else isn't allowed to run it down to the post office after the funeral.) But if the voter sent in the ballot, *then* died, before the votes were counted, that person's vote is still good and is tallied with the rest.

DROP DEAD BEAUTIFUL

What kind of makeup do funeral parlors use on corpses?

THE POINT of putting makeup on the dead is to make them look as lifelike as possible for the "viewing." This isn't always easy, as blood pools after death, sometimes from broken or clogged blood vessels, sometimes because the body has been left in one position for a while. The embalming procedure helps: since the fluid is colored pink, the skin takes on a "warm" look. To finish the effect, there is a special kind of makeup especially for use by morticians—but many funeral parlors use regular commercial products.

Why were pennies put on dead people's eyes?

COINS HAVE been used by many cultures to keep the eyes of the dead shut until rigor mortis sets in. Some cultures, including the ancient Egyptians and more modern African Americans, have also used coins on the eyes and hands of the deceased to share with relatives in the spirit world or to pay for admittance into eternity. In some Old World cultures, coins were used to keep the eyes shut for a specific reason: so that the living couldn't see their own death in the eyes of the deceased.

Today keeping the eyes of the dead closed is more for aesthetic reasons than any other, especially since "viewing the body" has become commonplace. Coins are rarely used, however. Nowadays, morticians employ one of two methods. One is to use a device called an *eye cap*, which resembles a contact lens and actually fits over the eyeball. On the other side there are tiny "grippers" that keep the lids shut. The other method is to place a thin line of adhesive on the lids to keep them shut.

How do morticians keep a dead person's mouth shut?

BEFORE EMBALMING, it wasn't uncommon to tie gauze or string around the chin and head until rigor mortis set in. Today undertakers pass a suture through the nasal septum and tie it to the lower lip. Or they use an injector needle gun to place wires into the lower and upper jaws; these are then twisted together to close the mouth.

DO YOU BELIEVE IN FERRIES?

Weren't coins used in ancient Egyptian burial practices?

ANCIENT EGYPTIANS (and other ancient peoples) believed—either literally or symbolically—that worldly goods were transported with the deceased into the spirit world. Sometimes material possessions such as coins, food, and pottery were used to appease the spirits beyond; sometimes, as in the Chinese culture, they were used to aid the departed in the afterlife.

How are mummies made?

In the afterlife mythology of the ancient Greeks, dead souls had to journey over the River Styx to meet Hades, the god of death. The ferryman, Charon, who would carry the dead in his boat, waited for new passengers by the riverbanks. If the departed had been administered burial rites and had a coin placed under their tongue, Charon would steer them on his ferry to the gates of the underworld to find Hades. If one or both of these things had not happened, the deceased was doomed to wait beside the River Styx for 100 years.

HEAD START TO THE AFTERLIFE

What role does a hammer play in a Hindu funeral?

ACCORDING TO Hindu beliefs, a hammer is an important tool in helping a spirit get to the afterlife. It is used to crack open the skull of the dead in order to "release the soul from entrapment." The practice stems from the Hindu belief that the soul resides in the skull.

WHAT DEAD PEOPLE CAN'T DO

Is it true that a person's hair and nails continue to grow after death?

NO, IT'S NOT TRUE. This myth is based on perception: When a person dies, the skin loses moisture and elasticity and begins to recede. This recession makes both hair and nails appear longer than they were prior to death.

Do dead people sometimes suddenly just sit up?

THIS IS ONE of those great, creepy stories kids tell each other, but it's not true, according to those who know. It is true, though, that dead muscles can go through slight spasms. Funeral workers sometimes massage the legs and arms to relieve spasms in the muscles while washing, cleaning, and dressing the body after death.

It is believed this myth began during a time when dying people were often pronounced dead before they actually died. The person "came to" long enough to sit up or raise their head toward the end. But as far as anyone knows, this can't happen postmortem.

OUR WORST NIGHTMARE

Have people actually been accidentally buried alive?

YES, IT HAPPENED with alarming frequency as recently as 100 years ago, when determining the moment of passing was more difficult. A universal fear of being buried alive inspired inventors to come up with several coffins designed with escape hatches.

Was Robert E. Lee's mother buried alive?

ANNE CARTER LEE, the Southern general's mother, suffered from cataleptic spells that caused her to fall unconscious and grow rigid with tremors. As the story goes, she was mistaken for dead during one of these spells and buried in the family plot in Virginia. Hearing a noise a while later, one of the servants called attention to it, and she was dug up—alive but traumatized. This supposedly happened in 1806, a year before Robert E. Lee was born.

| Where can I see a coffin with an escape hatch? |

This is a wonderfully gruesome and touching tale, but it's probably erroneous. There is no official record of it, nor is it alluded to in Robert E. Lee's biographies or those of his father, Henry, who was prominent in his own right.

MILITARY HONORS

What are the origins of flying a flag at half-mast?

IT BEGAN WITH ships. When someone passed away on a ship, or a country's leader died, all the rigging would be loosened so that it looked in disarray. This was a sign of mourning. Although the slacked rigging isn't practiced today, the tradition of lowering the flag to half-mast continues in many countries—both at sea and on land.

Why are cannons fired off a naval ship when someone dies?

BECAUSE SHOOTING a cannon at nothing left an entire ship partially unarmed, it was a sign that the ship was bereft. Back in the days when war was a gentleman's game, firing shots told the enemy to hold off. The practice, which began in the British navy, has come to be a respectful homage to the deceased, indicating the person's passing was important enough to unarm the ship so that the crew could mourn.

What is the significance of firing three shots at a military funeral?

THIS IS AN OLD custom once used during battle. The three shots would signify that both sides had finished clearing the dead off the battlefield, so the fighting could resume. The shots at a military funeral are usually carried out by seven people firing in unison three times.

THEY IS DONE, GONE THE SON . . .

How did "Taps" come to be played at funerals?

ACCORDING TO military manuals, it was once exclusively for use at the end of the day at what's called "lights out." This changed during the Civil War, when Northern and Southern camps were often in close proximity to one another. Out of fear of restarting the fighting, officers decided to temporarily dispose of the three-shot salute that was customary in wartime funerals (see previous question) and replace it with the playing of the lights-out song, "Taps." The custom remains today, sometimes in conjunction with the tradition of firing three shots.

> **Why do we embalm dead bodies?**
> Primarily as a disinfectant.

WHO TOOK THE "FUN" OUT OF FUNERAL?

What are the origins of the word "funeral"?

IT COMES FROM the Latin word *funus,* meaning "funeral," which comes from the Latin *funis,* meaning "torch." Using torches in death and burial ceremonies dates back to Neanderthal times, and the ancient Romans believed funeral torches showed the deceased the way to their eternal homes.

BASIC BLACK

Why is a funeral car known as a "hearse"?

IT ALL BEGAN with the huge, elaborate candelabras that the ancient Normans used in religious ceremonies. Because (upside down) they resembled a type of British plow used under Norman rule, these candlesticks were eventually given the same name—*herse.* The large candlesticks not only were used in churches, but were also placed on the backs of coffins being taken for burial. Eventually the whole cart that the coffin was transported on became known as a "herse." The English later added an "a."

The slow pace of funeral processions is said to be a remnant from the usage of the early candelabra. The slowness kept the candles from blowing out on the way to the cemetery.

Why is black worn for funerals?

SOME ANTHROPOLOGISTS say it comes from an ancient belief that the spirit of the deceased would try to enter the bodies of the living. In order to avoid this, everyone present would disguise themselves, believing their dead loved ones wouldn't take over their bodies if they couldn't recognize them. One method of concealment was to paint the body black. As society moved along and clothes became part of the cultural standard, the family of the deceased would don black not only at the funeral but for some time afterward to keep the soul at bay.

OF COURSE, THE REPORTS HAVE BECOME MORE ACCURATE WITH TIME

What did Mark Twain mean when he said, "Rumors of my death are greatly exaggerated"?

WHEN TWAIN was visiting England in 1897, newspapers in the United States reported that he had died. He received an inquiry about this and answered by cable with the now-famous line.

> **How can I find out if a celebrity is still alive?**

DEATH AT THE BOX OFFICE

What do they do in Hollywood when a star dies while filming a movie?

THAT DEPENDS. Sometimes the film is abandoned, as in the case of *Dark Blood* when River Phoenix died. But if the star has already completed many crucial scenes, directors can use doubles and other tricks to complete the project anyway. A recent example that you may remember is the 1994 Brandon Lee movie *The Crow.* Lee was killed accidentally during filming by a .44-caliber gun filled with blanks. Part of one of the blanks was shot from the gun, lodging in Lee's stomach with fatal results. There were only three more days of filming scheduled. The producer was able to digitally alter some of the remaining scenes but for others used body doubles. The doubles were asked to wear a mask resembling Lee's face but refused, claiming it was too creepy. So instead, the producer filmed them from a distance.

Another example: During the filming of *Saratoga,* Jean Harlow died of kidney failure, leaving co-star Clark Gable and the rest of the cast and crew in a lurch. They used Harlow's stand-in to finish the film, carefully lighting her from the back and using long shots. The stand-in was positioned looking through binoculars or peering out from under large, wide-brimmed hats. Ironically, this film was considered one of Harlow's best.

And then there's the notorious *Plan 9 from Outer Space,* in which director Ed Wood used a much taller extra to stand in for newly dead Bela Legosi.

IT'S VERY PEACEFUL HERE . . . AND, OH YEAH, COULD YOU PICK UP MY DRY-CLEANING?

Did Harry Houdini ever send a message from beyond the grave, as he promised?

BEFORE MAGICIAN Harry Houdini died, he promised his wife he would contact her if possible from the spirit world. During his life, Houdini had spent quite a bit of time running to psychics in an attempt to contact his dear departed mother, to no avail. He desperately wanted to find out once and for all whether it could be done. Because of his promise, Houdini's wife held séance after séance in attempts to receive the secret message he'd said he would try to convey to her. Alas, there were no positive results. Even the best escape artist ever wasn't able to escape the Great Beyond.

How did Harry Houdini die? Most likely from a ruptured spleen.

BONE VOYAGE

Where can I have a funeral service for my dog?

THERE ARE A number of services available for pets, including funerals, burial plots, cremation, and memorial services. Look in your local phone directory. If an online tribute is what you're looking for, this free service lets you pay permanent tribute to your beloved and departed Fifi or Snowball: *www.in-memory-of-pets.com/*

FOLK WISDOM AND FOOLISHNESS

Folklore says that people die in threes. Is that true, statistically?

AH, THE LONG-DISCREDITED Rule of Threes, which says that family members or celebrities "always die in threes." It's not true. Death folklore is not usually accurate, but it's easy to understand the appeal: folklore is one of the ways people make sense out of something that seems senseless and scary. However, the folklore itself is often confusing. For example, it's said that a person who wears the clothes of the dead will be unlucky, yet it's also said that a dead person's clothes must never be thrown away—they must be worn out by others to give eternal peace.

DEATH SENTENCES
Where can I find some famous last words?

HERE'S A BEGINNING:

"Never felt better."—Douglas Fairbanks, Sr.

"Why not? Why not?"—Timothy Leary

"Monsieur, I beg your pardon."—Marie Antoinette, upon accidentally stepping on the executioner's foot

"I am about to, or, I am going to die. Either expression is used."—Dominique Bouhours, a grammar expert

"Are you sure it's safe?"—William Palmer, condemned criminal, upon stepping up to the gallows

"Why yes, a bullet-proof vest"—murderer James Rodgers, when asked if he had a final request before being put before a firing squad

For a more thorough list, see the BBC's site of Famous Last Words
www.bbc.co.uk/education/archive/famous/index.shtml

TICK, TICK, TICK . . .
When will I die?

OH MY. Of course, it's impossible to predict, but there is a Web site that claims to know. Go to *www.deathclock.com* for a grim look at the Death Clock, which will help you try to guess the arrival date of the Grim Reaper. You can also send others their own personal death clock, as long as you know their birth date and e-mail address.

What's the leading cause of death in the United States? Heart disease.

As to *how* you will die, check out *www.thespark.com/deathtest/*. But whatever the results, don't worry. It's all meant as a joke.

Trains, Boats & Planes

No MATTER WHERE PEOPLE ARE, IT seems there's somewhere else they want to be. Transportation—from trains and ships to dogsleds and elevators to unicycles and subways—has always been a top human priority. And sometimes, getting there is half the fun.

NAUTICAL . . . BUT NICE

Which of Columbus's three ships didn't come back from his first journey to America?

THE *SANTA MARIA* hit a reef on December 5, 1492, and sank. Luckily, Columbus and his crew were able to scramble aboard the other two ships.

Ironically, the *Santa Maria* was the flagship, the one piloted by the Great Captain himself, and Columbus, a devout Catholic, had renamed the craft after Jesus' mother, hoping for good luck. Previously, the ship was called *Marigalente* ("Dirty Mary"), following a local tradition of naming ships after favorite dockside prostitutes. The *Nino* ("Little Girl") and *Pinta* ("Painted Lady") followed that earthier tradition . . . and both made it safely back to Spain. Perhaps that goes to show that it's better to be nautical than nice.

Why are the right and left sides of a ship called "starboard" and "port"?

HERE'S THE story of why sailors *started* using those terms. Why they *still* use them can probably be chaulked up to tradition.

What does "S.S." mean before the name of a ship, like S.S. Titanic?
Steamship.

The old Viking ships were steered by rudders on the right side, which the Vikings called a *styrbord,* Scandivanian for "steer side." The term was adopted into Old English as *steorboard,* which later became *starboard.* With the steering on the right side, the Vikings docked on the left side and so called it *ladebord*, "loading side," which the British turned into *larboard.* Unfortunately, *starboard* and *larboard* sound enough alike that British ships had some fatal confusions. The Admiralty ordered that the left, docking side be henceforth known as the *port* side.

Can people on ships feel earthquakes?

YES, BUT NOT nearly as intensely as people on land. Even a tsunami doesn't do damage until it hits land, because it's a long lateral wave that barely affects the ocean surface. People on a ship would experience it as an insignificant rise or fall of a foot or two, lasting five minutes to an hour.

Why do they call it a "poop deck"? Did they ever really use it for . . . um, you know?

A *POOP DECK* is just a partial deck near the stern (back) of a ship. The name comes from the Latin *puppis,* which means "stern," by way of the Italian *poppa* and then the Middle French *poupe.*

What is the difference between a boat and a ship?

ALTHOUGH A lot of landlubbers, and some seamen, use the terms interchangeably, the U.S. Navy defines a boat as "a vessel that can be hauled about a ship."

ON THE RIGHT TRACK
Where did the Orient Express train go?

FROM 1889 to 1978, the *Orient Express* was the most efficient and luxurious way to get from western Europe to the Middle

East. The train traveled through several different cultures and opposing sides in European alliances along the way, lending each trip a sense of adventure, espionage, and intrigue. The journey began in Paris and traveled through major cities in Germany, Austria, Hungary, Yugoslavia, and Bulgaria before ending at its final destination, Constantinople (now Istanbul), Turkey. Its *chef de train*, who spoke six languages fluently, would handle the passports and paperwork at each border crossing, leaving passengers undisturbed.

In 1982, a truncated version of the *Orient Express* began operating again to placate tourists who wanted to experience the famous line. One thing missing on the new train: King Boris of Bulgaria, who, as absolute monarch, often insisted that he be allowed to drive the famous train through his realm. Luckily, he was experienced at it and his stops and starts were as smooth as a professional's.

> **Where can I see pictures of the Orient Express?**

Somebody sent me an e-mail that says railroad tracks are based on the size of the ruts made by Roman chariots. Is this true?

AH, MY FRIEND, you've been hoaxed. But don't feel bad, you're in very good company—millions of people have gotten that same e-mail, and there are thousands of Web sites that carry the story as truth. You have to love the Internet: a piece of misinformation can get posted as a joke to a small mailing list in 1994 and take on a life of its own, believed by many to be true as it continues richocheting and reverberating through cyberspace nearly a decade later.

Here's how it began: On February 9, 1994, Bill Innanen typed out a reasonable-sounding essay about the "exceedingly odd" railroad gauge of the United States and Britain—4' 8½" between tracks—and claimed that the measurement was based on the ruts left by Roman war chariots. He sent it to the an e-mail mailing list composed mostly of military R&D engineers like him. It was a group he expected would appreciate his wry point that military project specifications live long beyond their practical usefulness.

The story was taken as gospel and spread like electronic wildfire among engineers and bureaucrats and then the world. It got picked up by news sources and book authors. It mutated into new stories. Meanwhile, Innanen sat by and watched, amused and powerless to stop the juggernaut he'd started.

When we asked Innanen about the story, he said, "The post was never meant to be a serious historical thesis. Never did I imagine that sending this to some friends would cause it to become a bona fide urban legend. I personally sent the message out only once. From there it took on a life of its own. Every once in a while someone would unknowingly send me a copy of whatever version was being passed around. It was like a prodigal child returning home, carrying the evidence of his travels with him in additions and modifications. It's always fun to be able to reply to the sender on these occasions saying, 'Yes I've seen this one before. In fact, I wrote it!' "

What's the truth about tracks? There were once dozens of track sizes used by railroads in both countries, but these eventually became standardized to the most popular gauge so that all trains could run on all tracks. But why 4' 8½"? It turns out it isn't so odd after all. Gauge is now officially measured from the inside of one track to the inside of the other, but it wasn't always that way. If you measure from the outside to the outside, you'll find that it equals just about 5 feet—not an odd measurement at all.

To see Innanen's original post, check out the VAL-L archive: www.marist.edu/htbin/wlvtype?VAL-L.1027

Do train whistles mean anything besides "get out of the way"?

THE WHISTLES used to mean a lot more back before phones, walkie-talkies, and other ways for the engineer to communicate with the rest of the crew. For example, one urgent *toot!* signaled the brakeman to jump from car to car, applying the brakes on each one, which at one time was the only way to stop the train. Other signals:

1. Bell while in station—Passengers take your seats.

2. *Toooot toooot*—Train ready to proceed.

3. *Too too too*—Backing up.

4. *Too too too too too toot*— Succession of short blasts means nothing to the crew, so used to scare cattle off the track.

5. *Toooot toooot ta toooot*—Approaching a public crossing.

6. *Tooot tooot tooot tooot tooot tooot tooot*—Train is one mile from the next station.

ONE-TRACK MINDS

What do trainspotters do?

LIKE BIRDWATCHERS keeping track of all the birds they've seen, trainspotters keep detailed lists of the various engines, cars, and equipment they've run across, including types, names, and identification numbers. The sport is particularly popular in parts of England. Unfortunately, the practitioners have been vexed by public ridicule, including a popular novel and movie about heroin addicts called *Trainspotting*. Even the *Oxford English Dictionary* reports that *trainspotter* has become a derogatory term for "a person who obsessively studies the minutiae of any minority interest or specialized hobby."

> **Where can I hear train whistles online?**

Who is the world champion trainspotter?

ACCORDING TO the *Guinness Book of World Records,* at last reckoning the best trainspotter is Bill Curtis of Clacton-on-Sea, England, who has spotted about "60,000 locomotives, 11,200 electric units, and 8,300 diesel units" during trackside vigils in several countries over the last 40 years.

A SUBWAY AIN'T JUST A SANDWICH

Where exactly is the breezy subway grate that Marilyn Monroe stood on in Some Like It Hot?

IT'S AN unforgettable image. Marilyn Monroe and Tom Ewell come out of a movie theater playing *The Creature from the Black Lagoon*. Monroe steps on a grate and a subway rumbles down below. Suddenly a blast of air lifts her skirt up, exposing her thighs. "Ooh, do you feel the breeze from the subway?" she says, smiling. "Isn't it delicious?" The theater used to be the Translux before it was torn down for an office building, but the subway grate at Lexington Avenue and Fifty-fifth Street is still there.

> How many stations does the New York subway have?
> 461.

What's the oldest subway system in the world? What's the longest?

LONDON'S Underground is not only the oldest (it opened in 1863) but the longest as well, with 244 miles of track.
For route maps and more history and facts about London's subway, see: www.londontransport.co.uk/underground/t_fact00.htm

CLANG, CLANG, CLANG!

How do San Francisco's cable cars go?

IF YOU EVER listen carefully to the streets of San Francisco, you'll hear a low rumble. No, it's not (necessarily) the San Andreas Fault acting up again, but the cables running under the tracks of the cable cars. Made of large metal strands, the cables travel between two huge pulleys, one motorized, at a speed of about nine miles per hour. One of the two workers on the car pulls a handle to grab onto the cable and start the car with a lurch. Later, when he wants to slow or stop, he releases the grip and the other worker pulls a brake lever that drags along the track. On any line there are several pulleys along the way, so the cable is released at certain intersections and the car allowed to coast until it reaches the next cable. The motors that run the pulleys are not incredibly powerful, so the cars are timed so that one coming down a hill helps balance the weight of another going up.

PLANE AND FANCY

Why did the Hindenberg *zeppelin catch on fire?*

THERE ARE a lot of theories about what actually started the fire—an electrical short, lightning, sabotage, somebody smoking in the bathroom—but we don't know for sure.

> **Where can I see a video file of the Hindenburg tragedy?**

What we do know is that if the airship had been filled with nonflammable helium instead of hydrogen, the fire wouldn't have been nearly as disastrous. So why was it filled with hydrogen? Helium, a natural gas, isn't common to most parts of the world—in fact, the United States has the vast bulk of the helium stores within its borders. In the 1930s, the United States wouldn't sell helium to the Nazis, so the Germans had to use the more dangerous gas, hydrogen, in their zeppelins.

What finally happened to the Red Baron? Did Snoopy get him?

MANFRED VON Richthofen was Germany's best pilot in World War I. In the red-painted Albatross fighter that gave him his nickname, he shot down at least 80 Allied planes. He was finally killed in action in 1918 when he was simultaneously

> **What are the words to "Snoopy vs. the Red Baron"?**

attacked by Canadian pilot Roy Brown in the air and Australian machine gunners on the ground. Both claimed credit for bringing him down.

What is the world's largest airport?

RIYADH AIRPORT in Saudi Arabia. If you think Chicago's O'Hare is bad—this one covers 87 square miles of the Arabian Desert.

Was Charles Lindbergh the first person to fly nonstop across the Atlantic? If not, who was?

LINDBERGH was the first to make a *solo* transatlantic flight, in his plane *Spirit of St. Louis* in 1927. However, eight years earlier, two British aviators flew nonstop from Newfoundland, Canada, to Ireland, for the first Atlantic crossing. They were Capt. John Alcock and Lt. Arthur Brown. And on May 21, 1932—five years to the day after Lindbergh's famous flight— Amelia Earhart became the first woman to fly across the Atlantic solo, following the same route as the Brits.

How did Lindbergh find his way to Europe without a radio or navigational equipment?

ON HIS nonstop flight across the Atlantic, Charles Lindbergh carried almost nothing but extra tanks of gasoline because he wanted to avoid adding weight. His navigation was pretty iffy in the dark. Near the end of his journey, he spotted a fishing fleet below. He dove to within shouting distance, cut the engine, and screamed to the fishermen below, "Which way to Ireland?" They pointed, and he restarted his engines and continued on.

Where is the "black box" on an airplane and why do they paint it black?

FIRST OF ALL, the black box isn't really black. It's fluorescent orange so it's easier to find. It's called the "black box" because it's associated with death.

The box is made to survive crashes and extreme temperatures (up to 2,000°F for 30 minutes). Inside are recordings of the pilots' voices and the aircraft's flight information from its cockpit on metallic tape. The tape is a 30-minute-long loop, so that if a plane crashes, the last 30 minutes before impact are recorded. The box is mounted in the back of the plane, which is the part most likely to stay intact in a crash.

When the Wright brothers made their first flights, how fast could their planes go?

ON THEIR first four flights, their average speed was a little over 30 miles per hour.

What do scientists think happened to Amelia Earhardt?

THE MOON'S A BALLOON

Is it possible to fly into the air with a bunch of helium balloons?

YES. ONE Larry Walters of California flew nearly three miles into the air with 45 weather balloons rigged to his lawn chair on July 2, 1982. The North Hollywood truck driver outfitted the chair with a BB gun, CB radio, giant bottle of soda, and water-filled milk cartons as ballast. He had hoped to slowly waft into the sky, but instead shot up to 16,000 feet, where he quickly began to go numb from the cold and thin air. After 45 minutes, he began shooting at the balloons in order to pop them and bring himself down. In the process he ended up dropping the gun, but hit enough balloons to start a slow descent. After about two hours, his balloons tangled in power lines, blacking out a Long Beach neighborhood for 20 minutes but allowing him to dismount from his dangling lawn chair. For his stunt, he appeared on David Letterman's show and was fined $1,500 by the FAA.

Can you fly with kids' toy balloons?

IN 1987, Britisher Ian Ashpole did exactly that. He used a hot-air balloon to get up to an altitude of one and a quarter miles. Then he jumped out, holding 400 extra-large toy balloons, each 2 feet in diameter. He floated as in the last scene of the film *The Red Balloon* and released one balloon at a time until he was plummeting toward the ground at about 90 miles per hour. Releasing the last of the balloons, he opened his parachute and landed safely.

How did the blimp get its name?

THERE ARE at least two stories about the origin of the word of the word *blimp*. One is that a British naval officer coined the term while trying to duplicate the sound the giant airbag made when he flicked his fingernail against it. The other story is that the early airships were marked AIRSHIP MODEL B-LIMP (meaning "uninflated").

BIG WHEEL KEEP ON TURNING

What's the fastest a bicycle's ever gone?

167 MILES per hour. The record was set in 1995 by Fred Rompelberg on the Bonneville Salt Flats in Utah, using an automobile mounted with a windshield to create a slipstream for the cyclist to peddle behind.

What's the top speed for a unicycle?

ONE WHEEL isn't even half as fast as two, alas. The world's record for a 100-meter sprint from a standing start is a little over 12 seconds, or about $18\frac{1}{2}$ miles per hour, set by Peter Rosendahl in Las Vegas in 1994.

GOING DOWN?

If you jumped straight up into the air at the last second, could you save yourself in a falling elevator?

NO. EVEN if your timing were impeccable and you jumped your hardest, you would not be able to move upward anywhere near as fast as you would be traveling down. The good news is that you'll probably never have to worry about it. Elevators have multiple safety features, including brakes to stop them immediately if a cable breaks. They are by

How many elevators does the World Trade Center have? 208.

far the safest form of transportation, boasting only one fatality every 100 million miles traveled. Stairs, in comparison, are five times more dangerous.

PUTTING ON THE DOG

I've got six big dogs and I live in a place with long winters. How fast can a dogsled go?

THE BEST dogs are those that are bred for the job—Siberian Huskies, Samoyeds, and Alaskan Malamutes. Some recreational mushers have even used Irish Setters, Dalmatians, and Golden Retrievers. A good sled with six to eight good dogs should get you blazing through snow in excess of 20 miles per hour.

How much does a good dogsled cost?

ABOUT $500; the harness, gang lines, and a snow hook (the Arctic equivalent of an anchor) will cost another $35; sled bags will cost $25; and booties for your dogs' cold feet will cost about $1 per paw.

For more information on dogsledding, go to www.ooowoo.com

Stupid Body Tricks

WHAT DOES YOUR SPLEEN DO? Why does your body smell? And what's that punching bag in the back of your throat, anyway? Whether it's hiccups, burps, or breaking wind, Jeeves gets a lot of questions about anatomy.

FIT TO BE DYED

What causes grey hair?

AS PEOPLE AGE, their bodies stop producing melanin, the pigment that colors hair. Without melanin, hair becomes transparent, so you can see through to the air inside the hollow hair shafts. The diffusion of the light through the air bubbles makes hair look white. Hair dye works to hide the white because it stains the outside of the hair shaft.

> **Who grows more head hair—redheads, blondes, or brunettes?**

ICE CREAM, YOU SCREAM

Why does eating or drinking something very cold make your head hurt?

THE REASON FOR "ice-cream headaches" isn't clear. They are caused by ingesting something very cold, and tend to strike migraine sufferers as a group more than the population at large. Some researchers think that ice-cream headaches are caused by the constriction of blood vessels in the mouth and throat: the vessels get smaller, so blood may get slightly backed up in the head, causing pain.

For more information on this and other intriguing body reactions, try: http://howstuffworks.com/

What can I do to stop an ice-cream headache?

THERE ARE MYRIAD folk remedies. Try using your tongue to warm up the hard palate at the roof of your mouth. Or place something cold across the bridge of your nose and your fore-head for a few seconds to restrict the blood vessels from the opposite direction while the other ones warm and reopen. Of course, the best defense is to avoid the headaches from the start. Eat cold things with the sides of the mouth instead of up against the roof of the mouth. Or next time you eat ice cream, get a cup of coffee to use as a chaser.

GREETINGS FROM THE INTERIOR

What's a hiccup, exactly? Why do we have them?

HICCUPS ARE muscle spasms in the diaphragm and throat. The large muscle at the bottom of the chest cavity sometimes con-tracts in a spasm (as do most muscles at one time or another). When this happens, air gets sucked in through the mouth. The air never actually reaches the lungs because the muscles of the throat contract at the same time. Any number of remedies have been suggested to stop hiccups—from swallowing dry sugar to standing on your head—but basically the same principle works here as with other muscle spasms: If you relax, calm down, take your mind off the spasms, and get on with your activities, your diaphragm and throat will settle down and the hiccups will stop.

Why does my stomach growl?

IT CAN BE embarrassing when stomachs make noises, but stomachs have their reasons. A lot is going on in there. When you are hungry and there's nothing in your stomach, your stomach acid churns and produces gases as it bubbles and waits, impatient for you to feed it. When food comes down the pipe and drops into the brine, your digestive juices make noises, too, as they work on the food.

How is it that people make themselves burp?

BURPS ARE CAUSED by air swallowed while eating or drinking, carbonation from drinks, and gases produced from digestion. Talented practitioners of grade-school hijinks are able to swallow air at will. Naturally, it mostly comes right back up in the form of a burp, grossing out Sally, Susie, and Janey and making Mummy cross.

Why do beans make you break wind?

BLAME IT ON oligosaccharides (or, if you prefer, the dog). Beans, like other fibrous foods—soybeans, cabbage, peas, cauliflower—are made up of a special kind of sugar called oligosaccharides. These sugar molecules are very large and are not digested by the small intestine, so they pass on, more or less whole, to the large intestine, where colonies of bacteria lie in wait. The bacteria absolutely adore these large sugar molecules and multiply like rabbits, releasing gases as they go. With no place to go but down, the gases invariably reach your colon the moment you step onto an elevator or meet your new boss.

> **What's it called when someone's eyes go in different directions?** Strabismus.

My brother told me that if you burp, fart, and sneeze at the same time, you might die. Is that true?

ONE OF THE best lessons of childhood is that brothers aren't the best source for reliable information on anatomy or death or much of anything else, for that matter. Surely you've done at least two of these things simultaneously. No? Then be assured that it isn't true. Some suggest that this preposterous anatomical myth was begun by *National Lampoon* in the 1970s.

Who was Le Petomane?

SOME PEOPLE can burp at will. Le Petomane (born Joseph Pujol in 19th-century France) could break wind at will. He used his talent to make a name for himself on the stage. He could control not only when and how much wind he broke but the pitch and tone as well. He could "whistle" or flute out tunes. He could imitate animal noises. He was also famous for his water tricks using the same part of his anatomy, but the air show is what people loved best.

After he blew into town, as it were, Le Petomane would make his entrance dressed to the hilt. Dignified, poised, and stylish, he'd then drop to his knees and run through his repertoire, explaining what character each fart represented. He was one of the most popular entertainers in Europe at the dawn of the 20th century.

Recollections on Le Petomane—his life and his career—by colleagues and his son, Louis Pujol, are featured at The Suitcase, a Journal of Transcultural Traffic: www.suitcase.net/pujol.html

Are farts really flammable?

YES. PEOPLE WITH more matches than sense try to prove this all the time. Many of them get their body hair singed, or worse. One statistic indicates that close to one-quarter of the people who try this get burned. Methane and hydrogen are both in farts and are both flammable gases. Word has it that the results tend to be yellow or blue flames; however, they can't always be easily seen.

> **What was Dopey's only utterance in Snow White?**
> A hiccup.

ORAL FIXATION

Can someone actually die from laughing?

SUPPOSEDLY, YES. According to record, the ancient Greek painter Xeuzis purportedly laughed himself to death looking at one of his own paintings. But did the laughing actually cause his death, or was it more likely asphyxiation, a heart attack, or stroke? I suppose it makes sense theoretically that you could die from laughing, but the chances are very, very low . . . so low as to be laughable.

> **How much does the human brain weigh?**

Why can't everyone roll their tongue?

IT MAY BE an inherited trait, but perhaps not. Studies over the last several decades have found that genetically identical twins do not necessarily share this trait, and that a tongue-roller or two had no parents who could accomplish the same muscular feat. Maybe it can skip a generation. Research continues.

What's going on when saliva squirts out of your mouth by accident?

SALIVA SQUIRTS because it sometimes builds up in glands under the tongue. When you compress the glands as you yawn or talk, suddenly the saliva is catapulted forward and you spray whatever (or whomever) is in front of you. Most people find it highly embarrassing.

YOU'RE GETTING WARMER . . .

What causes the body to shiver?

THE HUMAN BODY, being warm-blooded, has smartly devised ways of taking care of itself when things threaten to get out of whack. When you're too hot, your body will sweat. When your body needs to generate heat, it will shiver, expending energy and warming the blood. What's really happening? Very small muscles involuntarily contract and relax in quick bursts to generate heat and keep the blood flowing.

ALL IN VEIN

Why is human blood blue in the body and red when it comes out?

BLOOD IS ALWAYS RED—even blood in the body that is oxygen-deprived and heading back toward the lungs to refuel.

Veins close to the skin show through as purply blue or greyish blue because that's their color.

The term *blue blood* as it's used regarding royalty comes from the fact that royalty didn't get outside much. Peasants and regular workers were browned by the sun, so their blue veins were less likely to show. The white skin of European nobles showed off their blue veins, and people assumed their blood was blue as well.

IT'S FINGER POPPIN' TIME!

What makes the cracking sound when I pop my knuckles?

THE SOUND comes from air bubbles in the joint between the bones. Usually the air trapped in the cushioning fluid sacs between two bones dissolves. When the knuckle joint is "cracked," one bone is pushed out of or into a joint, letting a little pocket of air in.

How much does an eyeball weigh? About an ounce.

The jury is still out on whether cracking your knuckles causes damage. One major study suggested there was little significant damage done, that it was a harmless habit. However, another study found that knuckle popping wore down the fluid-filled cushion area between bones, causing more and more friction with time and leading to arthritis. In other words, your mother's warnings about getting big knuckles may be correct.

Note that the popping of hip or ankle bones when you stand up from a sitting position is caused by something else. That popping noise is a ligament that is passing over the joint, repositioning itself so the bones can move to a different position, sort of like a snapping rubber band.

What makes the sound when you snap your fingers?

THE FINGERTIP hits the pad of the thumb in the palm and makes a smacking sound.

POP CORNEA

Will my eyes pop out if they're open when I sneeze?

NOT TO WORRY. You can't keep your eyes open when you sneeze. Your body shuts them tight every time. If you attempt to hold them open, either the sneeze tends to subside or the strength of the muscles clamping the eye shut is greater than the fingertips' ability to hold the lids apart. What if you *could* keep your eyes open? It still isn't a problem—the pressure is in your nasal cavities, not your eye sockets.

JUST SAY "AHHH"

Does that little thing hanging in the back of your throat have a purpose?

YOU MEAN besides giving animated cartoonists an easy sight gag? Perhaps under the circumstances "gag" isn't the best word, because that little hanging thing is actually there to keep people from gagging. It's called the *uvula* and it helps guide food and liquid down the throat and away from the windpipe and nasal passages.

Do animals have uvulas, too?
Yes, some do.

The uvula's muscles also lift the roof of the mouth, again reducing the chance of choking. Unless, of course, you're laughing at the aforementioned cartoons—then even your uvula can't help you.

Why do people yawn?

NO ONE KNOWS, but there are several theories. Most say it is because our bodies run low on oxygen when we're tired and not breathing energetically. We involuntarily open up and suck some air in to catch up. Some believe it's also a way the body cools itself when it's getting too warm. People yawn when they are sleepy, and they yawn when it is warm and they are contented. Oftentimes when one person yawns, more people will follow suit, as if it is contagious. In fact, some of you may be yawning right now just from reading about yawns, thanks to the power of suggestion.

WHAT NERVE!

What exactly is the funny bone? Why is it called that?

WHAT WE CALL a "funny bone" isn't funny and it isn't a bone. It's a nerve called the *ulnar nerve,* which is entirely too exposed for its own good and yours. When it is hit, tingling, numbness, and pain strike the outer fingers and may take from seconds to minutes to subside. The name comes from a word play on the name of the bone that runs from the shoulder to the elbow. It's called the *humerus.* Now *that's* funny.

What's going on when my arm (or leg or foot) falls asleep?

IT'S NOT THAT you've cut the blood off to your limb, as most of us were told. It's a pinched nerve. When you bend your arm or leg, the muscles actually constrict nerves. If left in that position for a long enough time, then moved, your limb will feel like someone has come in the night and sewed someone else's limb to your body. As the nerve begins waking up, you will feel pricks like ant stings until the nerve is back up and running as usual.

> **Who's more likely to be colorblind, men or women?**
> Men.

If you sit for hours on end with a major leg nerve constricted, the nerve can actually become damaged and cause parts of the foot to stop functioning properly. However, uncrossing your legs, changing your sitting pattern, and keeping pressure off the damaged nerve will bring everything back to normal in a few days or weeks.

SOLAR ERUPTIONS

Why does looking at the sun make me sneeze?

THOSE WHO'VE studied the issue believe it is because the cranial nerves run very close to one another inside the head. When a stimulus as bright as the sun comes into the optic nerve through the eye, it stimulates a reflex reaction in the nearby olfactory nerve, triggering a sneeze. A portion of the population will sneeze every time they look toward the sun; a larger portion can help a sneeze along with sunlight. It gets more bizarre: Some people begin sneezing from the stimulation of a full stomach; some, from combing their hair; others, from tweezing their eyebrows or cleaning their ears with a cotton swab. Aside from the dangers of a comb or Q-Tip injury, there's no apparent harm from this cross-nerve stimulus.

> **What is happening when ears "pop"?**

YOU'VE GOT SOME SPLEENIN' TO DO

I've heard the phrase "Don't bust your spleen" and wondered what a spleen does. Is it crucial to staying alive?

THE SPLEEN is not crucial to life, and it was once thought not to do much of anything. Medicine has since learned, however, what a modestly important role the spleen does play. Located slightly under the rib cage in the left side of the body, the spleen is an important cog in the body's immunity machine. Although a person can make do without one—if it's lost to injury or disease—their chances of infection are higher, as are their chances of contracting pneumonia from a simple cold. The bug responsible for pneumonia is just one of many significant, death-causing germs that the spleen routinely filters out of the bloodstream in a healthy person. The germ causing malaria is another. It's not all doom-and-gloom without this organ, though. In an otherwise healthy adult who's living without a spleen, the chances of dying from an infection are about the same as the odds of dying from a house accident: 1 in 30,000.

For a picture of a spleen and other internal organs, go to the Cornell University Joan and Sanford Weill Education Center site at: http://140.251.5.102/Pathology_Images/

RAISE YOUR HAND IF YOU'RE SURE
Why do people sweat, and why does it smell?

SCIENTISTS KNOW that sweating is a cooling mechanism that keeps us from overheating, but they don't know why we sweat instead of cooling down in other ways. Other animals have sweat glands, but most of them go almost entirely unused because the animals have developed different methods to cool their blood and regulate their body temperature. Rabbits, for instance, rush blood through their ears to cool their body. Dogs pant. Some animals wallow in mud or water, and still others urinate on their legs.

Humans release two substances from over two million sweat glands in the skin, which tends to attract bacteria that smell bad. The explanation that seems most likely comes from the famous anthropologist Louis Leakey. His theory is that humans once used body odor as marking for their territory and to ward off predators. Eventually humans learned to defend themselves with weapons, but the strong smell lingered on.

Now human smell tends to ward off other humans, as well as anything else with a nose. As a result, societies have engaged in the war against body odor. Early weapons include perfumes, herbal concoctions, and sometimes even bathing. Late in the 19th century, scientists developed antibacterial solutions that killed germs growing in the armpits or on the feet, and in the 20th century, along came sweat-blocking agents called antiperspirants. So far, these substances are the most successful solutions to B.O. in the course of human history. Until we come up with something else or evolve out of our sweat glands, they'll just have to do.

Why do my feet smell bad? What can I do?

FEET SMELL because small microbes thrive in dark, damp places and sweaty feet seem like heaven to them. When these bacteria reproduce, they create gas, in much the same way intestinal bacteria reproduce and form flatulence. The two main microbes that like to party on feet are Corybacteria JK and Brevibacteria-linen, both of which smell pretty bad. Why are some people more prone to smelly feet than others? They may have more active sweat glands in their feet or more creases that moisture can stay in. Others don't expose their feet to the air often enough.

> **Where can I see a diagram of the human circulatory system?**

If you have a problem with foot odor, try carefully washing and drying your feet more often and leaving them out of socks and shoes to air-dry. Some experts suggest using an antibacterial substance like Betadine or Neosporin for a few days and seeing if that doesn't solve the problem. Keep your shoes clean and dry so bacteria won't grow. If these things don't help, there are prescription medicines available.

HUNKA BURNIN' FAT

Can I deliberately speed up my metabolism?

YES, YOU CAN take healthy steps to speed your metabolism. Everyone has a basal metabolic rate, defined as the lowest amount of energy exerted to keep the body at rest. Several factors contribute to this rate, with muscle mass playing a large role. Other factors include hormone output, anxiety, caffeine, nicotine, and overall body size. The larger the surface area, the more heat that is lost and the higher the metabolism. Artificial stimulants, although they work in small quantities, will also take a huge toll on your physical health. For a long-term, effective, and healthy way of increasing metabolism, lift weights and stop dieting: cutting calories to an unhealthy level slows metabolism as your body protects itself from starvation.

For more information, check out Eight Essential Exercises for Weight Training Newbies at www.thriveonline.com/shape/weights/weights.intro.html

SHRINKING VIOLET

Is it true that when a man gets cold, his penis and testicles shrink?

YES. THE TISSUE on the scrotum and the penis is a very pliable erectile tissue—like the tissue on nipples—designed so it can move. When a man gets cold, his testicles and penis often get pulled close to the body to maintain warmth. Sometimes the penis and testicles are pulled so close, it appears they're in danger of disappearing into the body. But don't panic! When the body warms again, they return to normal in a more dropped position.

SINISTER DESIGNS

What makes someone right-handed or left-handed?

IN A PERFECT world of chance, an equal number of people would have a right dominant hand or a left dominant hand. Oddly, most people are right-handed, and despite research about brain function, intelligence, and artistic talent, no one has been able to figure out why.

Do right-handed or left-handed people get injured more often?
Lefties do.

Is there any special support for "lefties" out there?

ABSOLUTELY. There's even a holiday to honor lefties. Left-handers Day is celebrated on August 13. For in-depth information for and about left-handed people, subscribe to *Left-Hander's Newsletter* at *www.lefthandpublishing.com/newsletter.html*

A WRINKLE IN TIME

Why do toes and fingers wrinkle in the bathtub?

ACTUALLY, THEY aren't wrinkling at all. They are puckering from swelling. The thick outside layer of skin called the *stratum corneum* takes on excess water when soaked—sort of like dried beans when soaked in water. The underlying skin and connective tissue don't absorb water and don't swell along with it. This anchoring of the skin-tissue layers makes the swelled area appear puckered.

It's not just the fingers and toes that do this, though they are easier to see because the stratum corneum in those areas is thickest. When you see your fingers and toes wrinkling, take it as a sign that your entire body is on guard to prevent water, soap, dirt, and germs from invading through your skin.

On the Farm

"HOWYA GONNA KEEP 'EM down on the farm after they've seen Paree?" asks an old postwar song. Sure enough, in the United States, traditional farm living seems almost a thing of the past. But as Jeeves can attest, people remain curious about this way of life.

BARNS, YET NOBLE

Why are barns painted red?

TYPICALLY, barns are not red, but more of a rust color. There's a practical reason. A barn is a big investment in both raw materials and labor, so early farmers looked for an inexpensive paint that would protect their wood from the elements. They discovered that a good base could be made from skim milk, linseed oil, and lime. Then they tried various ways of adding color to the mix. They wanted an intense dark color that would cover rough-hewn wood in one coat and not show every bit of dirt and grime. Eventually they tried adding iron oxide extracted from rocks or rusty iron for color. The resulting brick-red finish was cheap, good camouflage for stains, and quite durable. Red barns have become such an archetypal image that many farmers still paint their barns that color, even when they're using store-bought exterior paint and can have colors like Avocado, Frosted Lilac, Chartreuse, or Autumn Sun for no extra charge.

What famous ship was dismantled and made into a barn?

THE *MAYFLOWER*. Cut and planed lumber was hard to come by in the New World, and since the Pilgrims didn't intend to go back to Europe, they decided that they needed a barn more than they needed a ship.

THE BOVINE COMEDY

Why are there different kinds of cows? Isn't a cow a cow?

COWS COME in two different species: *Bos indicus,* from Asia (with a hump), and *Bos taurus,* from Europe. Together, the two species include (at last count) 274 different breeds. Nearly all North American cattle are from the European *taurus* type. For milk production, the most popular breeds are the Guernsey, Holstein, Ayrshire, Jersey, and Brown Swiss. The breeds not only all *look* different but they also produce different milk. For example, the Holstein has the classic-cow black blotches on white and gives the most milk per cow; a Guernsey has fawn coloring and distinctive yellowish milk; and a Jersey, also fawn-colored, has the highest percentage of butterfat in its milk. For beef, the most popular breeds are Angus, Hereford, Charolais, Shorthorn, Santa Gertrudis, Brahman, and Brangus (a Brahman-Angus cross). These breeds are known by varying physical characteristics. For example, the Angus is black and hornless, and the Hereford is recognized by its red body and white face. The Brahman is usually all white, with distinctive floppy ears, while the Charolais is more of a cream color and has typical ears.

> **Does a cow's milk taste different if she eats onions?**
> Yes. It tastes oniony.

For exhaustive information about all breeds of major farm animals, check out the Oklahoma State University animal breeds site: www.ansi.okstate.edu/breeds/

Were there ever wild cows?

WHEN YOU LOOK at their vacant stares, it's hard to imagine that a cow could survive in the wild. Pigs, sure, chickens, maybe—but cows? Apparently they did at one time, though.

Although the first cattle were domesticated over 6,000 years ago by the residents of what are now Asia and Switzerland, roving bands of wild cattle called *aurochs* were depicted on prehistoric cave paintings. These feral cows had the wits to survive in the wild until 1627, the year that the last known surviving *auroch* was killed by a poacher on a hunting preserve near Warsaw, Poland.

Is it legal to sell and eat horse meat in the U.S.?

How do you milk a cow by hand?

VERY CAREFULLY, of course. Cows can *kick,* my friend. Hand milking is a dying art but it's still done, despite the invention of the mechanical milker in 1894. If you're lucky, the cow you're hoping to milk has been hand-milked before and is used to being prodded and pulled in that delicate spot. If not, may Io, the goddess of cows, be with you.

1. Approach the beast with a confident yet insouciant attitude. It's best to use a stanchion around the cow's neck to keep her from turning and biting you or running away, and an antikicking device if you've got one. There's nothing more discouraging than having a nearly full pail kicked over—except, of course, getting kicked yourself. Cows have been described as having the temperament of a four-year-old child, so giving the cow some hay to keep her occupied is a good idea, too.

2. After you've got her settled in, wash the udder thoroughly with a mild veterinary disinfectant and dry the teats by patting them with a clean towel.

3. Before using your pail, take your thumb and index finger and squeeze a little milk from each teat into your hand. Inspect it carefully to make sure it looks like milk from the carton and not watery cottage cheese. It may take a few minutes of this before the cow relaxes and "drops her milk."

4. At that point, curl your index finger around the teat and back against your thumb and squeeze to simulate the effect of a sucking calf. It takes about 340 good squirts to fill a standard

milk pail (about five gallons), and most cows produce about one pail a day, so be prepared for your hands to get a good workout.

Do cows really have four stomachs?

NO. A COW has one stomach, but it has four chambers. That's because grass is hard to fully digest and cows need a lot of nutrients. A typical cow takes in 100 pounds of grass and 300 pounds of water a day. The food initially goes into the *rumen,* the first chamber of its stomach, where it is digested for a while. Then the cow regurgitates it as cud and chews it to break the grass up further. Then it swallows the mess into the second stomach chamber, the *reticulum.* From there, the food passes leisurely through two more chambers, the *omasum* and the *abomasum,* before cruising down the intestines and heading back to fertilize the meadow.

Do cowbirds and cowslips have any connection to cows?

COWSLIPS, a type of primrose, are so called because they are especially adept at growing in the meadow muffins that cows leave behind. Cowbirds, a small blackbird, used to ride on the backs of American bison and eat the bugs they stirred up while roaming the plains of America. However, once the buffaloes were all but killed off, the birds easily switched their allegiance and began riding on the backs of cows. The birds get a ride, and they eat the flies that bedevil the cows, so everyone's happy. The cowslips are happy, too. Life is good.

MILKING THE TOURISTS

I've seen several roadside fiberglass cows on my travels. Which is the world's biggest?

ACCORDING TO the editors of *Roadside America* (the book and its Web site), there are world-class giant cows all over America. Not surprisingly, most are centered around America's dairy heartland. The biggest, they say, is "Salem Sue" in New Salem,

North Dakota. Salem Sue stands 38 feet tall . . . tall enough that you can stand under her impressive teats without bumping your head.

For photographs and locations of Salem Sue and many other "Cow-lossus of Roads," see www.roadsideamerica.com/set/cow.html

SOO-EEE!

What's the difference between a pig and a hog?

IT'S POUNDAGE. In the United States, any swine below 180 pounds is called a *pig;* a pig that grows larger than that is called a *hog.* In England, all swine are considered pigs, whatever their weight. There are other specialized names for pigs in their various stages of life as well: At birth they are *piglets,* weaning after age two to five weeks; a young pig is called a *shoat* or *weaner;* a half-grown pig is a *barrow* (castrated male) or *gilt* (female); adults are *boars* (uncastrated males), *stags* (castrated males), or *sows* (females).

> **How do I make a pig look pretty for the State Fair?** Ask!

Are pigs mellow, or can they be dangerous?

DANGEROUS TO WHOM? Pigs are omnivorous, eating—well, like a pig—nearly anything they come across. Fruits, vegetables, mushrooms, bird eggs, rodents, earthworms, roots, carrion, lizards, small animals, and even occasionally parts of people all look like food to them. Ranchers say that rattlesnakes are a special treat for pigs—they will gobble one up before the rattler knows what hit it. Although it's true that more people are killed by pigs than by sharks every year, pigs are not usually hostile, just strong and persistent at times.

What happened to the pig that played Babe?

"PIG"? Make that "pigs"—48 of them, and that was for the first movie, *Babe,* alone. New piglets had to be trained continuously throughout filming, because they could only be filmed while they were 16 to 18 weeks old for size reasons. To make them all look alike (and to bring out their eyes), a makeup artist dyed their eyelashes black. By the second movie, *Babe: Pig in the City*, the filmmakers used fewer piglets and let realistic-looking mechanical pig puppets do more of the work.

The filmmakers assured the public that none of the Babes would be slaughtered for ham and bacon but instead would be distributed to agricultural colleges, universities, schools, and farms to live out the 15 to 20 years of their natural life spans.

HERE A GROIN, THERE A GRUNZ, EVERYWHERE A NEFF NEFF

What do pigs say in other countries?

IF YOU ASK PIGS, you'd find that there isn't a lot of variation from country to country—the sounds are similar worldwide for such pig sentiments as "Feed me," "Go away," "Let's make a little bacon of our own," and so on. However, how people interpret those sounds varies widely from country to country. Americans hear "oink oink," whereas Russians hear, "kryoo krool," the French hear "groin, groin," Germans hear "grunz!," and Swedes hear "neff neff." It gets stranger still. How about "hulu hulu" (Mardarin Chinese), "rok rok" (Serbo-Croatian), "buu buu" (Japanese), "crum crum" (Polish), "ood ood" (Thai), "hrju hrju" (Ukrainian), or "ut it" (Vietnamese)?

> How many varieties of cheese are there in the world?
> About 400.

What do chickens say in other languages?

A ROOSTER'S crow is so distinctive that there isn't much variation between "cock a doodle doo!" (English) and "ku ku ri ku!" (Hebrew), "ko ki ko ko!" (Japanese), and "ku ka rzhi ku!" (Russian). However, language differences appear when you start talking chicks and hens. Chicks say "twit twit" in Arabic, "pip pip" in Danish, "plep plep" in German, and "jiap jiap" in

Thai. While to English-speaking listeners hens "cluck cluck," the sound becomes "cot cot cot codet" in French, "gak-gak" in German, "gut gut gudak" in Turkish, "gaggalago" in Icelandic, and "pak pak pak" in Hebrew.

COSMIC YOLK

Which came first, the chicken or the egg?

A NUMBER of religions have legends about the creation of the Earth. If you believe that any of them are literally true, then you'll have to buck all evidence and believe that the chicken was created first. However, most likely the egg came first. Chickens have been traced back genetically to an earlier bird in Indochina called the red jungle fowl. At some point one of these jungle foremothers laid an egg that had enough genetic mutations so that what hatched would be considered more of a chicken than a red jungle fowl. So the best evidence indicates that the egg came first, about 8,000 years ago, then the chicken.

> **Where did the term "scapegoat" come from?**

Does a baby chick breathe inside the egg? How?

YES, IT DOES. An eggshell may look solid, but it actually has about 8,000 pores that are large enough for oxygen to flow in and carbon dioxide to flow out. John Davy of Edinburgh, Scotland, proved this in 1863 by pumping pressurized air into an underwater egg and watching thousands of tiny bubbles appear on the surface.

Why are some chicken eggs brown?

A FEW DECADES ago, when people came to the conclusion that brown bread, brown flour, and brown sugar were more nutritious than their white counterparts, many also extrapolated that brown eggs must be healthier, too. Conversely, many lovers of white eggs figured there must be something alien and weird about the brown ones. In reality there's no discernible difference in flavor or nutrition between brown and white eggs. The only difference is that brown eggs are laid by rust-red chickens, such as the Rhode Island Red, while white eggs come from white chickens, most notably the White Leghorn, which makes up about 90% of the North American egg-laying chicken population. So can't we all get along?

Can chickens fly?

BETTER THAN a penguin, emu, kagu, kiwi, and ostrich combined. However, not that well compared to most other birds. The world's record for a nonstop chicken flight is a little more than 230 yards.

How long would chickens live if we didn't eat them?

BROILER CHICKENS, the ones we eat, are usually butchered after seven or eight weeks of life. If kept away from the frying pan and Colonel Sanders, they will live about eight years.

IT SELLS LIKE HOTCAKES!

How much maple syrup does a farmer get from one tree?

A GOOD SUGAR MAPLE tree will yield about 35 gallons of sap in its winter harvest. Once the excess water is boiled away, the 35 gallons of sap become only about a gallon of syrup.

LEARN TO BE OUT STANDING IN YOUR FIELD

Why the four H's in the 4-H Club?

YOU'D THINK that the four H's would be something like "horses, hogs, hoes, and horticulture." But no. It's really "Head, Heart, Hands and Health," the idea being that farming promotes all of these things. The organization was set up in 1915 by the U.S. Agricultural Extension Service to teach youngsters the basics of good farming (and good living). The club is led by volunteers, and even in our citified time, about five million kids participate in its programs each year. The organization has links to similar programs in 80 countries around the world.

LONG AGO AND FARM AWAY . . .

Why do we have daylight saving time?

THIS ANNUAL TIME CHANGE—setting clocks one hour ahead of standard time—was started by Benjamin Franklin but became popular during World War I. The idea was to give more daylight to farmers without making them get up earlier. Another holdover from our rural past is the traditional school year, designed to make kids available for summer growing-season chores. And finally, there are November elections, timed to let farmers travel into town to vote after finishing their harvest but before snow makes roads impassable.

ALL CROPPED OUT

Is it true a bunch of farmers built a statue in honor of the boll weevil?

YES, THERE'S ONE in Dothan, Alabama. It seems a strange thing, since the weevils (a type of beetle) destroy cotton crops (a *boll* is a cotton pod). But a particularly bad year convinced local farmers to diversify into other crops—which turned out to be more profitable than cotton. In gratitude, they decided that the insect pest was a hero.

Are there any countries with no farms at all?

MONACO, Nauru, and Singapore, to name three. They are all tiny urbanized or resort countries. There is also no evidence that the nation-state Vatican City has farms of any sort, no matter how large the pope's worldwide flock is.

President & Accounted For

IS THE WHITE HOUSE HAUNTED? Did Richard Nixon really replace the swimming pool with a bowling alley? Whatever happened to George Washington's false teeth? Was James Buchanan gay? People worldwide have long had a peculiar fascination for what goes on in the White House. And some of those goings-on have been peculiar indeed . . . .

ALL IN THE FIRST FAMILY

How many presidents have been related to each other?

MORE THAN ONE might think. John Adams and John Quincy Adams were father and son; William Harrison and Benjamin Harrison were grandfather and grandson; James Madison and Zachary Taylor were second cousins; and Theodore Roosevelt and Franklin D. Roosevelt were fifth cousins.

PRESIDENTIAL NAME-CALLING

Was the president always called "Mr. President"?

NOT AT FIRST. Washington wanted citizens to call him "His Mightiness, the President," but to many people, that sounded too much like addressing the king they'd fought so hard to shed. The next president, John Adams, thought he should be called "His Highness, the President of the United States and

Protector of their Liberties," but even fewer people went along with that. Finally, Thomas Jefferson began shedding the trappings of imperialism that earlier presidents had insisted on. After his inaugural, he walked back to his boarding house instead of riding in a coach. He was also the first president to actually shake hands with ordinary people (previous presidents had greeted people only with a slight, dignified bow.) People began calling him "Mr. President," a good mix of respect and equality.

Wasn't there something funny about Eleanor Roosevelt and her maiden name?

FUNNY? That surely depends on one's sense of humor. Eleanor Roosevelt was the First Lady of President Franklin D. Roosevelt and a powerful force to be reckoned with in her own right. What many people don't realize is that she was a niece of President Teddy Roosevelt and a distant cousin of her husband. As a result, she didn't have to change her name when she married, because she was already Eleanor Roosevelt.

What's the most popular presidential first name?

JAMES. Six of the presidents have been Jims. Tied for second most popular, with four presidents each, are John and William.

THE FATHER OF HIS COUNTRY

How many children did George Washington have?

THE "FATHER OF HIS COUNTRY" wasn't quite as prolific in his immediate family. He remained childless.

How come that famous portrait of George Washington was never finished?

GEORGE WASHINGTON hated the tedium of sitting for days at a time when getting his portrait painted. When he retired from public office, he swore he'd never pose again . . . until his wife, Martha, suggested that both of them pose for portraits to be hung above the mantelpiece in their home. They chose Gilbert

Stuart, a celebrated portraitist who took the assignment gladly because he needed the money. A hopeless alcoholic and profligate spender, Stuart knew that not only could he collect the commission from the Washingtons but, if he could hang on to the original painting for a while, he could probably paint and sell an unlimited number of copies of it in those prephotographic days. Because Washington's image was in high demand and he had often refused to sit for portraits, the copies would be very valuable. Stuart had done the same thing with two earlier portraits he'd done of Washington—sold dozens of copies while he took his sweet time delivering the originals to their rightful owners.

> **How did the Republicans get to be known as the GOP?**

The problem was that Martha Washington was wise to him. She didn't want to wait for months and didn't want dozens of copies made, so she made Stuart promise that he'd deliver the paintings "the moment they were finished." He reluctantly agreed, then began trying to figure out how to get around the agreement. He finally found a loophole, and he exploited it to the maximum. He finished the important parts of the portrait, named *Athenaeum Head,* in 1796, but left off a few brush-strokes. Time after time, he turned away insistent messengers from Mrs. Washington with the completely truthful assertion: "It's not done yet."

Meanwhile, he used the original as a model to paint hundreds of copies, including one he eventually palmed off on Mrs. Washington as the original ("It is not a good likeness at all," she told friends). On a good day, according to his daughter, Stuart could pump out a portrait of Washington in two hours that he could sell for $100, a hefty amount of money at the time. The government got into the act a few centuries later, using Stuart's unfinished portrait as a model for Washington's portrait on the dollar bill. . . .

To view the "unfinished" portraits of George and Martha Washington, go to www.npg.si.edu/exh/gw/gwexh.htm

Where can I see George Washington's wooden teeth?

WASHINGTON had one remaining tooth at the time of his inauguration. Despite popular myth, however, he didn't have wooden teeth. His four sets of dentures, one crafted by Paul Revere, were made of hippopotamus bone, elephant ivory, and teeth from cows and dead people, held together with gold palates and springs. None of them worked well. In person, you can see his last tooth and dentures at the National Museum of Dentistry on the campus of the University of Maryland in Baltimore. Or you can see them online at *www.post-gazette.com/ magazine/19990112miller2.asp*

WHITE HOUSE ROOMS AND ALLEYS

Was the White House always white?

NOT ALWAYS. Back when it was called the "Presidential Palace," it was made of brownstone. However, in 1814 the British captured Washington, D.C., and burned many government buildings, including the Palace and the Capitol. So much of its shell was charred from fire that painting the building became necessary. White covered the burn marks well

> **Was Elvis the first rock star to visit the White House?**
> No. The Turtles two years earlier, in 1969.

and brightened the place up. It had never looked much like a palace anyway, and even less so with bright white paint, so people stopped calling it the Palace and started calling it "the white house." Teddy Roosevelt made the popular name official when he had "Theodore Roosevelt, The White House" printed on his presidential stationery.

Did Nixon really replace the White House pool with a bowling alley?

IT'S TRUE THAT Richard Nixon was a bowling fan, but so was Abe Lincoln, who played ninepins regularly. The postwar bowling craze that brought bowling alleys into every corner of the nation gave Harry Truman the idea of putting regulation bowling lanes into the basement of the White House. He, Bess, and daughter Margaret often unwound by bowling into the night. Nixon did have the pool covered over, but it was to expand the press room. And no, that isn't where the term "pool reporter" came from.

Does the White House have any poltergeists?

THERE'S BARELY a ghost of a chance of it. Some of the reported spirits include Abraham Lincoln pacing the hallways, Thomas Jefferson playing the violin, Abigail Adams hanging laundry, and Dolley Madison inspecting the rosebushes she planted.

How many rooms are in the White House? 132. Of these, 32 are bathrooms

SMART AND DUMB

How many presidents have won the Nobel Peace Prize?

ONLY TWO, Woodrow Wilson and Theodore Roosevelt. In comparison, one vice president and five U.S. secretaries of state have also won it. The only president to have won a Pulitzer Prize was John Kennedy, for his book *Profiles in Courage* (1957).

Who was the smartest president?

HARD TO SAY for sure, but James Garfield must be up there in the top percentile. He was a college professor in ancient languages and literature and once published a mathematical proof of the Pythagorean theorem. An ambidextrous man, Garfield also had a nifty trick that is probably the best example of presidential multitasking: He could simultaneously write Latin with one hand and Greek with the other. Another candidate for most erudite president is Herbert Hoover, who translated ancient texts from Latin. When he and his wife wanted to speak privately when other people were present, they conversed in Mandarin Chinese. What's interesting, though, is that neither of these men were considered great presidents, so it may be true that intelligence is not necessarily a requirement of the job.

Did any of the presidents invent anything?

ABE LINCOLN, 12 years before he became the 16th president, was granted U.S. Patent No. 6,468. The four-digit patent number is a telling indication of just how long ago that was. The device was intended to help grounded steamboats get off shoals and sandbars without jettisoning heavy cargo; it involved inflatable chambers designed to float the ship off obstacles. It was a promising idea, but was never tested or manufactured. This is the only known patent held by a U.S. president.

> **Which president said he believed the Earth was flat?**
> Andrew Jackson.

FREEDOM FOR ALL!
WELL, MAYBE NOT YOU . . .

How many of the presidents owned slaves?

SHAMEFULLY, most of the presidents who served before and immediately after the Civil War owned slaves. Thomas Jefferson, who wrote ringing proclamations about the equality of all people, owned 185 slaves at Monticello. When the Revolutionary War broke out, 22 of his slaves decided they had little chance of getting freedom from the Americans, so they ran away to fight for the British. A widower, Jefferson also apparently fathered several children with his slave Sally Hemmings. Here's a twist to the story: Thanks to a similar master-slave liaison, Sally Hemmings happened to be the deceased Mrs. Jefferson's half-sister.

Other slave-owning presidents: Zachary Taylor owned more than 300 slaves while in the White House. George Washington owned 216. Others included Madison, Monroe, Jackson, Tyler, Polk, Taylor, and Johnson. Most mystifying, though, was

Union general Ulysses S. Grant. He owned four while fighting Southerners over the issue of slavery, and he refused to free his slaves until after the Civil War ended, when he was forced to do so by law. Ironically, his counterpart on the Southern side, General Robert E. Lee, was morally opposed to the institution of slavery and never owned one. . . .

FIRST PETS

Have there been any unusual pets in the White House?

CALVIN COOLIDGE had a raccoon. Teddy Roosevelt had a badger. Herbert Hoover had a horned toad. Woodrow Wilson had a ram named Old Ike that visitors fed chewing tobacco to, so that it became hopelessly addicted. Abraham Lincoln's son Tad had a pet turkey, and Andrew Jackson had a parrot with language so foul the bird had to be removed from Jackson's funeral. But probably the most unusual pet was an alligator that John Quincy Adams kept because, he said, he enjoyed "the spectacle of guests fleeing from the room in terror." That John Quincy was such a fun fellow. . . .

> Is it true you can buy a flag that's been flown over the Capitol?
> Yes. Contact your congressperson.

EMBARRASSING ELECTIONS

Has any U.S. presidential candidate ever won every state in an election?

THAT'S HAPPENED TWICE. George Washington in 1792 and James Monroe in 1820 won all the states. Of course, they had it easier back then, because there were only 15 states in 1792 and 24 states in 1820. More recently, Richard Nixon and Ronald Reagan both won 49 out of 50 states in re-election bids.

Has a U.S. presidential candidate ever gotten most of the popular votes, but lost the election anyway?

IT'S ONE OF the maddening features of the American system that such a thing can happen, and in fact it *has* happened three times. In 1824, Andrew Jackson got 155,872 votes but lost to John Quincy Adams, even though Adams received only 105,321. In 1876, Samuel Tilden got 4,284,757 votes, but widespread fraud by Republican-controlled electoral commissions in three states got Rutherford Hayes elected with 4,033,950. Again in 1888, Democrat Grover Cleveland received 5,540,050 votes, yet lost to Benjamin Harrison's 5,444,337 votes.

PERSONAL STATISTICS

Were all the bearded U.S. presidents also Republicans?

WELL, NOW THAT you mention it, yes. All of the bearded presidents—Abraham Lincoln, Ulysses Grant, Rutherford Hayes, James Garfield, and Benjamin Harrison—were Republicans.

Has there ever been a U.S. president who didn't profess any religion?

HARD TO BELIEVE in a time when candidates attempt to out-pious each other, but Thomas Jefferson, Abraham Lincoln, and Andrew Johnson were not members of any church.

How are the others divided? John Adams, John Quincy Adams, Millard Fillmore, and William Taft were Unitarians. John Kennedy was Roman Catholic. All the other presidents belonged to various Protestant Christian denominations: Episcopal (11 presidents), Presbyterian (7), Baptist (4), Methodist (3), Disciples of Christ (3), Quaker (2), Dutch Reformed (2), and Congregationalist (1).

Was any U.S. president an only child?
No.

Are U.S. presidents taller than the average person?

ON THE AVERAGE, YES. The taller candidate has won in almost every presidential election. While presidents have ranged from 5' 4" (Madison) to 6' 4" (Lincoln), the average president has been 5' 10.5"—remarkable when you consider how short the average person was a century ago.

How many U.S. presidents belonged to Masonic lodges?

AT LEAST 15 have been members of that secret society.

Were any U.S. presidents really born in a log cabin?

FOUR OF THEM WERE. Abe Lincoln, Millard Fillmore, James Buchanan, and James Garfield.

Was Jackie Kennedy the youngest First Lady?

ALTHOUGH JOHN KENNEDY was the youngest president, Jackie was only the third-youngest First Lady—age 31—when her husband was elected. Younger First Ladies were Julia Taylor, 24, and Frances Cleveland, 21—both married to men more than twice their ages.

WAY-TOO-PERSONAL STATISTICS

I remember the uproar when a woman on MTV asked Bill Clinton if he wore boxers or briefs, but I don't remember what he said.

AFTER A SHORT pause, the future leader of the Western world answered, "Briefs."

Were any U.S. presidents gay?

OF COURSE, it's impossible to know for sure. However, our only bachelor president, James Buchanan, had that reputation in his lifetime. His longtime roommate, Senator and later Vice President William Rufus De Vane King of Alabama, also never married. According to historians, the two had an inseparable relationship for nearly 25 years, until King's death—in fact, King was called "Buchanan's better half," "James's wife," and "Miss Nancy" by some of his colleagues.

When the two were temporarily separated after King was appointed minister to France in 1844, King wrote Buchanan, "I am selfish enough to hope you will not be able to procure an associate who will cause you to feel no regret at our separation." Buchanan wrote to a friend, "I am now 'solitary and alone,' having no companion in the house with me. I have gone a wooing to several gentlemen but have not succeeded with any one of them. I feel that it is not good for man to be alone; and should not be astonished to find myself married to some old maid who can nurse me when I am sick, provide good dinners for me when I am well, and not expect from me any very ardent or romantic affection."

But that's not all. Hang onto your stovepipe hats, because a few rogue historians also claim that Abraham Lincoln was homoerotically involved with lifelong friend Joshua Speed. They shared private thoughts, fears, desires, and a bed for four years. Lincoln biographer Carl Sandburg wrote that their relationship had "a streak of lavender and spots soft as May violets."

Which U.S. officials are not allowed to travel together?
The president and vice president.

A TURKEY FOR THE PRESIDENT

Did Ronald Reagan and his wife Nancy ever appear in a movie together?

NOT JUST A MOVIE, but Reagan and the former Nancy Davis also appeared in a made-for-TV presentation. The 1957 movie was an unremarkable military drama called *Hellcats of the Navy*. The 1960 G.E. Theater holiday production on television was likewise unremarkable, but decades before Reagan had any political aspirations, the show sported an uncannily prophetic title: *A Turkey for the President* . . . .

POLITICS IS HARD, DEATH IS EASY

How many U.S. presidents have died in office?

EIGHT. Four from assassination, the others from natural causes.

Which U.S. president died at the youngest age?

JOHN KENNEDY. The youngest president died in office at the age of 46. The oldest surviving president so far was John Adams, who lived 90 years and eight months, long enough to see his son also become president. Adams beat out Herbert Hoover, who lived a mere 90 years and two months.

Have any U.S. presidents died on the Fourth of July?

INDEPENDENCE DAY has been unusually dangerous for presidents. Three have died on July 4, and one contracted a fatal illness on that day.

Former presidents John Adams and Thomas Jefferson died within minutes of each other on July 4, 1826, exactly 50 years after the Declaration of Independence was signed. Former president James Monroe died exactly five years later. In 1850, President Zachary Taylor celebrated a hot July 4th with speeches and too many picnic foods. He took to his bed that night with acute indigestion and died five days later, largely thanks to the medical "treatment" he received (bleeding with leeches and dosing with mercury compounds), passing the presidency on to Millard Fillmore. On the other hand, July 4th hasn't been completely unlucky for presidents, since Calvin Coolidge was born on that day in 1872.

What state has the most U.S. presidents' graves?

VIRGINIA WITH SEVEN, followed by New York with six and Ohio with five. On the other hand, every president ever named Andrew is buried in Tennessee (Jackson and Johnson). As is James K. Polk—not an Andrew, that is, but buried in Tennessee.

What were the last words heard by John Kennedy before he died?

SECONDS BEFORE shots rang out in Dealey Plaza on November 23, 1963, Nellie Connally turned to the president and, referring to the cheering crowds lining the street, shouted: "You can't say Dallas doesn't love you, Mr. President!"

What were the last words heard by Abraham Lincoln before he died?

"YOU SOCK-DOLOGIZING old mantrap!" It was a line from the comedy Lincoln was watching, a British satire of American manners called *Our American Cousin*. After actor Asa Trenchard delivered the line, the audience roared with laughter. John Wilkes Booth, waiting at the back of the president's box for audience noise to cover the sound of his approach, quickly stepped up, put a gun to the back of the president's head, and fired.

HOW TO SUCCEED A PRESIDENT WITHOUT REALLY TRYING

I remember an old National Lampoon *comic strip in which the secretary of transportation plotted the murder of everyone in the way of him becoming president. How many people would he have to kill?*

FOURTEEN. But it could be worse—if he had been secretary of veteran affairs, for example, he would have had to kill 17 people.

The line of succession for the U.S. presidency is vice president, speaker of the House, and president pro tempore of the Senate. If they all die, then the job passes to the president's cabinet in this order: secretary of state, secretary of the treasury, secretary of defense, attorney general, secretaries of the interior, agriculture, commerce, labor, health and human services, housing and urban development, transportation, energy, education, and veteran affairs. During the president's annual State of the Union address, in which all of the above would be likely to be in attendance,

Where can I see a floor plan of the White House?

one random cabinet member stays away each year to ensure that there'll be someone to take over the reins of government if the Capitol dome caves in.

Did anybody personally witness more than one presidential assassination?

HOW ABOUT THREE? Unlucky Robert Todd Lincoln was there as his father died in 1865. He was also present on July 2, 1881, when James Garfield was felled by an assassin while waiting for a train in the Washington station of the Baltimore and Potomac Railroad. And finally, he was also standing nearby the Pan-American exposition in Buffalo in 1901 when William McKinley was shot. After that, Robert Lincoln decided to stay away from state affairs.

For more weird trivia about U.S. presidents check out www.americanpresidents.com/

The Written Word

LITERATURE ENTERTAINS, INSPIRES, and offers a means with which to interpret the world. Good characters can inhabit our imaginations as vividly as the people in our real lives, and a good poem can open the doors of perception . . . .

POETIC LICENSE

Does anything rhyme with the words "orange" and "purple"?

ACCORDING TO poetry experts, no. That fact sometimes drives poets nearly loony. As a limerick puts it:

> I'll drink or I'll use a syringe
> I'll hang myself up on a doorhinge
> Not a belch nor a burp'll
> E'er match up with "purple"
> And no one can ever rhyme "orange."

What's the name of that beautiful 17th-century poem found in Old St. Paul's Church in Baltimore?

YOU MEAN "Desiderata," which begins, "Go placidly amid the noise and haste…"? It was on a lot of posters in the 1960s, attributed as "found in Old Saint Paul's Church, A.D. 1692." It may be beautiful, but it wasn't found in Baltimore's Old St. Paul's Church and it isn't from the 17th century. Its author was Indiana lawyer and businessman Max Ehrmann, and the copyright on the poem is 1927.

A genuine slip-up gave the wrong origins to the poem: In the 1950s, Old St. Paul's housed a clergyman by the name of Frederick Ward Kates, who liked putting inspirational phrases on his church bulletins for his congregation. He ran across a copy of Ehrmann's "Desiderata" and printed it. On the letter-head, there was also the founding date of the church: "Old Saint Paul's Church, Baltimore, A.D. 1692." The founding date of the church became confused with the authorship date of the poem, and because the poem was pretty, it got circulated into the heart of the Flower Power movement in San Francisco. Banners, framed cross-stitch patterns, posters, and T-shirts were created bearing the poem. Everyone thought the beautiful, cosmic piece ("You are a child of the universe / no less than the trees & the stars...") was ancient wisdom being passed from the 1690s to the 1960s.

In 1977, a local news writer for the *Washington Post*, Barbara J. Katz, began tracking down the history of "Desiderata" after hearing conflicting stories. She pinpointed the true author as hobbyist poet/playwright Ehrmann and discovered how the slip-up occurred at Old St. Paul's.

You can read the full article in the Washington Post *archives online for a small fee:* www.washingtonpost.com/

What does haiku actually mean in Japanese?

ALTHOUGH SOME people assume it means something like "incomprehensible nature poem," in actuality, the definition is far less interesting. The term comes from a combination of two other Japanese poetry forms: *haikai* and *hokku*. Haikai is a form of *renga* (linked-verse poem) that's humorous. Hokku is the first verse of a renga. It is used to set the tone of the rest of the poem but only has three lines in which to do so. In the 1600s, Japanese poetry enthusiasts started to appreciate the hokku standing on its own, without the following renga or haikai—just a poem in and of itself. The idea caught on and became a popular art form in Japan.

How did the Chinese poet Li Po die?

LI PO (A.D. 701–762), a distant relative of Chinese royals and sometime follower of Taoist principles, supposedly drowned in a lake while drunkenly trying to grasp the reflection of the moon in its waters. He was a wide-eyed, heavy-drinking romantic, and legend has it that he was granted all the wine he wanted by royal decree. The truth is, because he is China's most honored poet, much of what he did has now been romanticized and much of what is known about him is only guesswork.

How do you write love poems?

We do know that Li Po went off twice to Taoist monastaries, spent much of his time simply wandering about writing poetry on nature and wine (although he really wanted a job in the royal court), and several times got caught up in political intrigues. At one point, he had charges brought against him for aligning himself with the wrong prince in a power struggle, but he managed to have the charges dropped after a few years.

Many of Li Po's wandering sprees were preceded by official banishments for being too close to this or that segment of the royal family. Reliable sources suggest that his work wasn't fully appreciated until after his death and that no royal decree about wine or anything else would have been given while he was living. According to some historians, Li Po really died in seclusion at a friend's house at the age of 61.

FOR BETTER AND VERSE

How many of Emily Dickinson's poems were published during her lifetime?

SEVEN. She rarely showed her work to anyone, not even her family, and the seven were published by acquaintances without her knowledge or consent. It wasn't until four years after her death in 1886 that the first collection of her pieces was published.

Why was Samuel Taylor Coleridge's poem "Kubla Khan" never finished?

BECAUSE SOMEONE knocked on his door and interrupted him. This normally wouldn't have been a problem, but Coleridge was writing while high on opium. The interruption caused whatever train of thought he had going to be lost forever.

Do the e's stand for anything in the name of poet e. e. cummings?
Yes. They stand for Edward and Estlin, respectively.

PROFESSIONAL JEALOUSY

Who was known as "the drunken fool"?

THAT WOULD BE Shakespeare. According to some reports, Voltaire couldn't stand the great poet and playwright, so he called him "the drunken fool." Coincidentally (or not), Shakespeare pursued this theme for characters in many of his works. Most of his comedies had one main character that was portrayed as a drunken fool whose tricks, antics, and foolishness were key to unfolding the plot. Voltaire also supposedly called Shakespeare's work "this enormous dunghill."

How many famous writers have disliked Shakespeare's work?

MOST WRITERS have the highest regard for the writer from Avon. However, anyone can be a critic; for the sake of a good chuckle, here is what a few great artists have said of Shakespeare:

> I have tried lately to read Shakespeare, and found it so intolerably dull that it nauseated me. —*Charles Dickens*

> With the single exception of Homer, there is no eminent writer, not even Sir Walter Scott, whom I can despise so entirely as I despise Shakespeare when I measure my mind against his. The intensity of my impatience with him occasionally reaches such a pitch, that it would

positively be a relief to me to dig him up and throw stones at him. —*George Bernard Shaw*

Shakespeare never has six lines together without a fault. Perhaps you may find seven, but this does not refute my general assertion.—*Samuel Johnson*

Shakespeare's name, you may depend on it, stands absurdly too high and will go down. He has no invention as to stories, none whatever. He took all his plots from old novels, and threw their stories into a dramatic shape, at as little expense of thought as you or I could turn his plays back again into prose tales. —*Lord Byron*

Crude, immoral, vulgar and senseless. —*Leo Tolstoy*

Did Shakespeare ever mention America in his plays?

YES, ONCE. In *The Comedy of Errors,* during a discussion between Antipholus of Syracuse and Dromio of Syracuse, Dromio describes a woman—a rather large woman, who, in his mind, is globe shaped. During the course of the conversation, Antipholus urges Dromio to keep pinpointing geographic locations on her large body. Dromio says he found America "upon her nose all o'er embellished with rubies, carbuncles, sapphires, declining their rich aspect to the hot breath of Spain; who sent whole armadoes of caracks to be ballast at her nose." Ireland didn't fare so well...or so high up on her anatomy: Antipholus asks, "In what part of her body stands Ireland?" And Dromio responds, "Marry, in her buttocks: I found it out by the bogs."

How many words did Shakespeare coin?

SHAKESPEARE IS given credit for as many as 10,000 first-used words and phrases in his plays and poems. But did he actually coin them? Some of them, perhaps, but it's likely that most of the words were commonly used in his time and his plays are merely the earliest known written usage. Some historians give him credit for actually coining all 10,000, but others cut the number down to a few hundred. *Alligator, pander, hobnob, skim milk,* and *leapfrog,* for instance, are all first noted in his works. Phrases he's been credited with include "bated breath," "one fell swoop," "be-all-and-end-all," and "hoist with his own petar[d]."

Is it true that other people probably wrote Shakespeare's plays?

THERE HAS BEEN quite a bit of controversy over the original authorship of many of Shakespeare's works. William Shakespeare was a dramatic actor who owned a theater in Stratford, England. His name appears at the top of all plays performed there. Most experts believe this is ample evidence— knowing the traditions of the day—that they are his works. Others have come up with what they consider evidence that Shakespeare either stole most of his works or that someone else altogether was responsible for them. These other candidates have included the likes of Christopher Marlowe, Francis Bacon, the Earl of Oxford, Queen Elizabeth, and Ben Jonson. None of the theories have proved strong enough to rewrite history, however.

PLAYWRIGHTS, LAST RITES, AND STATES RIGHTS

Shakespeare's the first, of course, but who's the second most published playwright?

IN ENGLISH, that would be Neil Simon, with more than 16 plays, including *Barefoot in the Park, The Odd Couple, Sweet Charity, California Suite, Brighton Beach Memoirs, Biloxi Blues,* and *Lost in Yonkers.* In addition, he's written 18 books and 12 screenplays.

Who said, "I am dying as I have lived, beyond my means"?
Playwright Oscar Wilde, on his deathbed.

Was Tennessee Williams from Tennessee?

NO, HE WAS from Mississippi. He was born Thomas Lanier Williams III, but when his writing career began to take off in 1939, he moved to New York, got an agent, and began signing his plays Tennessee Williams.

ON THE BOOKS

What people first kept written records?

THAT HONOR probably goes to the ancient Babylonians. Clay books have been found containing land sales, business agreements, and judgments—dated at more than 5,000 years ago.

Who invented the modern book?

MOST PEOPLE credit the Chinese with inventing books as we know them today. Five hundred years before Johannes Gutenberg became famous for printing with movable type, the Chinese had begun doing so using porcelain or metal plates. In addition, the Chinese were creating covers and title pages and were binding manuscripts in a similar way to our modern book.

What is parchment?
Untanned sheep, goat, or calf skin, pressed flat.

Who was the first writer to submit a typewritten manuscript?

MARK TWAIN, with *Life on the Mississippi* (1883). A sucker for new gadgets, he was one of the first people to buy a typewriter, calling it a "curiosity-breeding little joker."

How much does the average writer or editor make in a year?

ACCORDING TO THE latest from the U.S. Bureau of Labor and Statistics, beginning salaries for writers and editorial assistants average $21,000, making them some of the lowest-paying jobs of all. After five years on the job, writers and editors make about $30,000. Senior editors at the largest newspapers can earn up to $67,000. These figures are for salaried positions; a large proportion of writers and editors freelance, making their job security virtually nonexistent. And you wonder why Jeeves went to butler school.

Who is the most successful book author writing in the English language?

WHILE THE RICHEST author is Stephen King, whose estimated worth is over $84 million, the top-selling author of all time is Agatha Christie. She wrote 78 mystery novels that have sold an estimated two billion copies.

Doesn't Isaac Asimov have a book in every category of the Dewey Decimal System?

ALTHOUGH THIS has been reported widely, it just ain't so. Even librarians have been fooled: the third edition of *The New York Public Library Desk Reference* states it as fact. Asimov has a book in nine of the ten major categories of the D.D.S—all except for Philosophy/Psychology. That, in and of itself, is quite amazing. So is the fact that he wrote over 300 books, deliberately covering a wide base of topics. Most can be found in Pure Sciences and Applied Sciences.

PLAYING DOCTOR

Is Dr. Seuss the author's real name?

SEUSS WAS Theodor Geisel's middle name. He initially used it out of necessity in college: When he was busted for having gin in his dorm room at Dartmouth during Prohibition, Geisel was forced to resign as editor from the school's humor rag as punishment. Instead, he called himself "Seuss" and stayed at the paper. Years later, after some success, he added the "Dr." to sound more scientific, he claims. But it became a legitimate title in 1957 when his alma mater awarded Geisel an honorary doctorate.

How did Dr. Seuss come up with his book ideas?

HERE'S THE rundown on a few Seuss classics:

- *Green Eggs and Ham* was written on a bet with the founder of Random House, Bennett Cerf. Geisel wagered that he could write a good book using only 50 words, and Cerf was sure it was impossible. Geisel won the bet but never collected on it. It was the only one of his books, the author claimed, that made him laugh.

- *Yertle the Turtle* was based on Adolf Hitler.

- *Marvin K. Mooney, Will You Please Go Now?* features a skulking character who is constantly asked to go away. The character was based on ex-president Richard Nixon.

- *The Cat in the Hat* was an answer to a 1957 report about children who were struggling to read in school. The study showed that children responded to illustrations and retained more from "fun" books than from traditional but boring readers like *Dick and Jane*. Geisel was hired by a publisher to come up with a book that would fit this bill. He was given a list of 400 words and asked to choose 220—the number of words kids were thought to be able to absorb at one time. Unfortunately, the word restrictions made the book difficult for Geisel to write. He found two words on the list that rhymed—*cat* and *hat*—then spent nine months writing the story.

How many kids did Dr. Seuss have?

THEODOR SEUSS GEISEL once said, "You have 'em, I'll amuse 'em." He was married twice but never had any children of his own.

FAIRY TALES CAN COME TRUE
How many fables did Aesop write?

DEPENDING ON the source, anywhere between zero and several hundred. According to some scholars, Aesop was a Greek slave who, between 620 and 565 B.C., wrote down folk tales he'd heard. His name became associated with tales that centered around the animal kingdom and always contained a moral. Tradition has it that Aesop's master eventually freed him and he met his end at Delphi.

However, it's now widely believed by most scholars that Aesop was as mythical as his talking beasts. It's quite possible that the name "Aesop" was invented in the Greek culture to associate these particular types of tales with one another and set them apart from other sorts of stories. The majority of tales called "Aesop's fables" are the work of two poets from the first and second centuries A.D.: the Greek writer Valerius Babrius, who combined oral tradition with tales from India, and the Roman poet Phaedrus, who translated them into Latin.

Why was "Little Red Riding Hood" banned in California?

A TRADITIONAL version of the classic tale was banned in the town of Empire, California, in 1990. Ironically, it wasn't because of the sexual undertones in the story of the beautiful young girl being seduced by the aggressive, conniving wolf, or the gory attack on the grandmother. Nor was it because the wolf is hacked open at the end. The book was banned because this particular version put a bottle of wine in Little Red Riding Hood's basket that she was taking to her sick grandmother. The local school board was afraid that the story encouraged drinking.

Who wrote "Little Red Riding Hood"?

"LITTLE RED RIDING HOOD" was a well-known fairy tale that was first written down by Charles Perrault. He retold "Cinderella" and "Puss in Boots" as well. A man of many diverse talents, he is also remembered for helping with the design of the Louvre.

Were the brothers Grimm the most prolific fairy tale authors?

THEY WEREN'T fairy tale authors; they simply collected them and wrote them down. Traditionally, fairy tales are passed on orally, which means they are always in danger of becoming lost. Jacob and Wilhelm Grimm were two highly regarded language scholars who were doing studies in comparative German grammar and philology when they began collecting and coding these tales in the early 1800s.

> **Where can I find Aesops Fables online?**

Who wrote "Mary Had a Little Lamb"?

NOW THERE'S A can of worms one might not want to open in polite New England company. There are two stories behind the origins of the poem and two New England towns divided.

We'll begin with the Sterling, Massachusetts, story and a little girl named Mary Sawyer, who lived there in 1815. This version has Mary's lamb following her to school one day and her classmate, John Roulston, writing the first verse of the poem about it. The townspeople and all of Mary Sterling's descendants swear the story is true and have erected a monument to Mary and her lamb in the town square.

In Newport, New Hampshire, the townspeople are livid over these claims. Local poet and publisher Sarah Josepha Hale is the first to have published the poem in books and magazines in 1820, and Newport citizens swear she is the one true author. (The people in Sterling admit she added verses, but say that the first verse is Roulston's.) Incidentally, Hale is also remembered for badgering President Lincoln into naming Thanksgiving a national holiday (see page 102). She wrote against slavery and was well known in her time for both her politics and her children's nursery rhymes.

REQUIRED READING

How long did it take Edward Gibbon to write *The History of the Decline and Fall of the Roman Empire?*

WE DON'T KNOW precisely, but we can make a good guess from the publication dates. It was published in six volumes between 1776 and 1788.

What was the original name of Jane Austen's *Pride and Prejudice?*

FIRST IMPRESSIONS. It was renamed and published—anonymously—in three volumes in 1813.

What book does Stephen King say inspired him to become a writer?
Dr. Doolittle by Hugh Lofing.

Where did the story of Frankenstein come from?

FROM A GHOST story party in 1816. Nineteen-year-old Mary Shelley, her husband, Percy Bysshe Shelley, her pregnant stepsister, Claire Clarement, Lord Byron (father of Claire's unborn child), and Byron's physician, John Polidori, were all staying together on holiday in Geneva, Switzerland. To fill the long, rainy nights during this stay, Lord Byron challenged them each to come up with a homespun ghost story. One evening while Lord Byron and Percy Shelley were arguing over whether human life could be artificially created, Mary Shelley was struck with an idea and stayed up to write her tale of Frankenstein. It was a hit the next night at story time—so much so that her fellow storytellers insisted she write a novel-length version for publication.

What was Dr. Frankenstein's monster's name?
Adam.

What is the full title of the book Frankenstein?

FRANKENSTEIN: The Modern Prometheus. Prometheus, you'll remember from Greek literature class, was the mythical Greek god who came down to Earth and helped mankind stay warm. As punishment, Zeus chained him to the Caucasus Mountains and came as an eagle every day to eat his liver for the rest of eternity.

Wasn't Sherlock Holmes killed off and then resurrected?

SHERLOCK HOLMES "died" in 1893. After 24 Holmes stories in six years, creator Arthur Conan Doyle had grown weary of the popular hero and wanted to focus more on his "real" work, his historical novels. The Holmes series was running in *Strand* magazine out of London, and so to end it, Doyle had Holmes plunge to his death from Switzerland's Reichenbach Falls, holding his archenemy, Professor Moriarty, in a mutual death grip. Public outcry was enormous, but Doyle was adamant about not bringing Holmes back.

So why was Holmes resurrected? Money, of course. In 1903, *McClure's* magazine in the United States offered Doyle $5,000 per story if he'd bring Holmes back to life. Doyle as much as said the editors were fools but couldn't resist the deal. To bring him back, Doyle had Holmes come out of hiding after 10 years. He then continued writing Holmes stories for nearly 25 more years, before retiring for good in 1927.

EIGHT WRITERS WRITING

What does the "F" in F. Scott Fitzgerald stand for?

FRANCIS. His full name was Francis Scott Key Fitzgerald, and yes, he was the second cousin, three times removed, of the Francis Scott Key who wrote the U.S. national anthem.

Where did Charles Dickens come up with the name Fagin for the villain in Oliver Twist?

HIS BEST FRIEND'S name was Bob Fagin. Whether his friend was honored or offended hasn't been determined.

How did Virginia Woolf die?

WOOLF PIONEERED the stream-of-consciousness novel and was an early feminist. But mental illness plagued her most of her adult life. She suffered from depression, voices in her head, violent mood swings, and tremendous sexual and emotional confusion.

On March 28, 1941, Woolf put on a long coat, filled its pockets with rocks, and walked into the Ouse River in Sussex, drowning herself. This was the experience Woolf had earlier labeled "the one I shall never describe."

Why did Samuel Clemens call himself Mark Twain?

FIRST, YOU HAVE to know that Clemens once wanted nothing more in life than to be a riverboat captain. Having someone measuring and calling out depth in a river was a must for any riverboat captain trying to navigate the Mississippi. The call *mark twain* means "two fathoms," or 12 feet deep. "Mark twain" was just barely deep enough for a boat to navigate, indicating somewhat unsafe waters—suggestive enough to suit humorist and satirist Samuel L. Clemens just fine.

What did Zane Grey do?

BESIDES WRITE about fictitious cowboys? He was a dentist in Ohio. Grey was one of the more prolific writers of the Western genre, paving the way for the likes of Louis L'Amour and others.

What other books did Margaret Mitchell write besides Gone With the Wind?

SHE DIDN'T write any. Mitchell worked as a feature writer for a few years at the *Atlanta Journal* under the name Peggy Mitchell and then began her long, sprawling novel. Ten years later, a friend told her she wasn't the type to finish a book, and in a rage, she packed up the handwritten manuscript and sent it to a publisher. She

How old was Stephen King when he had his first story published?
19.

received an advance of $500, not much even then, but the book quickly sold millions of copies.

Is it true that writer Rod Serling was planning another TV show like "The Twilight Zone" when he died?

WHEN SERLING, a chain-smoker, died during open-heart surgery in 1975, television lost one of its best writers and one of its most memorable on-screen narrators. His nervously terse delivery—sought after for commercials, documentaries, and "The Night Gallery"—was still being imitated decades after his death. Still, the last project Serling planned sounds dubious at best: a comedy-variety series named "Keep On Truckin'." One can imagine his introductions, delivered in his trademark monotone: "You're traveling through a land whose boundaries are of the imagination. Ladies and gentlemen, submitted for your approval: the Fifth Dimension!"

LIFE IMITATES ART

What's the story behind Agatha Christie's bouts with amnesia?

IN 1926, Agatha Christie had an episode of amnesia while under a great deal of stress. Her beloved mother had recently passed away, and her husband was in the middle of having a very open and outrageous affair with a woman named Nancy Neele. In December, Colonel Archibald Christie decided to tell his wife that he was leaving her to marry Neele. Over the course of the next week or so, Christie wrote several conflicting letters. To her brother-in-law, she wrote that she would be vacationing in Yorkshire; to the local chief constable, she wrote a note talking about fearing for her life. When her abandoned car was found at the bottom of a chalk pit, with no driver in sight and her fur coat left on the seat, foul play was instantly suspected.

> **Was Hemingway a pen name or his real name?**
> Hemingway was Ernest Hall's mother's maiden name.

The colonel became a prime suspect, particularly after confessing that he had announced his engagement to Neele at a dinner party the night his wife disappeared. He added that his wife had called the party and threatened to come and make a scene. As a result, he had sped off to their family home an hour away, only to find no one there, and so returned to the dinner party. Colonel Christie, with no solid alibi for two hours in a case that looked like murder, was told not to leave town, and the police began tailing him everywhere he went.

Meanwhile, Christie, true to her word to her brother-in-law, really did go to Yorkshire, where she checked into a hotel under the name Theresa Neele, the same surname as her husband's lover. She hid out as police launched a nationwide search for her and, when recognized, denied any ties to the famous missing author. She was discovered by police 11 days after she disappeared, thanks to a tip from hotel employees. Her husband was brought in to identify her.

Both Christies claimed amnesia on Agatha's part over those 11 days. Not even in her autobiography did she mention the ordeal, and to her death she claimed she never had any memory of what had actually taken place. The press accused her of a publicity stunt to sell her stories that cost taxpayers thousands of pounds. And still others think she may have been deliberately hoping her husband would be framed for her murder. Instead, the two divorced and Agatha eventually remarried.

A DARK AND STORMY PARENT-CHILD RELATIONSHIP

What is the book Children Are Wet Cement about?

CHILDREN ARE WET CEMENT, by Ann Ortlund, is a guide for molding children. Ortlund is known as an author of religious titles, including *Disciplines of the Beautiful Woman*.

Other books for your "funny titles" bookshelf: *How To Be Happy Though Married,* by E. J. Hardy (1885), *Life and Laughter* 'midst the Cannibals, by C. W. Collison (1926), *Sex Life of the Foot and Shoe,* by William Rossi (1977), and *Be Bold With Bananas* (1970s), a cookbook by the Australian Banana Growers Council.

What's the Bulwer-Lytton contest?

INVENTED BY Professor Scott Rice at San Jose State University, the contest challenges writers to come up with the best *worst* way to begin a novel. The contest derives its name from Edward George Earle Bulwer-Lytton, who began his novel *Paul Clifford* (1830) like this: "It was a dark and stormy night; the rain fell in torrents – except at occasional intervals, when it was checked by a violent gust of wind which swept up the streets (for it is in London that our scene lies), rattling along the house-tops, and fiercely agitating the scanty flame of the lamps that struggled against the darkness."

Here are two winning Bulwer-Lytton samples from years gone by:

Gail Cain, 1983 winner: "The camel died quite suddenly on the second day, and Selena fretted sulkily and, buffing her already impeccable nails – not for the first time since the journey began – pondered snidely if this would dissolve into a vignette of minor inconveniences like all the other holidays spent with Basil."

Robert Chappell, 1999 winner: "The oil made their skin glisten as their bodies moved in slow synchronous rhythm on the beach, the water gently flowing up around their legs, birds floating in the surf accompanying their moans with songs of pain and despair, otter and seal carcasses washing ashore around them, and it frightened her and exhilarated her at the same time that their love under the open sky might be discovered by a Sierra Club cleanup volunteer."

If you think you can write equally bad prose go to www. bulwer-lytton.com/

BAD ENGLISH

I know The Great Gatsby, *but what's the book* Gadsby?

ONE OF THE more interesting literary works in modern times. If you like challenges, that is. The book was written in 1937 by Ernest Vincent Wright, and the full title is *Gadsby, A Story of Over 50,000 Words Without Using the Letter "E."* Why? Wright claimed he wrote it because he read a four-stanza poem that had been written without using "e" and learned that "e" occurs five times more often than any other letter in the English language. For the novelist, the gauntlet was thrown, and he tied down the "e" key on his typewriter (literally) and set to work. After 165 days, the book was complete and certainly readable, despite the lack of "e." It was quite a feat, say most experts, but Wright didn't get to enjoy his glory: he died the day *Gadsby* was published.

THE GIFT OF THE MAGISTRATE

Why did writer O. Henry end up in jail?

LIKE MANY writers, the short story author wasn't very good with money. That was a problem, because before he began writing stories, William Sidney Porter (O. Henry's real name) was a bank teller by occupation. In 1894, some of the money that passed through his hands turned up missing. He lost his job, but at first it looked like the whole thing might blowover. However two years later he was indicted on four counts of embezzlement.

Porter fled to Honduras, but his wife was too sick with tuberculosis to join him. Six months later, he got word that his wife was dying, so he returned to the United States to be with her and face trial. She died; he was convicted and sentenced to five years in jail.

It was sad for him, but a great day for American literature. From his jail cell, Porter began writing short stories and a New York daily paper eagerly published them. Porter had taken the pen name O. Henry, fearing that as he got progressively more famous somebody would dredge up his past and publicly humiliate him.

While it didn't help support his proclaimed innocence that he had fled the country, his defenders depicted him as being basically honest, just not very good with money. There is some support for that claim. Read the first three lines of his most famous story, *The Gift of the Magi,* in which he describes an impossible set of change: "One dollar and eighty-seven cents. That was all. And 60 cents of it was in pennies. . . "

BOOKED SOLID

Why did FEMA suggest lining fallout shelters with books?

YOU'D THINK it would be to help while away a long nuclear winter, but no. The U.S. Federal Emergency Management Agency didn't actually suggest that books be used, but merely provided a general guideline for substitutions if concrete and other standard building materials weren't available. Here is an excerpt from the FEMA handbook *In Time of Emergency:*

Concrete, bricks, earth and sand are some of the materials that are dense or heavy enough to provide fallout protection. For comparative purposes, 4 inches of concrete would provide the same shielding density as:

- 5 to 6 inches of bricks

- 6 inches of sand or gravel or 7 inches of earth (may be packed into bags, boxes, cartons for easier handling)

- 8 inches of hollow concrete blocks (6 inches if filled with sand)

- 10 inches of water

- 14 inches of books or magazines

- 18 inches of wood

For the Birds

THEY HAVE PEA-SIZED BRAINS, yet discovered flight millions of years before humans. Our fine-feathered friends can be appealing, enthralling, and even sometimes downright perplexing.

IN THE PINK

Why do flamingo knees bend backward?

WHAT YOU are actually seeing in the middle of a flamingo's leg is its *ankle*, not its knee. Its knee is located high up on the leg and is usually not visible beneath its body and feathers. Its foot is part of the lower leg, and like most other animals, it walks on its toes. Humans are one of the few animals that walk on both their toes and feet.

Are there flamingos in different colors besides pink?

YES. FLAMINGO babies, for example, are born white with gray streaks and take one or two years to develop their pinkish color. And depending on which of the five flamingo species you look at, the color will vary in intensity to the point that some of the lighter species look quite white. The best-known species in North America is the greater flamingo, which has a very deep pink hue. The pink comes directly from things in the birds' diet that are heavy in carotene, a natural food color also found in carrots and other reddish vegetables. Their staples include small fish, insects, crustaceans, and certain types of algae. Some zoos give their flamingos carotene supplements to keep them "in the pink."

How does a big bird like a flamingo eat something as small as algae?

THE WAY in which a flamingo eats is unusual. It lowers its head into the water so that its beak is submerged upside down. It then swishes its beak back and forth, using its large tongue to sort out the food from the water. It's the only known animal to eat in this way.

Why are plastic flamingos so popular as lawn ornaments?

DECORATIONS with a flamingo motif originally became popular because they represented wealth. Back in the 1920s, only those with money were able to relocate for the winter to balmy Florida. Since people associated flamingos with Florida, the bird became linked to wealth and privilege. And like much that stands for wealth and privilege, it was adopted by the middle class.

What do you call a group of flamingos?
A *pat.*

In 1951, this middle-class chic hit a new level of absurdity. A young art student named Don Featherstone came up with the well-known bright, hollow, plastic yard flamingo. His first two designs were failures: first a flat model, then a 3-D flamingo made of construction foam. The latter might have worked except it disintegrated too easily and dogs enjoyed chewing on it. Finally, he hit upon the molded-plastic design, and the rest is history. Now Featherstone is the vice president of Union Products of Massachusetts, the same company that has made his bird for half a century. Today there are estimated to be more plastic lawn flamingos in the world than real ones.

WATER WINGS

Did the word loony come from the loon's laughlike call?

ALTHOUGH MANY believe this to be so, the word *loony*, or *looney*, is just a short version of the word *lunatic*. *Lunatic* has been in use for almost 1,000 years and comes from *luna*, the "moon," based on the belief that insanity was affected by the moon's phases. In contrast, the

Where can I hear a recording of a loon's cry?

bird was first called a loon little more than 300 years ago. The name probably comes from people confusing it with another diving water bird called a loom. The two had a couple of things in common and the name stuck, having nothing to do with the bird's call or any other specific characteristic.

Why is an albatross considered lucky but "an albatross around the neck" unlucky?

TRADITIONALLY, sailors on a ship consider seeing an albatross to be a sign of good luck. Probably this came from early days of navigation, when sailors mistakenly thought the bird sighting meant that land was near. Little did they know that an albatross can live for years on the sea without setting foot on land. It lives over the open ocean, even sleeping in flight.

The bad-luck "albatross around the neck" comes directly from Samuel Taylor Coleridge's famous poem "The Rime of the Ancient Mariner," published in 1798, which is about a young sailor on a ship who shoots an albatross. The sailor is forced by shipmates to wear the dead bird around his neck. The bird's death brings terrible luck: the winds stop, the ship is stuck, and the crew runs out of water. But wait, that's just the beginning. Along comes a ghost ship that kills all the sailors, leaving the one, albatross-laden man alone and dying. Finally, the lone sailor begins to pray, the albatross falls off his neck and into the sea, and he's rescued. But at great cost—for his penance, he must tell his story to anyone who will listen for the rest of his life.

AMERICAN AVIARY

Does a roadrunner go "meep-meep"?

DESPITE THE famous roadrunner cartoon, a roadrunner actually coos, very much like a dove. The coos come in a series of six or eight with each dropping a little in pitch like a soprano doing warm-up exercises. Part of the cuckoo family of birds, the roadrunner gets its name because, although it flies when necessary, it usually gets around by walking and running—as fast as 18 miles per hour.

Is the bald eagle really bald?

NO, ITS HEAD is covered with flat white feathers. From a distance it can appear to be bald, though.

What's the difference between a crow and a raven?

Do crows make good pets?
Yes. They bond well with humans.

ALL RAVENS are crows, but not all crows are ravens. There are a number of species of crows, and the ravens are one of these groups. Ravens are larger than most other crows, and have a distinctive croaking call as opposed to many other crow varieties' cawings.

THAT'S THE NAME!

What's an oxpecker?

NOT WHAT you might think. It's a tick-eating bird that's dependent on large animals for survival. A symbiotic relationship exists between the oxpecker and the rhinoceros: the bird eats mites and ticks from the rhino's back and gets free transportation; in return, the oxpecker alerts the nearsighted rhino to approaching danger.

DEAD AS A DODO

Why did the dodo bird become extinct?

IN PART, because of evolution. The dodo bird—related to the pigeon—settled on an island named Mauritius, just east of Madagascar, millions of years ago. Because the island housed no predators, the bird lost its ability to fly, yet lived in relative peace for over four million years. Occasionally, humans would land at the island, but not until the 1500s did sailors begin using it for frequent stops on their trade route. Not long after, the Dutch set up the first human colony, bringing pigs, dogs, rats, and other animals. The animals made quick meals of dodo birds and their eggs, wiping out the entire species by 1681.

It wasn't just the dodo bird that was affected, however. Dozens of other bird species were exterminated when the Mauritius Island forests were cut down for sugarcane plantations in the 1800s. In addition, the tree the dodo bird depended on for food became an endangered species because its seed had become dependent on being passed through the bird's digestive tract before it would germinate. The species, called the dodo tree, dwindled down to a handful of ancients with no new trees germinating for more than 300 years. Recently, though, scientists discovered that turkey gullets can also help this tree germinate new seedlings, so the dodo tree may not go the way of its feathered namesake after all.

COO-COO QUESTIONS

Why do I never see baby pigeons?

YOU DO SEE baby pigeons, just not newborns. This is because pigeons make excellent parents. To start with, they hide their nests well in crags and crannies. When the nests are well hidden and sturdy, they lay two eggs, then spoil their babies rotten when they hatch, until they leave the nest. As a consequence, baby pigeons quickly become plump and large, about the same size as their parents when they go off into the world alone. You've heard of the delicacy squab, I trust? That's a plump baby pigeon cooked just so.

If you want to spot the young in a flock, here are some hints: Look for them in the summer and spring months. If you're feeding a flock, watch the ones that don't aggressively go after your bread crumbs; you may find your babies there. Beyond that, there may be fluffy down sticking through their regular feathers; they may show a little bit of lip around their beaks from being recently fed by their parents; and their heads may not be as broad.

Where did the term stool pigeon come from?

BY THE EARLY 1800s, *pigeon* came to mean "decoy," and some decades later, *stool pigeon* was synonymous with "informer." It comes from the practice of using one pigeon to attract other pigeons into captivity. As anyone who has lived in a big city can tell you, pigeons love to gather in large groups. Instead of trapping pigeons one at a time, fowlers soon learned it was easier to tether just one to a stool and let it fly and hop around until others came to join the captive bird. It then became easy to drop a net and capture dozens at a time.

GOBBLE GOBBLE GOBBLE

Can turkeys fly?

How many wild turkeys are there in the U.S.?
About 4.5 million.

WILD TURKEYS can fly up to 55 miles per hour and can run up to 20 miles per hour. However, the domestic turkeys we eat at Thanksgiving are too fat and not strong enough to get their bodies aloft. Humans have bred them that way.

Were any other birds besides the eagle considered for the U.S. national bird?

BENJAMIN FRANKLIN lobbied heavily for the turkey to become the national bird, but it was never given serious consideration by anybody else.

Why do we say that people coming off addictions go "cold turkey"?

THIS PHRASE comes from an earlier phrase, *talk turkey*, meaning to talk honestly. So when people go *cold turkey,* they're cutting the excuses and getting down to business.

However, the origins of *talk turkey* are somewhat less clear. A jokey anecdote, traced to an employee of the U.S. Engineering

Department in the early 1800s, is usually given credit as the origin of the phrase: A white man and a Native American were hunting together and

What is "anting" and why do some birds do it?

killed a buzzard and a turkey. When they were finished, the white man tried to fool the Native American, saying, "You take the buzzard and I will take the turkey, or I can take the turkey and you can have the buzzard." The Native American responded, undeceived, that the white man had never offered him the turkey with either option: "You never once talk turkey to me."

Do turkeys really drown when it rains?

THAT'S A COMMON myth about how dumb turkeys are: When it rains, they supposedly open their mouths and hold their heads straight up in the air until they drown. This is so widely believed that even some turkey farmers swear it's true, citing the fact that they sometimes find turkeys dead after a rainstorm. The reality is that no one has actually seen a turkey behave in this way despite the dead turkeys after a rainstorm. The turkey's rain problem comes not from its intellect but from its coat. Young turkeys under nine weeks old don't have protective outer feathers, just down. Down is a good insulator when dry but loses most of its effectiveness when wet, so wet turkeys die from the cold.

BIRD TIDBITS

How does down keep a body warm?

DOWN IS THE soft, fluffy layer of feathers that is below regular bird plumage and helps insulate birds' bodies from cold. Down—whether on a duck or goose or in a sleeping bag—has tiny notches that hook together and trap layers of air. Trapped air is a good insulator.

Why do birds fly in a V formation?

THINK OF the V formation as the front of a boat cutting a path through water. The formation cuts through the air and blocks some of the air and wind resistance for the birds in the back, so they can save energy. In this way, the birds are better able to travel long distances during migration. When the front bird gets tired, another comes and takes its place in the front and the first one moves back. It's true that the birds could travel in a clump behind the front birds in the V and this would have the same effect, but the birds in the back wouldn't be able to see ahead.

How come birdseed is now thrown at weddings instead of rice?

THERE'VE BEEN rumors it has to do with exploding bird stomachs—that when birds eat uncooked rice, it supposedly swells up in their stomachs and kills them. This isn't true, however. A bird's stomach is made to crunch up hard things. It's filled with *grit*—swallowed stones and gravel—along with strong muscles to help grind up seeds and grains. If you can entice a bird to eat uncooked rice grains, it won't get sick and its stomach definitely won't explode.

Does a hummingbird eat only nectar?
No. It also eats insects.

The exploding-bird-stomach myth may well have been planted by church custodians. Birds aren't too enthusiastic about eating rice, so the grains are often left all over the front area of a church after a wedding, needing to be cleaned up. But birds naturally and quickly take care of the mess left by birdseed.

How deep should birdbath water be?

THE PURPOSE of a yard birdbath is to offer birds a place to bathe without danger. The safest depth to meet this goal, according to the Audubon Society of America, is 2½ inches. They say that any less is not enough to clean in and any more scares small birds.

Food for Thought

"THERE IS NO SINCERER LOVE than the love of food," said George Bernard Shaw. And yet it's a love that's unrequited, no matter how (literally) all-consuming it may be.

A FEW QUICK APPETIZERS

Which would kill you first, not sleeping or not eating?

MOST PEOPLE can last for nearly a month without food. However, 10 days without being allowed to sleep would kill most humans.

How much food will the average American eat in a year?

MORE THAN A TON. This includes 117 pounds of potatoes, 80 pounds of fresh fruit, 116 pounds of beef, and 100 pounds of vegetables.

How many people in the United States die of food poisoning each year? About 8,000.

What food has the longest shelf life?

HONEY, WHICH can last nearly forever if well stored. In fact, honey from ancient Egyptian burial chambers—left there to accompany the dead to the afterlife—has been found to be edible in modern times.

What happens to meat in supermarkets that hasn't been sold by the "sell by" date?

MOST OFTEN it goes to rendering plants to be transformed into tallow for pet food. It's also used as a base product for automobile tires, cosmetics, soaps, candles, detergents, lubricants, and plastics.

> **What is the most nutritious food in the world?**
> Blood.

How many edible plant species are there?

PEOPLE HAVE identified more than 30,000 edible plant species so far. Despite that rich variety, 90% of the world's grain and vegetable food supply comes from only 20 species.

I know it's a name for an appetizer, but what does hors d'oeuvre literally mean?

IT'S FRENCH for "outside of work." In other words, it's meant to mean a food that's moonlighting outside the regular main course menu.

Who invented the electric food mixer?

DR. LILLIAN MOLLER GILBRETH, who also invented the now-common kitchen trash can with a step-on, opening lid. She was a pioneering efficiency expert and incidentally was also the mother in the book *Cheaper by the Dozen*, written by two of her twelve children.

PIZZA = PI

Which has more pizza, a 10-inch pizza or two 7-inch pizzas?

NEXT TIME you hear someone complain about never being able to apply the math they learned in school in real life, remember this question. You'd think the two smaller pies would have more pizza, but they don't. You just need some pi with your pizza. Remember the formula: $A = \pi R^2$ (A = area; R = radius). The area of the pizza's circles is the same as half their diameters (5 and 3.5 inches, respectively) multiplied by itself (25 and 12.25) times 3.1416 (pi). So a 10-inch pizza has about 78.5 square inches of cheesy goodness, while two 7-inch pizzas have only about 77 square inches.

CREATURE FROM A BEIGE LEGUME
What's the story behind Mr. Peanut?
WELL, ACCORDING to comedian David Letterman, his real name is "Keith," he belongs to a private club that doesn't admit pistachios, and he was once arrested for wandering through New York City chanting, "Eat me!" Actually, though, the Planters Peanut Company was founded in 1906 by two young Italian immigrants, Amedes Obici and Mario Peruzzi, who chose the name Planters because it sounded "important and dignified." Ten years later, the company held a contest for a mascot, and 14-year-old Antonio Gentile from Suffolk, Virginia, submitted a drawing of a dandy peanut dressed in monocle, top hat, and tails. For his idea, Gentile won a grand prize of either $5 or $15, depending on which account you believe.

How many peanuts are in a jar of peanut butter?
IT TAKES an average of 548 peanuts to make a 12-ounce jar of peanut butter. The average American will eat an average of 3.3 pounds of peanut butter in a year.

What is a peanut, anyway—a pea or a nut?
NEITHER. It's a legume. The plant grows with its flowers above the ground and its fruits (the peanuts) below. More than half the peanuts grown in the United States are made into peanut butter, and a quarter are sold as roasted peanuts. Most of the rest are made into peanut oil.

GRILL OF MY DREAMS
Where does the word barbecue come from?
WELL, FIRST OF ALL, let's talk about where it *doesn't* come from. It's been reported by some "experts" that the word comes from the French *barbe et queue,* which translates literally

as "beard and tail," meaning everything from end to end. But that is apparently false. Even the definitive *Oxford English Dictionary*, which doesn't smirk lightly, can't resist out-and-out derision of this etymology: "This an absurd conjecture suggested merely by the sound of the word." Instead, says the *OED*, the word comes from the Spanish *barbacoa*, which means "a framework of sticks set upon posts," and it quotes from the earliest known English usage in 1661, recorded by a visitor to Jamaica: "Some are slain, And their flesh forthwith barbacu'd and eat." Since then, people have expanded the word to mean not only the device the meat is cooked on but also the meat itself.

PERSONAL FOWL

Why are they called "buffalo wings" when they're really chicken (I hope)?

YOU'RE RIGHT. They aren't really wings from bison. They're called "Buffalo wings" because that's where they originally came from—Buffalo, New York. An establishment called Frank and Teresa's Anchor Bar, to be exact. It's the only culinary product from Buffalo that's made it big worldwide. It's a good thing Frank and Terry didn't invent crisped potato snacks instead, or junk food gourmets would find themselves eating out of a bag labeled "Buffalo chips."

Of all the turkey eaten year-round in the United States, how much of it is eaten on Thanksgiving?

AMERICANS EAT 45 million turkeys on Thanksgiving Day, about 15% of the turkey eaten all year.

What was in the first TV dinner?

IN JANUARY 1952, in Omaha, Nebraska, the first TV dinner in history rolled off the Swanson Company's assembly line in a segmented aluminum tray shaped like a TV screen. It contained turkey, cornbread stuffing, gravy, buttered peas, and sweet potatoes in orange and butter sauce, and retailed for 98 cents.

WHOLE HOG

What is Spam exactly? Or do I really want to know?

SPAM ISN'T so bad—there isn't anything particularly strange in it. It's pork shoulder that's been chopped, spiced, and formed into loaves. Every meat packer runs into the problem that some parts of an animal are more popular than others. For the George A. Hormel Company in 1937, the unwanted part was pig shoulder. Too fatty to be sold as ham, not fatty enough to be sold as bacon, the shoulders were in a marketing limbo and piling up in the company's massive freezers.

Finally, a desperate executive got the idea to grind them up, add some gelatin to fill the leftover space, and create a canned product that could survive for months without refrigeration. Spam—the name came from compressing the phrase "spiced ham"—got a boost from the military during World War II, which liked its long shelf life and so put tons of Spam into mess kits and foreign aid shipments. Today, worldwide, 264 cans of Spam are eaten every minute of every day.

How do you make genuine Pennsylvania scrapple?

THERE ARE a number of recipes on the Internet for regional variations of scrapple, but the Pennsylvania Dutch version is supposed to be the most authentic. Bear in mind before you begin, though, that the name comes from the word *scraps*—in other words, the parts left over when you're done making ham, pork, bacon, chops, ribs, and

Where can I find scrapple recipes?

Spam. True scrapple recipes are not for the squeamish—you'll have to be willing to handle snouts, brains, and hearts (one recipe starts, "Begin with two pig heads . . . . ")—but there are also some upscale scrapple recipes that use more traditional supermarket pork parts.

What is Jell-O made of?

IF YOU MUST know, the parts of the pig that are left over after producing the traditional cuts of meat, then Spam, and finally scrapple. Hides, bones, and sinew from pigs and cattle are boiled down to make gelatin. Added to the colorless and taste-less result are coloring, flavoring, and sugar.

SMELL THAT DAIRY AIR

Besides cows and goats, what other animals' milk is made into cheese?

CHEESE HAS been made from the milk of a whole menagerie of animals, including the buffalo, camel, horse, llama, zebra, yak, reindeer, and donkey. May I suggest a nice fig wine with your yak cheese?

Where did Ben meet Jerry?

IN 1963, Bennett Cohen and Jerry Greenfield were both self-described "smart, nerdy, fat kids" at Merrick Avenue Junior High School on Long Island, New York, separately undergoing the humiliations that come with being overweight in junior high P.E. class. They ended up on the same running track, way behind the others. Recalled Greenfield to an interviewer: "We were the two slowest, chubbiest guys in the class. Coach yelled, 'Gentlemen, if you don't run the mile in under seven minutes, you're going to have to do it again.' And Ben yelled back, 'Gee, coach, if I don't do it in under seven minutes the first time, I'm certainly not going to do it in under seven min-utes the second time.' To me this was brilliance. This was a guy I wanted to know."

> **What's the milk fat content in 8 oz. of skim milk, whole milk, half-and-half, and light cream?**
> 0, 8, 28, and 46 grams of fat respectively.

It was the start of a firm friendship. Years later, when they decided to go into business together, they decided it should be food related because they were unabashedly into eating. They considered making bagels until they learned that startup costs would total more than $40,000; instead, they rented an abandoned gas station near the University of Vermont, signed up for a $5 correspondence course in ice cream making from Pennsylvania State, and began producing and selling ice cream.

IN THE KITCHEN WITH DINER

Can you tell me where the term blue plate special comes from?

A PLATE with separate sections—like a TV dinner tray—came off the dishware assembly line sometime during the Great Depression. Because the plates were cheap and cleanup was reduced from three plates (or more) per meal to one, diner owners began using them to serve their daily specials. For some reason, those first plates were colored blue, and *blue plate special* became synonymous with diners' low-cost daily meals.

Was diner lingo invented because it was faster than giving the real order?

WELL, LET'S try it and see. First a little lingo: *"Noah's boy with Murphy carrying a wreath, splash of red noise, frog sticks, and an MD, hold the hail!"* Now the order, straight: "Ham with potato and cabbage, tomato soup, French fries, and a Dr. Pepper, no ice." You'll note that the colorful version is longer, so efficiency wasn't the issue. Or was it? Diner lingo accomplished two things: for one, it amused the cook and customers as waitresses made up new and obscure variations. For another, the word pictures suggested by the phrases made it easier for a cook and waitress to remember a complete order without continuously consulting paper documentation. So perhaps the lingo actually did make things more efficient, even if it added a few extra syllables.

Where can I find a list of diner lingo and what it means?

HERE'S SOME to get you started:

Noah's boy = Ham (in the Bible, Noah had a son named Ham)

Warm a pig = Ham

Pig between the sheets = Ham sandwich

Adam and Eve on a raft = Two poached eggs on toast

Radio sandwich = Tuna (a pun on "tuner")

Wrecked hen fruit = Scrambled eggs

Cow juice = Milk

Nervous pudding = Jell-O

Betsy in a bowl = Beef stew

Axle grease = Butter

Belch water = Soda water

Mug of murk = Coffee

Mystery in the alley = Hash

A bowl of birdseed = Cereal

An order of down with mama = Toast with marmalade

Keep off the grass = No lettuce

Burn the pup = Hot dog

A brunette with sand = Coffee with sugar

Fish eyes = Tapioca pudding

A cold spot = Iced tea

All the way = With everything

High and dry = Plain

THAT MELBA, SHE'S A REAL DISH

Who or what is the "Melba" in Melba toast and Peach Melba?

BOTH DISHES are the result of a chef's infatuation with an opera singer. Australian Helen Porter Mitchell took the stage name Nellie Melba from her hometown, Melbourne, when she traveled the world's stages in the late 1800s. In London, she stayed at the Savoy Hotel, where head chef Auguste Escoffier poured out his love for her and her art by creating a peach and ice cream dessert inspired by the swans in *Lohengrin*, the opera

Melba was performing in. The next morning, overstuffed from the night before, the opera singer ordered only plain toast, sliced extra thin. One can't help but imagine that if she'd stayed longer at the Savoy, we'd now also have Chicken a la Melba, Melba Eggs, Melba Oatmeal, Melba Fish and Chips, Melba Bangers, and Grilled Cheese Melbas.

IT'S THE YEAST YOU CAN DO

What is baker's yeast? Can vegetarians eat it?

BAKER'S YEAST is a fungus, and when you buy it, it's still alive. Yes, vegetarians can eat it but be very careful. One gram of yeast contains about 10 billion cells, which, given a chance, will quickly multiply. Yeast manufacturers, using ideal conditions, can take that one gram of yeast and get it to grow into 15 tons in five days, enough to make about a million loaves of bread.

> How many calories do you burn while watching TV?
> One to two minutes.

How did people discover yeast for baking?

IN ABOUT 4000 B.C., Egyptian bakers discovered that kneading the dough with their feet made the dough rise instead of staying flat and hard, because of the natural yeasts between their toes. (It's believed that the discovery of cheesemaking had a similar "foot" note in history.) Yeast cells eat the sugars in dough and release alcohol and carbon dioxide, making thousands and thousands of small bubbles that get trapped. As a result, yeast-risen dough is soft and fluffy instead of flat and hard.

BURNING CALORIES

How do nutritionists determine how many calories a food has? Do they feed them to people and see how much weight they gain?

CAN YOU IMAGINE the volunteers they'd get to test the chocolates? But no, that's not how they do it. Although we associate calories with weight gain, a scientist hears "calories" and knows it refers to how much heat a food will generate if burned. In fact, the word *calorie* comes from a Latin word that means "heat" and is defined as the amount of energy needed to raise the temperature of one gram of water by one Celsius degree. Your digestion process is, in a sense, a slow-motion fire. As in a real fire, the energy of the food you eat is released by digestion. The released energy can be used to move muscles or generate heat; or if you're taking in more fuel than you can use immediately, your body stores it for later. That's fat— energy waiting to be used. For millions of years, fat was the equivalent of an emergency fuel tank to draw on in hard times. Then it became "ugly."

So how do scientists measure the calories in food? They burn it, using something called a *bomb calorimeter,* which measures how much extra energy comes out compared to how much went in. Now here comes the confusing part: what is commonly called a "calorie" is actually a *kilocalorie*—a thousand of the scientists' calories. So that glazed doughnut doesn't have just 235 calories; it's *really* got 235 kilocalories, or 235,000 calories. And you wonder why you're having trouble keeping the weight off!

HOLE FOODS

I understand the "dough" in doughnut, but why the "nut"?

IT WASN'T always called a nut, and when it was first called a nut, the name actually made sense. First of all, let's dismiss one spurious but widespread legend reported by otherwise reputable sources: that the name was invented during World War I because the fighting "doughboys" went "nuts" over the doughnuts and coffee that were routinely distributed to soldiers by the Red Cross.

Actually the name goes much further back, to a time before doughnuts had holes. Washington Irving described in his *Knickerbocker's History of New York* in 1809 "an enormous dish of balls of sweetened dough, fried in hog's fat, and called dough-nuts or *olykoeks*." In the late 15th century, Dutch bakers origi-nated *olykoeks* ("oil cakes"), a ball named for the amount of grease absorbed in the deep-frying process. When the Pilgrims left England in the early 1600s and took refuge in the Netherlands, they learned the secrets of making olykoeks. Before the little group of religious fanatics left for America on the *Mayflower*, they gave the cakes a new name, dough nuts, because the little balls looked like walnuts.

So, ironically, little round "doughnut holes" aren't anything new—they've simply gone back to the original format.

Why do doughnuts have holes?

DO YOU want the practical answer or a popular mythical answer? Oh, okay—let's do them both. The mythical answers include one popularized in Plymouth, Massachusetts, which claimed that an Indian shot an arrow through a window and punched a hole through oil cake

> **How does food have to be prepared to be 'kosher'?**

dough (see previous question). Another myth involves a Maine sea captain named Hanson Gregory, who needed his hands free while steering through a storm. He impaled the fried cake he was eating on one of the spokes of his wheel and decided the invention was so practical that the ship's cook should make the holes on purpose from then on. An alternative version of the story has it that Gregory was 15 years old when he suggested adding the hole to his mother as she made oil cakes. (Downtown Rockport, Maine, has a bronze plaque commemo-rating Gregory.)

The real answer is that a hole in the center of fried baked goods solves the problem of uncooked, doughy centers. The Pennsylvania Dutch discovered this method, but so did south-western Native American tribes centuries earlier: petrified doughnuts—or at least fried cakes with holes in them—have been discovered among their artifacts.

Who invented the bagel?

THIS IS A tough one. It's hard to imagine now, but just a few decades ago, bagels were an obscure ethnic food that relatively few people outside New York City had even heard of. (In fact, the 1976 version of Webster's unabridged dictionary doesn't even list the word *bagel*.)

Some food historians, in fact, say that—like chop suey in Chinese cuisine—the bagel as we know it is a New World invention masquerading as an Old World tradition. They point to the fact that the word *bagel* didn't even appear in print until 1932, from *Beigel*, German for any ring-shaped bread. In fact, bagels are thought of as "American food" in Israel.

Still, whether a true bagel or merely a ring-shaped bread, the modern bagel has at least some roots in European Jewish culture. A romantic story has it that a now-unknown Viennese baker wanted to honor the horsemen of Polish king John III Sobieski for driving the Turks out of his city in 1683. (Reportedly, the Turks left so hurriedly that the hundreds of sacks of coffee they left behind spawned dozens of coffee houses and spread the new fad of coffee-drinking throughout Europe, leading inexorably to Starbucks...but that's another story.) Anyway, the perhaps-mythical baker took dough for a popular bread called *Kipfel* and shaped it into a stirrup shape, supposedly creating a new pastry called a *Beugel*—Austrian for "stirrup."

But there are a few problems with the story. For one, a stirrup shape is more like a triangle than a circle. And decades before, in 1610, the community regulations in Kracow, Poland, referred to bringing "*beygls*" to pregnant women. Bringing O-shaped breads continued to be a tradition in some parts of the world as an expression of good luck during pregnancy. Finally, what we do know is that Harry Lender built the first modern bagel factory in 1927. When Lender's Company began to freeze bagels and distribute them throughout the country in 1962, they set the stage for making bagels as American as chop suey.

ACCEPT THIS COOKIE?

How many different animals come in circus-animal cracker boxes?

FIRST INTRODUCED as Barnum's Animals in 1902 by the National Biscuit Company (today's Nabisco), the cookies have always come in a circus-wagon package. A century ago, the package was made of tin and designed to hang on a Christmas tree, and the animals were just cookie-cutter silhouettes instead of a more detailed design. Over the years, 37 different animals have been represented. Today the 22 crackers in your cardboard box are randomly selected from a pool of 17 animals: bear, bison, camel, cougar, elephant, giraffe, gorilla, hippopotamus, hyena, kangaroo, lion, monkey, rhinoceros, seal, sheep, tiger, and zebra.

How do they get the fig inside a Fig Newton?

THE EASIEST way to visualize it is to think of a funnel inside of a larger funnel. Put fig paste into the inner funnel and cookie dough into the outer funnel. Take a plunger and force both out through the small end of the funnel at the same time. You'll get a rope of fig jam surrounded by cookie dough. Flatten it out, bake it, and then splice it into small pieces—that's the basic idea of how fig and cookie are extruded together to make a fig cookie.

What's Matzo?

An unleavened (without yeast), kosher cracker used during Passover.

Was the Fig Newton named after Isaac Newton?

NO, FIG NEWTONS were named for Newton, Massachusetts. It was the tradition of Boston-based Kennedy Biscuits (which later got absorbed into Nabisco) to name their prototype cookies and crackers after nearby towns. The Newton survived, but others—for example, the Beacon Hill, the Brighton, and the Quincy—did not.

Do you have a recipe for sauerkraut cookies?

BUT OF COURSE! Known for their ways with kraut, the Pennsylvania Dutch have improved almost every dish with a dash or two of pickled cabbage. From them to us and now to you:

Old-Fashioned Sauerkraut Cookies

> 1 stick butter
> ¾ cup sugar
> 1 tablespoon milk
> 1 egg
> ½ teaspoon lemon extract
> 1¼ cups flour, plus more if needed
> ⅛ teaspoon salt
> ¼ teaspoon baking powder
> ⅛ cup drained and chopped sauerkraut (to taste)

Preheat the oven to 350°F. Cream the butter and add the sugar slowly, beating until light. Add the milk, egg, and lemon extract and beat thoroughly. Mix the flour, salt, and baking powder together, then add to the wet mixture and blend well. Stir the sauerkraut into the dough. Add more flour if the dough is too sticky. Drop the dough by the teaspoon, 1 inch apart, on a cookie sheet. Bake until lightly browned, or about 8 to 10 minutes. Makes 3 to 4 dozen cookies.

THE NAME ON THE PACKAGE

Which of these food people are real and which are not: Colonel Sanders, Orville Redenbacher, Betty Crocker, Duncan Hines, Aunt Jemima, Paul Newman?

BETTY CROCKER was created to answer letters from consumers for the Washburn Crosby Flour Company. Aunt Jemima is a character named from a minstrel song. Duncan Hines, on the other hand, was a famous food and hotel reviewer who sold his name to the cake mix company. Sanders and Redenbacher were also real, even if they looked like fictitious characters. Joanne Woodward's husband, Paul? He's definitely real.

Who was Kellogg of the cereal company?

THERE WERE two of them, brothers Harvey and William. By 1886, Dr. Harvey Kellogg had become director of a religious health spa in Battle Creek, Michigan. A crusader for healthy food and total sexual abstinence, he believed eating whole-grain cereals would reduce sexual urges. He and his brother, William, developed a process of rolling whole grains to make them into flakes. William was the spa's bookkeeper and a good businessman who believed he could make a good profit from the Corn Flakes cereal the two invented…but only if he added malt and sugar for flavor. Harvey was horrified at that perversion of a good thing, believing sugar to be an aphrodisiac. Lawsuits flew, William eventually won control of the Kellogg company, and the two brothers remained estranged for the rest of their lives.

What cereal was originally called Elijah's Manna?

POST TOASTIES. C. W. Post originally wanted to give his new cereal a biblical name, but the government refused to give him a trademark on the name Elijah's Manna, because it sounded irreverent. Post had to settle for Post Toasties.

NAMES YOU CAN EAT

Most of the bread names, like "rye" and "wheat," describe what's in the bread. So what the devil is "pumpernickel"?

THE DEVIL is exactly right. The bread comes from Westphalia (now part of Germany) and was apparently pretty notorious in its earliest form. Travel writer Fynes Moryson wrote in 1617 that the dark brown bread was popularly called *cranck Broat*— "sick bread." Another adventurer, Thomas Nugent, in 1756 became the first writer to record the bread by its modern name: "Their bread is of the coarsest kin, ill baked, and as black as a coal, for they never sift their flour. The people of the country call it pompernickel." *Pumpern* is German for "fart" and *Nickel* is "the devil." (As an aside, the metal nickel was likewise named after the devil because of the difficulty of extracting it from the ore.) The name is meant to imply that the bread is so difficult to digest that even the devil would get gaseous after eating it. Pumpernickel is made with rye flour, with the dough fermented before baking.

Can you tell me what all those pasta names mean?

THE WORD *pasta* itself means "dough paste." Some popular pastas and their meanings:

> spaghetti—little strings
> vermicelli—little worms
> ravioli—little turnips
> linguine—little tongues
> fettuccine—small ribbons
> cannelloni—large reeds
> farfalle—butterflies
> manicotti—small muffs
> tortellini—small twists

ALWAYS USE A CONDIMENT

What are the most popular condiments for hot dogs?

MUSTARD, ketchup, onions, relish, chili, sauerkraut, and mayonnaise—in that order. About 70% of connoisseurs like multiple toppings, and 7% prefer no toppings at all.

Does ketchup always contain tomato sauce?

NOWADAYS PRETTY much so, but that hasn't always been true. In fact, *ke-tsiap* was originally developed by the Chinese in 1690 from pickled fish, shellfish, and spices. The tangy sauce spread (slowly, of course, and with great anticipation) to Malaysia and Singapore, where British sailors discovered it being eaten under the name *kechap*. When the Brits brought back samples, English chefs tried to duplicate the sauce's texture and flavor with mushrooms, walnuts, cucumbers, and whatever else they had available. But ketchup still had no tomatoes, which were believed by much of the world to be poisonous. Finally, in 1792, a recipe for "Tomata Catsup" appeared in a New England cookbook, *The New Art of Cookery* by Richard Brigg.

What exactly is in mayonnaise, anyway?

USUALLY RAW egg yolks, oil, water, vinegar, and some optional sweeteners, preservatives, and thickeners. Mayonnaise got its name from Port Mahon on Minorca, one of the islands of Spain. When the Duc de Richelieu brought it back to France in the 18th century, the exotic *mahonnaise* sauce was used only for the best cuts of meat.

Where can I find a recipe for home-made mayonnaise?

Can you shine silverware by soaking it in mayonnaise?

NO. IN FACT, mayo can dull knives and stain some metals if left on them too long. However, some people swear you can use it to polish furniture and moisturize skin.

A TOAST TO GOOD FOOD

What were the original flavors of Pop Tarts?

WHEN THEY were first distributed in 1964, there were four, three of which are still with us: Strawberry, Blueberry, and Brown Sugar–Cinnamon. The fourth—Apple Currant—went to a graveyard that has since also been populated by other marketing mistakes, including Chocolate Peppermint, Frosted Peanut Butter and Jelly, and Chocolate and Cherry Chip.

When I was a lad, I remember bacon you could make in a toaster. People won't believe me. Help me regain my credibility, Jeeves!

GLAD TO OBLIGE. After the success of Pop Tarts in the early 1960s, other manufacturers tried to jump onto the toaster-cuisine bandwagon. One of the products was ReddiWip's Reddi Bacon. If you consider the potential for disaster represented by grease in close proximity to electricity, you can guess why it didn't last long. Other long-dead toaster products from the time include Downyflake Toaster Eggs, Toaster Chicken Patties, and Electric French Fries, which one critic said "looks like a picket fence, tastes like a picket fence."

Beer & Wine

TINY BUBBLES IN THE WINE

Does champagne get you drunk faster than non-bubbly wine?

YES, AND there are two reasons for it, not even factoring in the fact that many people think it tastes better and therefore drink more of it. The first is chemical: The carbon dioxide in the bubbles of sparkling wine moves alcohol more quickly into the bloodstream. The second reason is contextual: People don't usually drink champagne unless they're celebrating something, so the giddiness of the moment can have them half-drunk even without the direct effects of the alcohol.

How much pressure is there inside a champagne bottle? Can they explode?

HAVE YOU ever had a blowout with a high-pressure bike tire? It sounds like a gunshot and can lift the wheel right off the ground. A champagne bottle has about the same amount of pressure—roughly 90 pounds per square inch, or almost three times the pressure in a car tire. True, you have to be careful when popping the cork, but the danger from sparkling wine bottles is virtually nonexistent these days.

Back in the days of hand-blown bottles, however, it was pretty much a given that 15% to 20% of all champagne bottles would spontaneously explode in storage, propelling jagged glass shrapnel in all directions. And that was in a normal year. In 1828, unusual weather conditions resulted in grapes with a higher than usual sugar content, increasing fermentation, and as many as 80% of the bottles from that vintage exploded, making the job of wine steward quite dangerous. Shortly after that, a French chemist invented a device for detecting the amount of sugar in grape juice, which—along with wire masks for workers in wine cellars and stronger bottles—helped solve an epidemic of champagne bottle–induced injuries.

IT MAY BE RICE WINE TO YOU, BUT IT'S SAKE TO ME

How long should Japanese sake be aged?

IT SHOULDN'T be aged at all. Unlike most wines, which mellow with age, rice wine loses flavor. The fresher it is, the better it tastes.

12 STEPS TO BETTER COOKING

When you cook with wine in a microwave oven, does the alcohol evaporate away?

NO. MICROWAVES heat with little escape of moisture compared to convection ovens, and bring foods up to temperature much more quickly, giving less time for the alcohol to turn to vapor. So go easy on the wine sauce.

CORK DE VIN

Help, Jeeves, I'm going to a fancy restaurant and don't want to make a fool of myself— what are you supposed to do when a wine steward hands you the cork?

Who invented champagne? French monk Dom Perignon, in about 1660.

AH, THE PITFALLS of ordering a bottle of wine in a restaurant. First of all, trying to figure out whether to go with red, white, or Blue Nun, and then what type, label, year, and price. Just when you think you're home-free, the sommelier arrives, opens the bottle, and hands you the cork. What are you to do—lick it? Pass it around the table? Put it in your pocket for the next time you go to the ol' fishin' hole? Nope. And for heaven's sake, don't sniff it!

What you're supposed to do is simple: read it and feel it.

"Say what?" you ask. First some background: A hundred years or so ago, it was a common trick for restaurants to refill wine bottles that had impressive labels with mediocre wine and recork them, or to take cheap wine and glue an expensive label on it. To counteract the practice, wineries began printing their names on their corks and sealing the ends with foil, wire, or wax. By bringing the bottle to the table unsealed and opening it in front of your eyes, the restaurant is assuring you that the bottle has not been tampered with. Your job is to check the label, then read the cork when it comes out of the bottle. The information on both should match what you ordered.

Why do you fondle the cork at the same time? You're checking that the end of it is wet. If bottles are not stored on their sides, corks can dry out and let air in, spoiling the wine. If your cork is dry and brittle looking, the next step becomes more critical.

The next step is also a potential pitfall: The waiter pours a splash of wine into your glass and waits expectantly. It's his little trap, just when you think you're out of the woods. Unless you want him and others in the restaurant to think you're an ignorant boob, *don't drink it.* That would be rude, to be drinking before your guests. Instead, swirl the wine around in the bottom of your glass, bring it up to your nose, and take one long, dramatic sniff. Pause for a moment to build suspense. Unless it smells like vinegar—which happens, though rarely—you exhale, look the server in the eye, and nod once with a significant air. The server will then go around the table, pouring wine into the glasses of all. Then and only then do you sip.

What do you do if the wine *does* smell like vinegar? Discreetly tell your server, "I believe this wine has 'turned.' " The server will apologize profusely, whisk it away, and bring another bottle, beginning the process all over again.

EARLY VINTAGES

What was the first alcoholic beverage?

PROBABLY WINE, but beer goes way back, too. An archaeological dig in Mesopotamia, for example, yielded beer-brewing instructions on stone tablets dating from about 7000 B.C., and we know that Neolithic man grew wheat, barley, and millet 3,000 years before that. However, wine most likely came first. Beer, after all, has to be brewed while wine will often just sort of happen if you leave a fruit juice out long enough. Persian poet and astronomer Omar Khayyám (A.D. 1050-1122) claimed wine was discovered by a member of a Persian king's harem. According to his story, grapes were stored in jars in the king's palace for eating out of season. One jar developed foaming grapes and a strange smell, so it was set aside as probably poisonous. A harem woman, suffering from excruciating "nervous headaches," decided to use this poison to commit suicide and free herself of the constant pain. However, after she drank it, her headache disappeared. She became the life of the party and then sank into a restful sleep. Historian Hugh Johnson, however, believes that wine was discovered two million years ago, long before there even was a Persia.

How many books of the Old Testament mention wine?

THEY ALL DO, except one: the book of Jonah. In all others, wine plays a part, even if just metaphorically. The book of Isaiah not only talks about wine, but also gives helpful advice about how to plant a vineyard.

> **How do you pronounce sauvignon blanc and pinot noir?**
> "So-veen-YAWHN blawhn" and "PEE-no nwahr."

FERMENTING MUTINY

Did the Pilgrims drink alcoholic beverages?

NOT ONLY DID they drink alchohol, but their drinking may have affected why they landed in cold Massachusetts in the dead of winter instead of traveling farther south as planned. A passenger wrote in a *Mayflower* journal about why they landed with much haste at first sight of land: "We could not now take time for further search, our victuals being much spent, expecially our beere."

AND THE FOAM OF THE BRAVE

I heard that the "Star-Spangled Banner" was written to the tune of a drinking song. Which one?

A CATCHY little number called "To Anacreon in Heav'n." Lawyer and amateur poet Francis Scott Key wrote the first drafts of the song as a poem while temporarily detained on a British ship during the War of 1812, after which he immediately sought refuge in a dockside saloon. It was there that he finished off the verses and got the idea of putting them to the theme song of the Anacreontic Society, a London drinking club—the song was perhaps sung around him as he worked on his poem. (When you sing the "rockets red glare" high notes, you can see why a little alcohol would help in the performance of the song.)

The original tune, coincidentally, was written by Anacreontic Society member John Stafford Smith, who also wrote "God Save the Queen"—another British tune recycled into an American patriotic song, in this case "America (My Country 'tis of Thee)."

The first words to the Anacreontic drinking song, by Ralph Temlinson, Esq., run some six stanzas and choruses. Here are the first stanza and chorus followed by the last, as sung at the Crown and Anchor Tavern in the Strand, circa 1780:

> To Anacreon in Heav'n, where he sat in full glee
> A few Sons of Harmony sent a petition
> That he their Inspirer and Patron would be;
> When this answer arrived from the Jolly
> Old Grecian:
> "Voice, Fiddle, and Flute, no longer be mute,
> I'll lend you my name and inspire you to boot,
> CHORUS:
> And besides I'll instruct you, like me, to intwine
> The Myrtle of Venus with Bacchus's Vine."
>
> Ye Sons of Anacreon, then join hand in hand;
> Preserve Unanimity, Friendship, and Love!
> 'Tis yours to support what's so happily plann'd;
> You've the sanctions of Gods, and the Fiat of Jove.
> While thus we agree, our toast let it be:
> "May our Club flourish Happy, United, and Free!
> CHORUS:
> And long may the Sons of Anacreon intwine
> The Myrtle of Venus with Bacchus's Vine."

IF YOU CAN MAKE WINE HERE, YOU CAN MAKE IT ANYWHERE

Obviously, California is the number 1 state in wine production. Which is number 2?

NEW YORK. But it's not exactly neck and neck with the Golden State. California produces 87% of the United States' total and

New York, 6%. Of the California wine, only 9% comes from Napa and Sonoma counties, the most famous wine regions. And here's a sobering statistic: Of all the wine made in the United States, fully a quarter is manufactured by the E & J Gallo Winery working, under various names, out of Modesto, California.

Where can I find drinking games for parties?

How can I learn to make wine?

WELL, ERNEST and Julio Gallo learned from a pamphlet they found in the local library, and they did all right. Or try this site, which has a 12-step system for making wines: *www.portland. quik.com/batwood/homebrw.htm*

HAVE A FIRKIN ON ME

What's a firkin?

A SPECIALIZED unit of measurement used in winemaking. It amounts to about a quarter of a barrel. Others you may run into include *runlet, tierce, pipe, gill, tun,* and *puncheon.*

DRINK TO THEE ONLY WITH MINE EYES? FIRST I NEED GLASSES . . .

Why are there so many different shapes of glasses made for wine?

ONE GLASSWARE manufacturer sells a completely different glass for each type of wine—23 in all, at last count—ranging in shape and size from a long tall, narrow champagne flute to a wide, squatty burgundy glass. Different shapes are designed to emphasize a wine's bouquet or bubbles, then deliver the liquid to the appropriate portion of the tongue for that particular wine. For example, a tart wine might be served in a glass flared at the top to direct the wine to the tip of your tongue, which is the part that tastes sweetness best.

TREAT DAT CARPET WITH DIS STAIN

How do you lift a red wine stain?

CATCH IT quickly and blot it up (don't rub!) with a clean towel and cool water. Rubbing on salt helps. If the stain is still visible, sponge on 91% pure alcohol. If none of these things work, bleach or dye the material back to its original color. Good luck.

LAND OF HOPS AND GLORY

Who drinks the most beer per capita?

WELL, DESPITE their reputation, it isn't the Germans. That's pretty amazing, considering that they down nearly 39 gallons for every person, nearly double the per capita consumption of U.S. citizens (who drink 22 gallons, roughly 235 cans or bottles of beer a year). No, the most beer-sodden place in the world is Australia's Northern Territory. The average person there soaks up 62.4 gallons of brew a year.

When was beer sold in cans for the first time?

JANUARY 1935. It was three decades before the pop-top came into use, meaning you'd have to make sure you had a "church key" can opener with you if you wanted to drink beer. Before that, beer was available in bottles . . . and before that, you'd go down to your local tavern and have them fill a pail for you.

What's a canologist?

A BEER CAN collector. If you are one, you might want to join the Beer Can Collectors of America. Despite the name, the Beer Can Collectors of America is an international organization and it concerns itself with more than just beer cans. Four thousand active members in over 45 different countries collect what they call "breweriana"—just about everything pertaining to beer advertising and packaging, including "bottles, cans, coasters, crowns, glasses, labels, lights, mats, openers, posters, signs, steins, tap knobs, etc."

For more details, check out the BCCA Web site: www.bcca.com/index.html

HISTORICAL FOOT NOTES

Does anyone still step on grapes with their feet to make wine?

A HUNDRED years ago, most red wine was made this way, but not so anymore. Foot treading is now used for only a small quantity of the best port wines. The rest of the grapes are pressed by machines.

Where can I find microbreweries around the world?

How hard is it to tread grapes with your feet? Sounds like fun!

IT'S HARDER than you'd think. For example, keeping your footing is difficult in the slippery pulp. Ancient Egyptians invented a grid of overhead hand bars for treaders because they kept falling in and drowning: while a little "body" is considered a good thing in wine, an actual body is not. Also, over long days and nights of treading, grapes would ferment, releasing carbon dioxide, and treaders sometimes died from asphyxiation.

If treading grapes still sounds like fun to you, despite these hazards, perhaps this description of a visit to a Spanish winery in 1877 will change your mind:

> The treaders, with their white breeches well tecked up, form three separate rows of ten men each . . . and placing their arms on each other's shoulders, commence work by raising and lowering their feet . . . varying this, after a time, with songs and shoutings in order to keep the weaker and the lazier ones up to the work, which is quite irksome and monotonous. . . . Taking part with them in the treading is a little band of musicians . . . who strike up a lively tune. . . . The grapes become pretty well crushed and walking over the pips and stalks, strewn at the bottom of the lagar, becomes something like the pilgrimages of old when the devout trudged wearily along,

with hard peas backed between their feet and the soles of their shoes. The treaders move slowly in a listless way. . . . The fiddle strikes up anew, and the overseers drowsily upbraid. But all to no purpose. Music has lost its inspiration and authority its terrors, and the men, dead beat, raise one purple leg languidly after the other.

Or this from an American visiting a Burgundy winery at about the same time (the American later turned down his host's offer of red wine, electing to drink an untreaded white wine instead):

Ten men, stripped of all their clothes, step into the vessel and begin to tread down the floating mass, working it also with their hands. This operation is repeated several times if the wine does not ferment rapidly enough. The reason is that the body heat of the men aids the wine in its fermentation.

NOT-SO-NEAR BEER

Why is root beer called "beer" when it isn't beer at all?

THE NAME is pretty much consumer fraud, pure and simple. In the early 1870s, Charles Hires was served a root and herb tea at a country inn on his honeymoon, and liked it so much he decided to market it as a soft drink. As an anti-alcohol prohibitionist, Hires hoped that drinkers would abandon demon rum in favor of his root tea. A friend, fellow prohibitionist and president of Temple University, Dr. Russell Conwell, convinced him that no hard-drinking Pennsylvania coal miner was going to abandon Jack Daniels for "Hires Herb Tea." Why not call it a "Root Beer" instead?

The ploy worked well. In fact, too well. The success of the root "beer" brought down the well-organized wrath of the Women's Christian Temperance Union, which called for a boycott of the soft drink and deplored the fact that Hires was advertising it as safe and healthy for children: "Soothing to the nerves, vitalizing to the blood, refreshing to the brain, beneficial in every way," said one ad in those pre-Truth in Advertising times. Added another, "Hires Root Beer gives the children strength to resist the enervating effects of the heat, bridges the convalescent over the trying part of a hot day, and helps even a cynic see the brighter side of life."

From 1895 to 1898, the war against root beer was waged in streets and newspapers, nearly destroying the Charles E. Hires Co. Finally, an independent lab decided to join the fray. It analyzed samples of the soft drink and concluded that root beer contained "less alcohol than a loaf of bread." The WCTU apologized and went off to find other dragons to slay, and sales of Hires Root Beer rebounded to past levels.

ANYBODY FEEL A DRAFT?

What is "cold-filtered" beer?

AN ADVERTISING term. All beer is "cold filtered"—it just means using fine screens to remove particulates, including microbes. If combined with sterile handling, the filtering eliminates bacteria, which means that the beer doesn't have to be pasteurized. Unpasteurized beer can legally be labeled "draft" beer, even though it comes in bottles and cans instead of being drawn from kegs.

Why do beer steins have covers on them?

THERE WAS a law passed in 19th-century Germany mandating lids on beer steins. It was based on the idea that swallowing flies could cause serious disease, including the plague. Since Germany has a number of outdoor beer establishments, especially during Oktoberfest, the government decided that adding lids would keep bar flies out of the beer, and Germany safe from the plague.

YOU DON'T BUY BEER, YOU RENT IT

Why do you have to pee so much when you drink beer?

BESIDES TAKING in the extra liquid, it's because alcohol is a diuretic, actively flushing the fluids out of your body. It's this dehydration that causes hangovers. Best preventative is to drink water as a chaser and to down a few glasses of water every time you get up in the night to go to the bathroom.

Is it true that heavy beer drinkers don't often get diarrhea?

SO SAY DOCTORS. The beer irritates their stomachs, which produce more acid, which kills the microbes that cause diarrhea.

I'VE GOT A TEAR IN MY BEER FROM CRYIN' FOR YOU DEAR . . . .

Does country music make people drink more than rock or jazz?

A STUDY BY anthropologist James M. Schaefer claims that country music fans drink more, when listening to their favorite music. Even allowing for the differences in culture and class among listeners, he found that the slower the tune, the faster the drinking, and specifically that there was a direct "tears to beers" ratio—sad, sentimental songs trigger heavier drinking.

WHAT'S A PAGODA? DID JESUS KILL anyone? And what makes a cult a cult? Since the dawn of time, people have turned to religion for the answers to life's most difficult questions. For those setting out on a long (or short) spiritual trek, Jeeves says, luckily, there's the Internet to help you in your quest.

CONGRATULATIONS!

Why do people say "God bless you" when some-one sneezes?

SUPERSTITIONS and traditions surrounding the sneeze have a long history. Ancients from around the world have believed that a sneeze holds significant messages—of either danger or health, depending on the time and culture. Arabs traditionally bow in response to a sneeze. Germans say *"Gesundheit!"* (Your health!). Ancient Romans responded with "Good luck to you!" and "Congratulations!"

During a nasty bout of plague in sixth-century Europe, when a sneeze often accompanied severe pain and death, Pope Gregory the Great demanded that everyone wish the sneezer well with a blessing from God Almighty. "God bless you!" was the ordered response to overhearing another's sneeze. If no one was around when the sneeze occurred, the sneezer was to beseech the good Lord himself with a loud "God help me!"

That plague came and went, as did others, and science finally caught up with religion and explained the reasons for sneezing in more concrete terms—but the phrase stuck and continues to be used today.

IT'S IN THE BOOK

How many words are in the shortest Bible verse?

TWO. John 11:35 simply states, "Jesus wept." Jesus had just arrived to find Mary, Martha, and other members of their village mourning the loss of the women's brother Lazarus. Jesus cried, too, and then raised his friend Lazarus from the dead.

What happened to Lot in the Bible?

A LOT, as it were. Like so many Old Testament characters, he lived a long and eventful life. However, his wife didn't fare so well, and his daughters seemed to be pawns in a terribly twisted tale. The story began when God decided that the town of Sodom—Lot's hometown—was so evil that it must be destroyed. Since Lot was a good person, God sent angel messengers to get his family out before He rained fire and brimstone on the wicked little burgh. Seeing the visiting angels in Lot's home, the men of the town demanded Lot turn the angels over to them so that they could "have their way" with them (sodomize them). Instead, Lot protected the angels and offered his virgin daughters to the debauched men of the town. Fortunately for the girls, the men refused and the angels eventually smote the men with blindness.

Who was Jesus' brother?
John (not John the Baptist).

The angels gave Lot's family these instructions: Get out of town, run to a safe place, and *don't look back*. Evidently, they meant every word to be taken literally. When Lot's wife turned to watch the city go up in flames, she was instantly turned into a pillar of salt.

With no husbands and all the marriageable men in their lives up in smoke, Lot's daughters decided to sacrifice themselves for the good of Lot's family name. On successive nights, they got their father drunk and had sex with him until they got pregnant. Funny, you don't hear this one much in Sunday school, do you?

NAME IN VAIN

What does the "H" stand for in Jesus H. Christ?

NO, JESUS' middle name was not Harold. His last name wasn't Christ, for that matter. The phrase "Jesus H. Christ," meaning the equivalent of "for crying out loud," probably morphed from similar phrases like "holy Christ," or "for Christ's sake." If the H. stands for anything at all, it just as well could stand for "Holy," as in "Jesus Holy Christ," to make the exclamation sound even more severe or shocking. Most likely, though, it doesn't stand for anything but just feels satisfying to say.

Why is the fish a symbol for Christianity?

THE GREEK word for "fish," loosely, *ichthus*, is the same as the initial letters of the phrase "Jesus Christ, Son of God, Savior": (*Iesous CHristos, THeou Uios, Soter*). Since Jesus was already associated with fishermen and fish, it worked well. Later, when persecution became widespread, Christians were able to greet one another with a drawing of a fish to keep from giving themselves away to authorities. It became the universal symbol for Christianity.

NOW AND ZEN

What's a pagoda?

A PAGODA is a temple in Asia and India—usually built on sacred ground—that consists of several levels, one on top of another. It is a place of worship and meditation built in the traditional Asian style. But the word can also represent an idol that is worshiped in parts of Asia. And at one point, India had a coin called a pagoda, as well.

What does the "Zen" in Zen Buddhism mean?

THE WORD *Zen* comes from the Sanskrit word *dhyana*, meaning "thinking meditation." And that is exactly what Zen Buddhism is about. It came out of India many centuries ago and has become a common religion in Japan. Zen Buddhists practice enlightenment through meditation and intuition, as opposed to many other Buddhist sects that use Buddhist scripture as their way to enlightenment.

What does "Nirvana" mean?

IN SANSKRIT, it literally means "going out." It's the state of bliss that Buddhists work to attain. Many Buddhists describe it as a state of being completely devoid of desire and want.

WE VISHNU WELL

What's an avatar?

AN AVATAR is the human form of a god in the Hindu faith. Some avatars of note are Rama, Buddha, and Krishna, all of whom are considered incarnations of Vishnu. The gaming industry has adopted this label for heroes in role-playing and fantasy games.

Is it Brahman or Brahmin?

IT'S BOTH. A *Brahmin* is a Hindu priest. *Brahman* is the "world spirit," or the guiding force of the world and beyond. The Brahman cattle breed—originally from India and noted for a hump between the shoulders—derives its name from the latter.

DON'T MOST CATS LIKE SALMAN?

Is it true that Cat Stevens wants to kill Salman Rushdie?

THE *SATANIC VERSES*, Rushdie's controversial 1988 book, made the mistake of poking fun at the origins of Islam by suggesting that their prophet, Muhammad, was just as human as anyone and just as easily persuaded with money, fame, and sex. As a result, the Islamic part of the world rose up in arms. Sometimes literally: The Ayatollah Khomeini put out a death warrant against Rushdie. At the time, ex-pop-singer-turned-fundamentalist-Muslim Cat Stevens (now Yusuf Islam), expressed enthusiastic support for the Ayatollah's action. When asked about it in more recent days, though, he has refused to answer, saying that his views were "misrepresented" at the time.

What's the start date of the Muslim calendar?

IT'S MARKED by the date that Muhammad and his followers left his hometown of Mecca to escape persecution. They made their *hijrah* (journey) to Medina on July 16, 622, so the Muslim calendar begins with that day. The Muslim calendar is based on lunar cycles and therefore is either 354 or 355 days long every year. A solar year, in contrast, is based on Earth's movement around the sun. The solar calendar has 30 or 31 days per month and is 365 and one-quarter days long. A lunar month typically has 29 or 30 days. What that means is that what were summer months several years ago are now spring months . . . and will become winter months over the next several years. In some countries that use a lunar calendar, an extra month is observed every three years to prevent the months from drifting too far into other seasons. Most cultures associate celebrations and holidays with certain times of year and want to keep it that way.

> **What are the Five Pillars of Islam?**

What does "Islam" mean?

THE MEANING of the Arabic word is "surrender." The idea is that one who practices Islam—a Muslim—is "one who surrenders" to God.

What do Muslims use prayer rugs for?

A PRAYER rug is a special rug that Muslims use to kneel on when performing *salat*—their prayers. The pattern on the rug consists of a niche in the design at one end, called a *mihrah,* that must always point toward Mecca (the holy pilgrimage city) during prayer. Prayers are performed five times a day: at dawn, noon, midafternoon, sunset, and night. The rug allows a Muslim to pray anywhere.

Which day is Sabbath for Muslims?

MUSLIMS BELIEVE God doesn't sleep, and therefore never needs to rest, and so they don't celebrate Sabbath in the same way that Christians and Jews do. What they do celebrate is

Yawm-Al-Jumau'ah. Literally this means "the day of congregation." Yawn-Al-Jumau'ah comes every Friday—a sermon is held
in the local mosque, followed by group prayer.

OUT OF THE DESERT

How is Islam related to Judaism and Christianity?

THEY ALL originated from the same faith—a monotheistic
one—have the same forefathers, and have many of the same
stories in their holy writings. How they differ may be a better
way to approach this question.

Briefly, the Muslim version of the story goes something like
this: Islam and Judaism split from each other back in the time
of Abraham. This forefather of both faiths
bore two sons: the first, Ishmael,
with a servant named Hagar, and
the second, Isaac, with his
wife, Sarah. Hagar and
Ishmael were sent away from
the family, and the Koran has it
that Ishmael's descendants are
Muslims, whereas Isaac's descendants are Jews. Ishmael and
Hagar are highly revered in Islam and are deeply ingrained in
the stories of the religion.

How many Christian denominations practice in North America?
Approximately 1,200.

Jesus came along thousands of years later and started
Christianity. The Christian faith has its foundation in Judaism.
Islam, in turn, builds upon aspects of the earlier two faiths. It
doesn't believe Jesus was God, but holds that he (along with
Abraham, Moses, Noah, and Adam) was one of the five great
prophets of god, or Allah.

The angel Gabriel plays an important role in all three faiths
as well. Everyone knows Gabriel–the heavenly interpreter sent
to Daniel in the Old Testament scriptures. Christians say he
was the messenger who told Mary she was going to have the
Son of God. Muslims say he was also the angel that delivered

the Quran (Koran)—the Muslim holy book—to the last prophet, Muhammad, in the seventh century.

LET MY PEOPLE GO

Will I have to be circumcised if I convert to Judaism?

IT DEPENDS on which branch of Judaism you are converting to. There are four: Reform, Reconstructionist, Conservative, and Orthodox. The latter two require that an uncircumcised male be circumcised at the time of conversion. This is done in a ceremony called a *brit* (pronounced *briss*) *milah*. If the candidate has already been medically circumcised, the Orthodox and Conservative rabbis will perform a ceremony called *hatafat dam brit*, in which a small drop of blood is drawn to represent a religious circumcision.

Although female converts don't have to go through anything like circumcision, all four branches require—or in the more liberal branches "strongly advise"—immersion in a ritual bath called a *mikveh*. The ceremony is called a *tevillah* and involves totally immersing your body in the waters as blessings are said over you by representatives of the faith.

What is the origin of the Jewish custom of placing small stones on graves?

FLOWERS ON gravesites were strictly forbidden by Orthodox rabbis for a long time because of Talmudic rules that nothing can be used for the dead that's really for the sake of the living. Pebbles became a more acceptable way of honoring the dead at their grave. They may have served a dual purpose: the Talmud implies that the soul stays in the grave for a while before going to the afterlife. The stones could have represented the desire of the living to make sure the souls stayed where they were for a while, by symbolically holding them there.

However the practice began, most agree that the stones represent a more permanent reminder of the deceased than flowers or wreaths, which also die eventually.

What is Yom ha-Shoah?

YOM HA-SHOAH VE'HA-GEVURAH is Holocaust Remembrance
Day. Directly translated, *Yom* means "Day," *Shoah* means
"Holocaust," *ve* means "and," *Gevurah* means "Heroism." It's a
day to remember the survivors, victims, heroes, and acts of
humanity of the Holocaust, not just to mourn and pray for the
dead. It's honored in Israel on the 27th day of the month of
Nisan, which falls between Passover and *Yom ha-Atzmaut,*
Israel's Independence Day. The date was chosen in part to
commemorate the Warsaw Ghetto Uprising on April 19, 1943,
which ended on the 27th day of Nisan. Generally, the holiday
falls in April or May of the Western calendar.

What do the characters on a dreidel say?

A DREIDEL is a four-sided spinning top that is used in a game
played during Hannukah. The letters on it are directives to the
players of the game. They're the Hebrew letters N (*Nun*), G
(*Gimmel*), H (*Hay*) and SH (*Shin*). The game goes something like
this: Kids gather around, and each gets the same number of
coins, or *gelt* (chocolate coins wrapped in gold foil). They put
one coin in the middle of the table, and each child gets a turn
to spin the dreidel. Whatever letter the dreidel stops on, the
player must do what it directs. N/*Nun* stands for *nisht* and
means you do nothing. G/*Gimmel* is *gahntz,* which means
"all"—the player gets to take everything from the middle.
H/*Hay* represents *hahlb,* or "half," so the player may take half
of the pile. SH/*Shin* means *shtel,* or "put in" one item.

POSSIBLY APOCRYPHAL

Did Jesus ever kill anybody?

IN THE New Testament Apocrypha—books not deemed
sacredly inspired by most Christian faiths, but still used by
some—there are stories of Jesus killing many people, one after
the other, when he was a child. The Gospel of Thomas, translated from the Greek, details stories of Jesus' childhood before
he made his famous trek to the temple at the age of 12.

Reading the Gospel of Thomas, one doesn't wonder long why it was stricken from the official version of the New Testament: children can be cruel, and the Savior was no exception. According to this gospel, when Jesus was five, he "withered" a kid who broke a small dirt dam that he had made after a rainstorm. At the same age, another kid running somewhere accidentally collided with Jesus, who killed him instantly, saying, "Thou shalt not finish thy course." At one point, his father, Joseph, was so despairing about the string of victims that he commanded his wife Mary, "Let him not forth without the door, for they all die that provoke him to wrath!"

Jesus calmed down with age and reportedly healed and resurrected more people than he supposedly killed.

Even in the official New Testament Bible, though, Jesus wasn't above doing some tree smiting when his temper flared. In Mark, chapter 11, Jesus was walking along and became very hungry. He came upon a fig tree that was in off season and so was bearing no fruit. He cursed it and went on his way. When the disciples came back by later, they saw the withered tree and questioned Jesus about why he had cursed the thing. Jesus changed the subject and talked about faith moving mountains.

What are the seven deadly sins?

THE SEVEN deadly sins (or cardinal sins), according to the Roman Catholic faith, are the sins that are most serious and can result in the death of one's soul: pride, lust, gluttony, anger, envy, sloth, and covetousness.

In their original form, as put forth by Avagrius of Pontus, an early Greek theologian, there were eight deadly sins. In order of increasing sinfulness, they were gluttony, lust, avarice, sadness, anger, acedia (apathy), vainglory, and pride. Along came Pope Gregory the Great, who gave us the Gregorian calendar and Gregorian chants. In the sixth century, he decided vainglory and pride were the same and combined them; added envy and reversed the sins' order of severity. Later, the Church decided sadness couldn't be labeled a sin and replaced it with a new deadly sin, sloth. After ordering and reordering the deadly sins over time, the Church finally decided that sin couldn't be measured and eliminated degree of sinfulness completely. Today the seven deadly sins remain numbered for tradition and identification only.

On the flip side, there are acts of moral distinction that sometimes offer a way of behavior to counter the seven deadly sins. The seven virtues are faith, hope, charity, fortitude, justice, prudence, and temperance.

What are rosary beads for?

ROSARY BEADS have been used for thousands of years in many different cultures, long before Christianity began using them as a method of counting how many prayers have been said. The beads have been made of wood, glass, stones, knots, and anything else that can be strung together. In the 1100s, St. Dominic of Spain, founder of the Dominican Order, made them popular tools for the Catholic Church, to keep people from "heresy and sin." The word *rosary* itself may have come from either a popular material for beads—rosewood—or the word for bead in French: *rosaire*.

What is the Hail Mary?

IT IS A PRAYER in the Catholic Church to Mary, the mother of Jesus, who intercedes on behalf of the person praying to Jesus and to all of the departed saints. Priests in confessionals often prescribe a number of "Hail Marys" that must be done in penance for a person's sins.

The beginning of the prayer comes from the Bible, when the angel Gabriel told Mary she was going to give birth to the Savior. "Hail Mary, full of grace, the Lord is with you" was the way the angel greeted her. The second part of the prayer is also taken from the Bible, from the story in which Mary tells her cousin Elizabeth about her divine conception. Elizabeth says, "Blessed are you among women and blessed is the fruit of your womb." The last part was added sometime in the 1400s by the Church: "Holy Mary, mother of God, pray for us sinners now and at the hour of our death." Saying the prayer in this order constitutes one Hail Mary.

"MOM! SHE'S STARING AT ME!"
What is the Evil Eye?

THE SUPERSTITION of the Evil Eye goes back centuries, and can be found in societies throughout the world. Ancient Romans claiming to possess the Evil Eye could be hired to charm enemies. Ancient India revered and feared the phenomenon, as did cultures in the Near East. For hundreds of years, gypsies were accused of possessing the Evil Eye and were persecuted by many cultures.

The Evil Eye was an especially terrible thing to be accused of in the Middle Ages. People with epilepsy, those having sneezing fits at the wrong time and place, even some simply caught daydreaming were accused of possessing the Evil Eye and were burned at the stake. Anything that was deemed out of the ordinary or inappropriate was attributed to the Evil Eye.

What is a jettatore? In Italy, it is someone with the Evil Eye.

But what exactly is the Evil Eye? It's a stare that can entrance and bewitch, that has the power to steal another's soul, possibly causing death. Depending on the culture and time, others could make a person get the Evil Eye, as could the Devil himself. Therefore, penalizing those who had the Evil Eye with death seemed an appropriate response, to keep the Devil and evil away.

Some anthropologists believe that the superstition is based on an observation: the mirrored reflection of one person in another person's pupils. The word *pupil* comes from the Latin word meaning "little doll." Seeing a reflection of oneself staring out from someone else's eyes could easily have led to the belief that one's soul had been snatched away and placed in that person's eye.

In order to combat this reflection effect, some folklorists theorize that the Egyptians thought up black eye makeup—for both men and women—to reduce the amount of light reflected in the eye, therefore lowering the chance a person's reflection could be seen in the pupil. (The other theory, of course, is simply that they worked in the hot desert sun and wanted to keep glare down to a minimum.) There's no doubt, however, that the English language has been impacted by this superstition. A number of everyday sayings come from the old and widespread belief in the Evil Eye: "if looks could kill" and "withering glance," to name two.

EVERYTHING YOU WANTED TO KNOW ABOUT SECTS (BUT WERE AFRAID TO ASK)

What is kabbalah?

KABBALAH IS a religious philosophy developed by a group of rabbis using a mystical method of interpreting Jewish scripture. Because Hebrew is a language without vowels, the word "*qblh*" can be spelled kabala, kabbala, cabbala, or caballah. Considered occultism by the traditional Jewish faith, kabbalah purports to find hidden meanings and prophecies in scripture by combining numerology and other mystical practices.

What's the difference between a cult and a religion?

THAT DEPENDS on the person you ask. For instance, some Christian denominations still believe that the Mormons—the Church of Jesus Christ of the Latter Day Saints—are members of a cult, even though most, at least grudgingly, consider them an offshoot of Christianity. Here's a loose rule of thumb: Every religion starts as a "cult," and if it lasts more than a century, it's considered a religion.

Who are the Gideons?

THEY'RE A Christian denomination with a very targeted mission. For over a century, they've operated a nonprofit, mostly male missionary business that works to place Bibles all over the world for people to read. The Bible in your hotel room? Odds are, the Gideons put it there. According to Gideons International, 86 Bibles are placed somewhere, worldwide—in a hotel room, jail, hospital, airport, or bus station—every minute of every day.

WITCH IS WITCH

How do I find practicing witches in my area?

YOU CAN try a phone directory search under Pagan Churches or Wiccan Groups, or send $2 and an SASE for a listing of organizations to:

> What do pagans believe?

> COG Correspondence Officer
> P.O. Box 1226
> Berkeley, CA 94701

COG—Covenant of the Goddess—is a U.S. umbrella group that aids and assists local pagan chapters all over the country. You can also contact them through e-mail at *info@cog.org* or visit their site on the Web: *www.cog.org/*

How many of the Salem witches were burned at the stake?

NONE. Twenty-five people lost their lives during the hysteria: 19 were hanged, 1 was crushed to death with stones, and the others died while in prison, but none were burned at the stake.

National Geographic Interactive has an illuminating illustration of the Salem witchcraft trials. Put together as a first-person account, it walks you through the 17th-century process in Salem, Massachusetts. Take a peek, if you dare: *www.nationalgeographic.com/features/97/salem/*

From the Ground Up

PLANTS FORM THE BASIS OF ALL LIFE on Earth—providing the oxygen we breathe and the food we eat (whether we consume the plants or the animals that eat plants). With their unique ability to convert sunlight into sugars, plants are also the source of medicines and poisons, pleasure and misery. They stimulate all our senses: we smell them, taste them, admire their beauty, enjoy their shade, and even listen to them as they rustle in the breeze.

INCREDIBLE EDIBLES

How many different varieties of corn are there?

THERE ARE thousands of corn hybrids, but almost all fall into six general groups. The most common variety grown in the United States is *dent corn*, used for chemicals and animal feed. *Sweet corn* is the kind most people consume, on or off the cob; its sugar doesn't convert to starch, so it is sweeter than most varieties. *Flint corn* has more moisture and is easily grown in extreme climates. It is used in the United States as animal feed. A subvariety of flint corn is popcorn. It has a higher moisture volume that causes it to explode when exposed to heat. *Flour corn* is used primarily for cornmeal—it is easily ground because the starch is softer and less packed. Finally, *pod corn* is a decorative plant.

Besides the tomato, what other vegetable-y thing is technically a fruit?

"VEGETABLE-Y" fruits include the cucumber (and the gherkin), eggplant, pumpkin, okra, zucchini, and squash. Rhubarb, on the other hand, although traditionally used in desserts like a fruit, is technically a vegetable.

How heavy is the largest pumpkin on record?

LAST TIME we checked, a pumpkin named Moonie, grown by Larry and Gerry Checkon of Spangler, Pennsylvania, topped the scales at 1,131 pounds in 1999. Moonie was over 3 feet high and well over 13 feet around.

> **Does eating broccoli make your urine smell funny?**
> No, but eating asparagus does.

Where does saffron come from?

CROCUSES, and lots of them. It requires thousands of these flowers to produce just one ounce of saffron. That's why it's so expensive.

THE GARDEN OF GOOD AND EVIL . . . AND WEIRD

What does "nasturtium" actually mean?

NASTURTIUM comes from two Latin words, nasus and tortum, which together mean "to twist the nose," a reference to the flower's rather overpowering scent. Many people don't know that nasturtiums are more than a feast for just the eyes and nose—they're edible, too. The flowers taste like watercress and make a nice addition to salads (be sure they're pesticide-free!).

I heard that the orchid was named after female genitalia. Is this true?

DESPITE ITS perceived resemblance to the outer female reproductive organs, apparently noticed by very lonely gardeners, it was actually named after male genitalia. The name orchid comes from the Greek *orkhis*, meaning "testicle." It was adopted because of the orchid's testicle-shaped root. This resemblance may have led to the belief that orchids were aphrodisiacs.

Where can I see pictures of giant flowers online?

What's the largest flower in the world?

A PARASITIC plant called the *rafflesia* holds that honor. Popularly known as the corpse lily, it attaches itself to other stems and vines, and produces large, five-lobed flowers measuring up to three feet wide and weighing as much as 15 pounds, with petals an inch thick. These flowers are native to Malaysia and Indonesia and are known for their putrid odor. Carrion flies pollinate them, so in order to attract the flies, the flowers mimic the smell of dead meat when in bloom.

How does the poison in poison ivy work?

ITS "POISON" is not really poison at all; it's a highly allergenic oil called *urushiol*. Coming in contact with it causes contact dermatitis (itchy, painful skin) in almost everyone. (Statistically, 85% of the population develops an allergy to the oil at some point in their lives.) You can come in contact with urushiol by brushing up against poison ivy, touching an object or person who's had contact with the plant, or by being in the vicinity when the plant is burned. The oil travels well in smoke and causes serious medical problems if it gets in the throat and lungs.

The Japanese sumac or lacquer tree contains urushiol as well. Urushiol is an ingredient in all Japanese lacquers. When the lacquer is completely hardened, urushiol's poisonous characteristics are lessened significantly, but highly sensitive people will sometimes react to Japanese lacquered products.

If you come in contact with poison ivy, you have 15 minutes to wash it off your skin with cold water before it binds with the skin surface and causes problems. Don't scrub and don't use a cloth; just rinse with copious amounts of water.

THE GIVING TREE

Where does aspirin come from?

SINCE ABOUT 200 B.C., willow tree bark has been chewed to relieve aches and pains. The active element is salicylic acid, which reduces pain and fever. In the 1890s, Felix Hoffman, an employee of Bayer & Company, figured out how to dilute the acid, and the Bayer Company began selling it under the brand name Aspirin. The name was a derivative of the Latin name for another good source of salicylic acid, the plant called queen of the meadow. Today most asprin is synthetic.

What's the biggest tree in the world?

THE GENERAL Sherman Tree in California's Sequoia National Park has the greatest mass. It stands at 274' 11" and is 102' 8" around. Its largest branch measures almost 7 feet in diameter. There are taller trees, heavier trees, and older trees, but none that are larger. It is estimated to weigh about 1,400 tons.

What's the oldest tree in the world?

THE OLDEST living tree is a bristlecone pine in the Great Basin area of the United States, which stretches from Colorado to California. In recent times, one of these trees, named Prometheus, was dated at 4,950 years old. Unfortunately, a graduate student accidentally killed it while performing date studies on it. Another bristlecone pine, named Methuselah, has been dated at 4,766 years old and is now considered the oldest tree. Jeeves hopes that graduate students are keeping away from it.

How much wood is used to make an average book?

ABOUT ONE cord of wood is used to produce 1,000 copies of an average-sized book. A cord is equal to a stack of logs measuring 4' x 4' x 8', or about 70 to 100 cubic feet. For a single book such as this one, it takes a block of wood just a little bigger than the book itself. Definitely worth it.

What part of a hemlock tree does the poison come from?

NONE. IT COMES from the poison hemlock herb, *Conium maculatum.*

Where does cork come from?

Cork comes from an evergreen oak, *Quercus suber.* Commonly called cork oak or cork tree, it is native to the Mediterranean area. The average tree grows to a height of about 30 feet. At 15 to 20 years old, the tree's outer bark is stripped and used for cork products. Every 10 years thereafter, the bark is ready for harvest and can be stripped again. With age, the bark becomes smoother and less coarse; a tree will produce cork in this way for about 150 years. Most of the world's cork comes from Portugal, Spain, and Algeria.

How can I grow my own bonsai tree?

Creepy Crawlers

THERE ARE FEW THINGS THAT BUG people more than bugs, whether mosquitoes, flies, ants, wasps, or spiders. And yet without bugs pollinating plants, clearing away dead things, and conditioning soil, life as we know it would be impossible. So let's show a little respect for our 6- or 8- or 28-legged friends.

MARCHING ONE BY ONE

How many different species of ants are there?

THERE ARE about 10,000 known ant species throughout the world, and about half that number have been well documented. Scientists believe there are at least twice that many species undiscovered at this time, the majority of them in South America. With the ongoing destruction of South American rainforest land, many of those species will probably never be identified before they are extinct.

Do ants really "farm" aphids?

YES. APHIDS, bark lice, and scale bugs are bred and reared by ants. The normally carnivorous ants protect, groom, and care for these bugs as we do farm animals. Why are these garden pests so valuable to ants? They want their "milk"— an excreted honeylike substance called honeydew.

> **Where can I buy an ant farm?**

This may sound odd, but if you consider the ant's habitat, it makes perfect sense. Food runs out from time to time when you have thousands—sometimes millions—of mouths to feed, so these bugs provide an ant colony with a ready food source. If the colony sets up a few good cowboy ants to tend herds of li'l ant cattle, there's a guaranteed supply of food when other pickin's get slim.

In exchange, the ants protect the insects from other bugs that will eat them. Ants are so protective, they will carry them in their jaws like a mother cat with kittens when rain comes, then carry them back to their plant again afterward.

Ants are also known enslavers. Some ant species will take over another colony and make them an offer they can't refuse. Ownership of the aphids, lice, or scale bugs of the enslaved colony also gets transferred with the hostile takeover.

For a Web cam of a homemade ant farm, check out www. channelu.com/AntCam/

ANTY-HERO

What happens to the ant in Aesop's fable?

THE STORY goes something like this: On a beautiful summer day, the grasshopper asked the ant to come and play, but the ant said he couldn't because he needed to lay up food for the winter. The grasshopper went on his merry way, but come winter he began to starve. Seeing the ants with plenty of food to pass around, he then learned his lesson: It is best to prepare in times of plenty for days of necessity.

This is not the only Aesop fable starring an ant. To hear Aesop's fables as read by children, go to http://rsts.net/home/audiovideo/ aesops.html

HUSH, MY DARLING—
DON'T FEAR, MY DARLING

What is an ant lion?

ANT LIONS are the larvae of a type of fly. Varying forms can be found in countries all around the world. The most common North American genus is about the size of a fingernail in its larval stage. Often called "doodlebugs," ant lions form pits in sand or dirt, leaving trails of squiggly "doodles" as they dig. When an ant lion has completed its pit, it lies quietly in wait for ants and other insects to fall in, and then it eats them.

Some ant lions live under logs and rocks, where they are concealed to unsuspecting insects. Others actually flip sand or dirt out of their pits, causing ants

> **Where can I order chocolate-covered ants online?**

and other insects to wobble and be knocked off balance. At this point, the ant lion can lunge forward and snatch the stunned insect into its lair. Eventually the larva passes through its antisocial teen stage and turns into a fly. Similar to a dragonfly, it's about an inch and a half long.

To see an ant lion capturing an ant, check out: www.eantlionpit. com

DESIGNING AND MAINTAINING
WEB SITES

Do all spiders spin webs?

NOT ALL DO; the world of spiders is very diverse. There are some spiders that catch their meals by hiding and attacking when an unsuspecting victim comes close. Others literally run after their prey until they catch them. And of the spiders that do spin webs, there are those that weave nests, spin circular webs, or even make parachutes for flying through the air.

Why don't spiders stick to their own webs?

SOME SPIDERS DO. A spiderweb is constructed of two types of silk: *anchor* and *snare* threads. The anchor threads are used to construct the basic web; the snare threads are sticky and are used to trap insects. A spider, in moving around its web, uses the nonsticky anchor threads. Once in a while, though, it will inadvertently catch a leg or two in a snare thread. When this happens, it will simply secrete an oily solvent to free itself. Some spiders have special claws at the bottom of the hind legs, called *scopulas,* that can slide along the sticky snare strands and help them escape from their own homespun death traps.

If a spider starts spinning a web at 6 a.m., when will it be completed?

IF IT'S A traditional-looking round web, it will be done before breakfast, at 7 a.m. Sounds quick, but building a web is not the hard part—maintaining it is. After a few days, the web is not only damaged from ensnaring supper but it also has lost most of its stickiness. A spider does construction renewal, gathering up damaged threads with its front feet while trailing new silk behind. In this way, a spider continuously keeps its web up and running.

What's a cobweb?

IT'S ANY spiderweb, as *cob* comes from the Middle English word *coppe* for spider. Apart from that, there is also a group of spiders specifically called "cobweb spiders." Cobweb spiders build messy webs in corners and usually have a bulblike body and clawlike legs. Black widows fall into this category.

CONSUMING PASSION

Do female black widow spiders really eat their mates?

SOMETIMES. This isn't at all unusual behavior for a spider, though, so it seems odd that the spider *Latrodectus mactans* was the only one to get labeled "black widow." Perhaps it was fear of her bite to humans that stirred the souls of the name-givers.

Do female praying mantises eat their mates?

YES, THE females are known to sometimes bite the heads off their mates, often during copulation (the act can continue on, sans head, by the way). They're also notorious for eating their sisters, mothers, children, or the boys in the band. Their eyesight is poor, and they usually prey on anything that moves.

ARACHNOPHOBIA

Can you die from a black widow spider bite?

IT'S POSSIBLE, but most people don't. Although a female black widow is not particularly aggressive, she is quite poisonous and will bite to defend herself (males are harmless). Her bite is painful and frightening, and there isn't much that can be done to reverse its effects. However, the symptoms can be somewhat alleviated, and a medical professional can monitor the victim.

> **Is there a test that can tell me if I have arachnophobia?**

Symptoms start with a stinging pinprick at the location of the bite. Numbing pain soon follows, often accompanied by some swelling. Within 30 minutes, usually, severe stomach pains and clenching of the abdominal muscles begin. After a while, spasms and severe pain in the arms, legs, and often the feet set it. The most frightening aspects are temporary paralysis, chest constriction, and difficulty swallowing. If you are bitten, it's a good idea to seek out a doctor. Those at risk of dying are the very young, the very old, and those with illnesses or allergies. A black widow spider bite has about a 1% fatality rate.

Are there black widows in New York?

YES. THEY are found in desert areas, central and eastern states, and Canada. What to look for? They make nonsymmetrical cobwebs in dark places. Logs, sheds, woodpiles, and cellars are prime real estate for black widow spiders. The poisonous female's body is usually black and shiny, about a half inch long, with a red hourglass-shaped marking on the underside of her abdomen. She mostly hangs upside down in her sloppy, but sturdy, web.

Do spiders suck blood?

NOT JUST blood, but guts too. Most spiders bite their prey, then inject a venom that contains paralyzing toxins. Then they pump digestive juices into the victim and either suck out all the victim's juices (blood and organs both) right away, or wrap up the live-but-paralyzed casualty to eat at a later time.

BUGS IN THE SYSTEM

What is entomophagy?

IT'S THE EATING of bugs, and there are more people than you might suspect who do this deliberately. Read all about it at *www.eatbug.com/*

How many insect parts are allowed to be in peanut butter before it's legally considered unsanitary?

HOW MUCH do you want to know? Unfortunately, growing and storing food is not a completely sterile industry; some impurities will sneak in on tiny feet and wings. Peanut butter, by federal safety standards, may have up to 210 or more insect fragments per 700 grams, an average-size jar of peanut butter. But wait, that's just the insect part. That same average jar of peanut butter may also contain up to seven whole rodent hairs at no extra charge before it's considered unsanitary.

For a complete listing from the FDA's Food Defect Action Levels Handbook, *see* www.cfsan.fda.gov/~dms/dalbook.html

Weren't spider eggs found in Bubble Yum a while ago?

NO. BUBBLE YUM never contained spider eggs or legs or any other arachnid part. This myth is almost as old as the gum itself and caused quite a stir in the late 1970s and early 1980s, when it spread inexplicably from playground to lunchroom among the younger set.

For a detailed account of the rumor and how it was handled by the Life Saver Company, go to www.snopes.com/horrors/food/bubblyum.htm

I'VE GOT YOU UNDER MY SKIN

Can spiders lay eggs in skin?

NO. OTHER insects may do this, like the mites that create the skin disorder scabies, but spiders are far too concerned with the well-being of their offspring to entrust them to the likes of us. Warmth isn't necessarily what mother spiders are seeking for their egg sacs; security is.

GOT LEGS, KNOW HOW TO USE THEM

My teacher says it isn't a spider, so what exactly is a daddy longlegs?

THE "GRAND-DADDY" or "daddy" longlegs is also called a *harvestman*. Although it is an arachnid, it isn't technically a spider.

What's the name of the little bugs that live in people's eyebrows and eyelashes? Follicle mites.

Spiders are just one type of animal that belongs to the class arachnid. Arachnids include spiders, daddy longlegs, scorpions, mites, ticks, and a few other invertebrates. If you've ever seen a harvestman up close, you'll remember a simple, round body without the typical body segments that spiders have. Its long legs enable it to walk right over potentially dangerous insects—like ants—that prey on such harmless creatures as the harvestman. Daddy longlegs eat insects, dead or alive, and fruit.

TASTES LIKE CHICKEN

Do people really eat chocolate-covered crickets?

YES. HERE'S an easy way to prepare them:
   Ingredients:
   Approximately 25 live crickets
   Several squares of semi-sweet chocolate

First, feed the crickets for three days on fruit and cooked rice or breads and give them fresh water—to make sure they're well-fed and healthy. On Reckoning Day, preheat oven to 250°F, then put the crickets in a closed container in the freezer for 30 minutes. Rinse the dead crickets and pat them dry. Then remove the barbed legs and heads and place them on a cookie sheet. Bake until crispy. In a double boiler, heat the semi-sweet chocolate until melted. Dip the toasted crickets into the chocolate. Set aside to cool.

Bon appetit!

If your baking skills aren't up to it or you simply don't have the time, you can order crickets already dipped from Fluker Farms in Louisiana: *www.flukerfarms.com/*. When you order their chocolate-covered crickets, you will receive an I ATE A BUG CLUB button.

A new candy company, Hot Lix, has recently received notoriety for their lollipops with crickets inside. The candy is transparent, so you can see the actual dead cricket in the middle. They also sell tequila-flavored suckers with a worm in the middle. They're online at *www.hotlix.com/*

DOO BEE DOO BEE DOO

Are killer bees more poisonous than regular bees?

"KILLER BEES," properly known as Africanized honeybees, are not more poisonous, but they are much more aggressive. In 1956, a geneticist named Warwick Kerr brought African honeybees to Brazil to crossbreed with European honeybees because they are such prodigious producers of honey. Unfortunately, the offspring turned out to be just as aggressive as the African bees. Worse, they escaped from captivity and have been moving north ever since, crossbreeding with native wild honeybees from South America to the southwestern United States.

Unlike the more docile native bees, Africanized bees will actually chase and attack other creatures in a swarm. Victims, ranging from small animals to humans, may be stung hundreds of times, and it is not uncommon for dogs and other animals to die as a result. Even a few people, notably those with heart conditions, have been killed by the bees.

What do bees see?

A BEE SEES relatively clearly up close. Its field of vision is oblong, with images stretching at the top and bottom. If a human could look at a picture the way a bee processes it, the image might be compared to a football standing on one end. The surface is like that of a round Christmas tree ornament and warps whatever the bee sees. Of course, to the bee, this is normal.

For more on how and what scientists believe honeybees can see, try this site designed by a neuroscientist: cvs.anu.edu.au/andy/beye/ beyehome.html

How do bees tell each other where flowers are?

THEY USE A bee dance: dancing or moving inside the hive in a figure-eight shape, facing in a specific direction, waggling periodically, and flapping their wings. What tells the story is the speed of the bee, the direction the bee points, and the sounds she makes with her wings (all worker bees are female).

Say a bee finds a sweet, flowering bush about 50 yards from the hive. She will bring some of the scent home on her legs and position herself on the wall of the hive. Using "up" to stand for the sun, she will point her body in the direction of the bush. This shows the other bees where the bush can be found. The bush is

Where can I see pictures of bee dances online?

only 50 yards away—pretty close for a bee—which means the bee will waggle frenetically to indicate that it is close. She will flap her wings to make noise and draw other bees to watch.

The bees watch all these directional/distance indicators and then go and find the dancer bee's bush. If they find it's worth dancing about, too, they will collect from it and come back and perform in the same way.

How do I start a bee colony?

BY OPENING your local phone directory. Try contacting a local beekeeper in your area for advice on when, where, and how to begin. Each location has varying conditions. You will also need to check out local laws—some locations forbid beekeeping and others require that you register as a beekeeper with your city or county.

For information about beekeeping and online support, read Bee-Culture Magazine: http://bee.airoot.com/beeculture/index.htm

How does "smoking" bees calm them down?

BEEKEEPERS use smoke to get bees to calm down and not sting them. When bees encounter smoke, they begin a feeding frenzy, thinking their hive is in danger from fire, and prepare to flee. When they are fully fed, their bellies are distended and they do not sting as easily or readily.

RAISING CRICKETS ON THE CHEEP

How do I raise my own crickets?

VERY CAREFULLY. Crickets that get loose can wreak havoc on a house, and it's almost impossible to get rid of the infestation once it starts. But if you have a secure area and a good aquarium with a tight mesh lid, it's not too hard.

1. Put a half inch to an inch of soil on the bottom of a dry aquarium. Spray it with water until it's moist. Put several moist cotton balls in a corner or two.

2. Locate several empty paper egg cartons and lean them up against the sides so the crickets will have a place to perch.

3. Then put about 100 crickets in, put the lid on securely, and let them do their thing.

4. They will need a constant supply of fresh fruit and/or vegetables. If you are going to use them in recipes, they'll need clean grains (bread, cooked rice, oatmeal) as well. If you are using them as reptile food, a good enriched tropi-

cal fish food works well, as does a calcium-enriched food made especially for crickets.

For more information, go to *www.geocities.com/Heartland/ Bluffs/1921/*

BUG LIGHTS

What's in a lightning bug's lighter?

LIGHTNING BUGS (or fireflies, if you prefer) produce light in their abdomens by a chemical reaction in cells called photocytes. The substance *luciferin* is in the body of the insect. When the enzyme *luciferase* is also present, the substances oxidize, creating a lot of energy. As the substances settle back down, they make a spark of light.

It is still unclear why fireflies actually have this mechanism. It could be for mating purposes, to serve as a warning, or to attract prey. It could be all three. The lightning bug is actually capable of controlling the speed and length of the flashes, which may change the meaning of the flashes entirely. The female of some species has been observed changing her signals to attract a male lightning bug of another species. Once he's close, she eats him.

What are glowworms? *Baby fireflies.*

THAT'S WHY THE LADY IS A BUG

I have aphids in my garden and want to use ladybugs to eat them—but won't they just fly away?

ALMOST ALL of the ladybugs will leave, but 5% to 10% will stay and do their job on aphids. It helps to have readily available water near where they are released—some experts suggest watering the yard the night before you release. An average ladybug purchase for your yard should be about 3,000 ladybugs for about a quarter of an acre. And because of aphid breeding cycles, some experts say a second spreading of ladybugs may be necessary fairly soon after the first.

To order ladybugs, try www.natpestco.com/garden.html, *a site that offers a wide variety of gardening products.*

POST NUCLEAR PEST

Will cockroaches survive a nuclear holocaust?

IF ANYTHING can survive, it's the cockroach, but even its chances of surviving a nuclear blast are slim. For starters, although there are a few roach varieties that are the exception, cockroaches don't live well in temperatures much below freezing. That is why they are a household pest in so many places: they move into human dwellings to find warmth, as well as food and water. Without these three things, the cockroach won't survive.

But did you know that a cockroach can live without its head for a time? A headless roach can't drink, though, so it dies within a week or so from dehydration.

For a "scrapbook" of several varieties of cockroaches, see www.nj.com/yucky/roaches/index.ssf?/world/

THEY DON'T LIVE LONG, BUT COME TO A BEAUTIFUL FINISH

How is shellac made?

FROM BUG RESIN. The lac insect (scientific name *Laccifer lacca*), related to the scale bug, sticks its mouth into the branches and bark of certain types of trees, then secretes a resin that covers its entire body.

After this bug resin is crushed (almost always along with the bug itself), washed, and melted into flakes or thin layers, it makes up what we call "shellac." It used to make a type of varnish, as well as sealing wax, lacquer, and phonograph records.

IS THIS WHAT INSPIRED THE ROCKETES?

Do millipedes have more legs than centipedes?

YOU'D THINK something named "milli" (thousand) would have more legs than something named "centi" (hundred). Although we think of them as insects, centipedes and millipedes are more closely related to crustaceans—lobsters and shrimp. Millipedes often do have more legs than a centipede, but technically that depends on the varieties you're talking about.

There are thousands of types of both worldwide. As a rule, millipedes have two pairs of legs per body segment; their total leg count ranges from 36 to 400. Centipedes just have one pair per segment; their total leg count falls between 24 and 200. So if a millipede and a centipede have equal numbers of body segments, the millipede will have twice as many legs.

> **Where can I see giant cockroaches online?**

There are other differences between the two. Centipedes all sting, causing swelling and pain at the site. All of them have poison in their front pincers, and some in *all* of their legs. Millipedes, on the other hand, are generally not poisonous, but can emit a smell that might cause an allergic reaction. It is recommended that you wash your hands if you touch a millipede.

WHAT'S THE BUZZ?

I've heard that only female mosquitoes suck blood. So what do male mosquitoes eat?

THEY EAT fruit and other juicy decomposing items.

BEFORE THERE WERE HMO'S

Weren't maggots once used to treat diseases?

MAGGOTS WEREN'T used to treat diseases, but they were used to heal wounds during World War I. Some doctors caring for

the injured during the war noticed that certain patients'
wounds healed more quickly and were more resistant to infection than others'. At closer look, they realized those patients
had flies landing on their open sores. "Fly-blown" wounds
seemed to contain some healing and antibiotic properties that
medical professionals couldn't ignore, especially during war.

To make the conditions a bit more safe, doctors took flies
and sterilized their maggots before placing them on open sores.
Thankfully, scientists discovered the healing substances—allan-
toin and urea—and extracted them, bypassing the menacing
go-between, the fly. Despite their war effort, flies are still
known carriers of typhoid, cholera, salmonella, dysentery, lep-
rosy, tuberculosis, and many other life-threatening diseases.

Comics & Cartoons

WHETHER MOVING OR STILL, COMICS and cartoons reflect basic human truths, even when they're ostensibly about animals. As caricatures, the drawn figures both zero in on and exaggerate people's most identifiable foibles. Oh yeah, and they make us laugh, too.

WHERE IT ALL STARTED

Where did the Republican and Democrat cartoon mascots come from?

THE ELEPHANT was created by political cartoonist Thomas Nast in 1874, four years after he popularized the Democratic donkey. The donkey and the elephant were both chosen for their negative traits: The stubborn donkey had first been adopted decades earlier to depict President Andrew Jackson and his policies, but Nast revived it for his cartoons. The elephant was chosen because one day when Nast needed a political symbol, a mass animal escape from a New York zoo was in the news. He merged rampaging elephants with the opinion that Republicans were practicing random destructiveness in their policies. Eventually, both parties put a spin on the negative animals they'd been saddled with, officially adopting their animal mascots and giving them positive characteristics.

What's a Rube Goldberg device?

IT'S A CONTRAPTION that accomplishes a straightforward goal through a series of complicated and unnecessary steps. The term comes from award-winning cartoonist Rube Goldberg's newspaper comics in the 1920s and '30s in which simple household problems like sharpening a pencil are solved with outlandish technological solutions:

Open window (A) and fly kite (B). String (C) lifts small door (D) allowing moths (E) to escape and eat red flannel shirt (F). As weight of shirt becomes less, shoe (G) steps on switch (H) which heats electric iron (I) and burns hole in pants (J). Smoke (K) enters hole in tree (L), smoking out opossum (M) which jumps into basket (N), pulling rope (O) and lifting cage (P), allowing woodpecker (Q) to chew wood from pencil (R), exposing lead.

For examples of Rube Goldberg's cartoons, see www.rube-goldberg.com/

Who was the first comic strip character?

RICHARD OUTCAULT'S "Yellow Kid" is considered the first, appearing in 1896 in Hearst's *New York Journal*. The Kid was a bald, floppy-eared, buck-toothed, grinning kid in a huge yellow shirt. Barefoot and pigeon-toed, he appeared center stage to the goings-on of the other characters in fictitious Hogan's Alley. Outcault was later the creator of the famous cartoon character Buster Brown.

Are any comics from the 1800s still being published?
Yes. "The Katzenjammer Kids." First published in 1897.

Where did the term heebie-jeebies come from?

IT WAS CREATED in the early 1940s by cartoonist Billy DeBeck, who created Barney Google and Snuffy Smith. He also added *sweet mama* and *horse feathers* to the American vernacular.

CELEBRITY PICKS

What cartoon doll did Charles Lindbergh take with him on his trans-Atlantic flight?

FOR THAT historic 1927 journey, Lindbergh carried a Felix the Cat doll for luck and comfort.

Which comic star appears in every episode of Seinfeld?

IF YOU KNOW anything about comedian Jerry Seinfeld, you should know that Superman is his all-time favorite comic book hero. On the set of his show (in Jerry's apartment), he had Superman paraphernalia that appeared in every episode.

IT'S A BIRD, IT'S A PLANE

How old is Superman?

SUPERMAN FIRST appeared in Action Comics in June of 1938.

Who was Clark Kent named after?

ACTORS CLARK GABLE and Kent Taylor. But Superman's teenage creators, Jerry Siegel and Joe Shuster, fashioned Kent's nebbish personality after themselves. Siegel said he was never able to "get the girl" and always felt inadequate handling life. If Kent personified their fears, though, the character's super-persona fulfilled the adolescent boys' dreams: he was invincible, handsome, and always got women's attention.

Was Lois Lane fashioned after anyone real?

SUPERMAN'S CO-creator, Joe Shuster, had a crush on a girl in high school named Lois Amster, who became the inspiration for the Lois Lane character. Although he lost that Lois, he gained another: Joanne Carter, the woman hired to model for sketches of Lois Lane, ended up becoming Mrs. Shuster.

ELEMENTARY, MY DEAR ROBIN

What was the inspiration for Batman?

A VILLAIN from the 1926 movie *The Bat*. Creator Bob Kane was taken with the bat costume but wanted his character to be like his literary hero, Sherlock Holmes. He put Holmes in a bat costume and created a comic strip hit.

Where did Robin, the Boy Wonder, come from?

BOB KANE wanted a "Robin Hood-like" sidekick for his Caped Avenger, Batman, so Robin was born. He once said, "In my subconscious mind I longed to be like Robin when I was his age, fighting alongside his idol Batman—or in my case, Douglas Fairbanks, Sr. as Zorro."

WOMEN IN TIGHTS

Who was the creator of the comic strip "Wonder Woman"?

WILLIAM MOULTON MARSTON, who also invented the systolic blood pressure test and the lie detector. During the course of his experiments with the lie detector, he became convinced that women were more tireless and honest than men. Seeing how few strong female models there were for young girls, he came up with Wonder Woman to fill that void.

Where did catoonist Lynda Barry get her start? In college, with the help of friend Matt Groening.

I've seen the creator of the strip "Cathy". She's thin, so who's the cartoon character fashioned after?

IT'S HER CREATOR, after all, Cathy Guisewite. The story goes that at the age of 26, she was miserable and 50 pounds overweight. While waiting for a date to call, she began to doodle pathetic, self-loathing caricatures of herself eating and waiting by the phone. After several years of self-effacing doodles, she put them into comic strip form and submitted them to United Press Syndicate. The timing was good—women's issues were hot, so UPS bought the strip and named it "Cathy" after its creator.

GONE BUT NOT FORGOTTEN

Who are Calvin and Hobbes named after?

HOBBES IS NAMED after gloomy philosopher Thomas Hobbes. Calvin is named after the famous theologian John Calvin.

What did "Far Side" creator Gary Larson do before he drew comic strips?

BIOLOGY-TRAINED Larson had several jobs before his cartoon took off, including acting as an animal cruelty investigator for the Seattle Humane Society. Right before his first big sell to the *San Francisco Chronicle*, Larson was pursuing a career as a jazz guitarist.

FAT CATS, UNDERLINGS, SECURITY BLANKETS

Who was the inspiration for Garfield the cat?

JIM DAVIS'S grandfather, James Garfield Davis, who was, in Davis's own words, "big, opinionated, and stubborn."

Where does Scott Adams get his ideas for "Dilbert"?

FROM A COUPLE of different sources. Adams was first a corporate cog in both the banking and the utilities industries, so a lot of fodder for his strip comes from personal experience. But the "Dilbert" strip is known for soliciting ideas from its readership, and today it's estimated that up to 20% of the story ideas come from reader e-mail.

Where did the phrase "security blanket" come from?

FROM CHARLES SCHULZ and his "Peanuts" gang. Linus was the owner of a crumpled, tattered security blanket that became the subject of many a Sunday strip over the years. Schulz and his "kids" also popularized the phrase "Good grief!"

LAUGHING ACHIEVEMENT
Which comic strip first won the Pulitzer Prize?

GARRY TRUDEAU'S "Doonesbury" did in 1975. It was the first comic strip to win the prestigious prize for editorial cartooning.

ANIMATION EVOLUTION
Who was the first animated cartoon character?

GERTIE, THE TRAINED DINOSAUR stomped onto the screen in 1909, laboriously animated frame by frame by cartoonist Winsor McCay, well known for his classic comic strip "Little Nemo." Discussing the new invention of motion pictures, a cartooning colleague, George McManus ("The Newlyweds" and "Bringing Up Father"), bet that McCay couldn't draw all of the 10,000-plus drawings needed to make an animated version of the movie. McCay went ahead to prove him wrong and figured out how to get his sketches one by one onto film. He opened *Gertie* for vaudeville audiences with a show like this: Dressed up as a lion tamer, he issued orders so it looked like he was taming the animated creature. Meanwhile, Gertie the dinosaur ate everything in sight. Despite the limited plot line, the technology amazed everyone and began an animation revolution.

What were the big technological advances in animation before computers?
Transparent cels and the copy machine.

STRONG TO THE FINICH

When did Popeye first get on the big screen?

ALREADY POPULAR in newspaper comics, Popeye made a guest appearance in an early-1930s "Betty Boop" short film. His animated career took off, and it was only a few years before he picked up his first Oscar. That was for his 1936 performance in *Sinbad the Sailor*.

I've heard there's a large statue of Popeye somewhere. Where is it?

THERE'S ONE in Crystal City, Texas, the self-proclaimed Spinach Capital of the World.

OF MICE AND SUPER MEN

What was Mighty Mouse's original name?

IN 1942, at the height of the Superman craze, Paul Terry of Terrytoons created a leotard-and-cape-wearing superhero mouse named, what else? Super Mouse. To avoid lawsuits, the popular Superman-like mouse had his name changed to Mighty Mouse.

ALLOW ME TO INTRODUCE MYSELF . . . .

What was the first cartoon created specifically for TV?

IN 1948, 11 years before there was "Rocky and Bullwinkle," there was "Crusader Rabbit" from the same creators, Jay Ward and Alex Anderson, made in black and white specifically for television.

How did Jay Ward and Alex Anderson come up with Rocky and Bullwinkle?

FIRST, IT HELPED that Jay Ward was lying in a full-body cast in a hospital, because it gave him a lot of time to think. He had been hit by a lumber truck, and after the accident he brainstormed cartoon ideas with boyhood friend Alex Anderson. (Anderson had cartoons in his family. His uncle, Paul Terry, was founder of Terrytoons and creator of "Mighty Mouse" and "Heckle and Jeckle.")

During this time, Ward and Anderson came up with "Crusader Rabbit" (see previous question). The rabbit's pun-filled adventures also featured a dumb tiger sidekick named Rags and other "Frostbite Falls" sidekicks, including Rocket J. Squirrel, Bullwinkle Moose, and Dudley Do-Right. (Frostbite Falls, home to these rag-tag characters, was based on the town of International Falls, Minnesota.) Although "Crusader Rabbit" was a success, TV was like the Internet in the 1990s—promising but not yet profitable. Ward drifted back to real estate, and Anderson ended up in an advertising agency.

A decade later, television had become very profitable, so Ward decided he wanted to be back in animation. Anderson was settled in his career and decided to let Ward go it alone. Ward decided to expand upon some of the minor characters of the last series and found a talented partner, Bill Scott. Scott was a good choice and ended up writing most of the "Rocky and Bullwinkle" stories, as well as "Fractured Fairy Tales" and "Mr. Peabody" time-traveling adventures, and he did the voices of Mr. Peabody, Bullwinkle, and Dudley Do-Right, too. For years, Ward and Scott created successful cartoons, creating new characters like George of the Jungle and the characters and commercials for a line of Quaker Oats cereals, including Captain Crunch, Quisp, and Quake.

Where did the name Bullwinkle come from?

FROM A FORD dealership in Berkeley, California. When Jay Ward walked to his office every day, he passed a Ford car lot owned by local Republican bigwig Clarence Bullwinkel (back when there were still Republicans in Berkeley). Ward never met the man, but was struck by the name as good for someone large and doltish. When he came up with a moose character, he used the name, spelled a little differently.

DOH!

What does the "J" in Homer J. Simpson stand for?

MATT GROENING, creator of "The Simpsons," says he gave Homer his middle initial as a tribute to Rocket J. Squirrel from "Rocky and Bullwinkle." Eventually, the show revealed that the J. stood for...Jay, just as it does in the name of the "Rocky and Bullwinkle" creator, J. Troplong Ward (a.k.a. Jay Ward). Groening used that "J" for all of his main male characters: Homer J. Simpson, Bartholomew J. Simpson, and Abraham J. Simpson (Grandpa).

Who does the voice of Marge Simpson?

JULIE KAVNER is responsible for the distinctive voice of the blue-haired lady and also for her sisters and mother. Kavner is most noted for her roles as Rhoda's little sister in "Rhoda" and the "Mary Tyler Moore Show" and also for co-starring on the "Tracey Ullman Show."

What is Marge Simpson's maiden name?

BOUVIER. Her mother's name is Jacqueline Bouvier, a little joke on a former First Lady.

> **Where can I find cartoon art museums?**

Where is Springfield, the Simpsons' hometown?

MISSOURI? Ohio? Who knows? The writers of the show have deliberately made it ambiguous, a sort of Anywhere, U.S.A., and the town itself seems to change geographically to fit individual plots. It's been Hollywood-like, a port town, a gritty metropolis, a gambling mecca, a historical colonial town, and just about everything else. Its radio station starts with K, which in the real world would mean that it's west of the Mississippi River. It has a nuclear power plant, a Russian ethnic section, and its own baseball team, yet it's small enough to hold town meetings in a town hall.

THE NOT-SO-ANIMATED WORLD OF HANNA-BARBERA

What was the first primetime-television cartoon sitcom?

"THE FLINTSTONES," debuting in 1960.

Were the Flintstones based on anyone real?

THE CARTOON wasn't initially based on anyone: it was about a couple, their child, and a dog living in prehistoric times. However, as the show progressed, Hanna-Barbera company founder Joseph Hanna thought it looked too much like the comic strip "Blondie," so he added a working-class spin by blatantly copying the look, voices, and personalities of Ralph and Alice Kramden of "The Honeymooners." It still didn't mesh, so he took it a step further—he added Barney and Betty Rubble to mimic the roles, personalities, and voices of Ed and Trixie Norton, too. Now he had a hit, and "The Flintstones" ran in a primetime slot for six years and has been in syndication ever since.

Wasn't Yogi the Bear based on Yogi Berra?

IT WOULD seem that way: the connection was as clear as pie to most people, including Berra himself. But when the baseball great and mixed-metaphor king threatened to sue Hanna-Barbera for defamation of character, the company swore the bear was, like Barney Rubble, fashioned after Art Carney's Norton character on "The Honeymooners."

THAT'S ALL, FOLKS!

When was Daffy Duck's screen debut?

IN THE 1937 cartoon *Porky's Duck Hunt*. The story of Daffy's voice is legendary. According to director Chuck Jones in his autobiography, *Chuck Amuck*, the animators were brainstorming to complete the duck character, and someone imitated the distinctive, lisping voice of Leon Schlesinger, their boss. The director and animators laughed and jumped on the idea of using their much-hated boss's voice and personality for the duck, not really thinking out the ramifications of what they were doing.

As they got further along with the project, though, they started to realize that a day of reckoning was coming soon: Schlesinger, after all, was going to have to see and approve the cartoon. While the animators and director were feverishly writing out just-in-case, you-can't-fire-me-because-I-quit resignation letters, Schlesinger appeared for the showing. The projector started and the animators all sat quietly through the show, nervously anticipating the boss's reaction. Finally, the lights came up. Schlesinger stood up and shrieked, "Jesus Crithe, that's a funny voithe! Where'd you get that voithe?" not realizing for a minute it was his own that they'd mimicked.

Who did the voice for Woody the Woodpecker?

MEL BLANC did originally. In his autobiography, *That's Not All Folks!,* he recounts being 15 years old and running through his Portland, Oregon, high school's echoing halls, practicing what would later, speeded up, become that red-headed woodpecker's trademark laugh. But when Blanc signed an exclusive contract with another production company, Warner Brothers, it left Woody voiceless. Grace Stafford auditioned for and got the part of Woody in 1952.

Is it true that Mel Blanc, the voice of Bugs Bunny, was allergic to carots?

HE WAS very allergic to them. He says he tried apples and celery and all sorts of alternatives to get the sound just right, but nothing worked as well as carrots did. So he chewed carrots when he needed to, spitting them out and watching for signs of anaphylactic shock.

In the Bugs Bunny cartoons featuring the tortoise-and-the-hare theme, what's the turtle's name? Cecil.

Who's behind the nasally voice of Marvin the Martian?

MARVIN MARTIAN, created in 1948 by famous Warner Bros. artist Chuck Jones, debuted in Bugs Bunny's *Haredevil Hare* under the name Commander-X-23. His voice, like so many of the Warner Brothers characters, was done by Mel Blanc. When Blanc died in 1989, Joe Alaskey took over the Marvin Martian role.

Earth, Space & Microwave Ovens

SCIENCE IS A REFUGE FOR THOSE who don't have enough imagination to believe in the outlandishly impossible. But in times when most people seem ready to believe just about anything, it's reassuring that scientists demand proof of even simple, self-evident things. Here are some of Jeeves' favorite science questions.

AUDIOS, AMIGOS

When a car goes by with its windows up and the driver is playing loud music, why do you hear only the bass?

HIGH NOTES HAVE short wavelengths, so they tend to bounce when they hit a solid wall. Low notes have long wavelengths, so they vibrate into and through solids. This explains not only why low notes go through car windows and apartment walls, but also why music in an empty room sounds shrill and tinny and the echo of your voice sounds like a younger you.

Why can't phone scientists make voices sound better on the phone?

THEY CAN; they just haven't. Many years ago, scientists at phone company labs studied how many of the frequencies they could take out of the human voice and still have clear comprehension. They then deliberately cut out all the "unnecessary" tones (the highs and lows mostly), which dramatically reduced the amount of power and phone-line bandwidth needed to transmit a phone conversation. Will sound quality improve over time? Maybe, but despite huge strides in audio quality in recordings, radio, movies, and television, consumers have gotten used to that tin-can quality on phones and apparently don't seem to mind it—at least not enough to complain to phone manufacturers.

What makes the sound when you crack a whip?

IF YOU FLICK it just right, the tip of the whip gets propelled faster than 700 miles per hour, breaking the sound barrier and creating a small sonic boom. That also explains why a snapped towel hurts so much.

BLOWHARDS ON THE EAST COAST

Why does the East Coast get hurricanes all the time, but the West Coast almost never does?

THERE ARE TWO reasons for this, not including West Coast good karma. The main reason is that hurricanes form in tropical waters, and in the northern hemisphere tend to travel toward the west-northwest. As a result, Pacific Ocean hurricanes tend to head *away* from North America, off toward the Pacific Islands and Asia, while Atlantic Ocean hurricanes tend to head *toward* the North American coast, stepping onto land now and again to scatter some mobile homes.

The second reason is that the water temperature is too cold on the West Coast to maintain hurricanes for long. The Gulf Stream along the East Coast comes from the tropics, and hot air rising off the warm waters feeds hurricanes and increases their power. The currents along the West Coast come from the Arctic, so the water is about 20°F colder. Even in the rare occurrence that a Pacific hurricane reverses itself back toward the mainland, the cool air saps its energy pretty quickly.

PLAY MISTY FOR ME

If clouds are made of tons of water, how do they float?

DESPITE THE façade of unbearable lightness, clouds are actually heavy. Take even a small, fluffy cloud measuring a mere cubic kilometer. The water in that cloud would typically weigh about a million kilograms, about the same as 550 SUVs. So how does all that weight stay up in the air? Well, it turns out that the air in that same cloud is also heavy—about a thousand times heavier than the water. Furthermore, clouds are usually formed in air that is moving upward. So, as long as the water is in the form of tiny droplets, it floats in the warm up-currents. It's only when the air cools that the mist condenses into large drops and the downward pull of gravity trumps the upward push of rising air. Then rain falls.

Since clouds are made of air and water and both are clear, why are clouds white? For that matter, why is the sky blue, since air is clear?

IN BOTH CASES, it has to do with the size of the particles and the length of light wavelengths. Air has small particles, so most of the sun's light just passes straight through it. However, blue light has a short wavelength, so some of it goes careening off the small particles and bounces

> **Where can I see the different kinds of clouds?**

around the air above you before reaching your eye. As a result, the sun looks more orange on Earth than it looks in space, and the sky looks more blue. In the case of clouds, the water mist adds larger particles to the mix, so that all colors, not just blue, are scattered in all directions. All colors combined make the clouds look white.

STOP THE WORLD, I WANT TO GET OFF

How fast is the Earth careening though space?

IT DEPENDS ON what you're comparing it to. The Earth is moving in several different directions at the same time, each at breakneck speed. Rotating on its axis, the Earth goes 460 meters a second (roughly 1,000 miles per hour) at the equator. Going around the sun, the Earth moves about 30 kilometers per second (roughly 67,000 miles per hour). Our solar system whirls around the center of our galaxy at about 220 kilometers per second (about 490,000 miles per hour). Meanwhile, our entire galaxy is traveling at a speed of about 1,000 kilometers per *second* (620 miles per hour) toward a region of space called the Great Attractor, which is about 150 million light years away. Hold on tight!

I live in Ohio—on what day during the year are daylight and darkness both exactly 12 hours? What day is it for my friend in Brazil?

FOR YOUR friends all over the world, no matter where they live, the answer is exactly the same. Twice a year, all over the world, everyone has the same length of day and night—on the spring equinox and autumn equinox, roughly March 20 and September 20. These are the two days that are exactly between the summer solstice and winter solstice, and they are the two days that the sun appears to pass directly over the equator.

DAILY PLANETS

What are the names of the Martian moons?

PHOBOS AND DEIMOS. Or, in English, Fear and Panic. Why the scary names? Their discoverer—astronomer Asaph Hall—was poking fun of the fear he had of his wife. On the night he discovered the two moons, he was tired and going to bed. His wife badgered him into getting back up and continuing to search the night sky. Lo and behold, cursing under his breath, he spotted the moons and was in his wife's debt for her nagging.

What does a sunset on Mars look like?

A BIT MORE red, but not much different from a sunset on Earth. For actual pictures, see *http://image.gsfc.nasa.gov/poetry/ask/a11418.html*

Would the Earth burn up if it were 1,000 miles closer to the sun?

NO. THE EARTH could actually move a lot closer to the sun before total damage took place. In the summer, the Earth is 94.5

million miles away from the sun. In the winter, it's over 3 million miles closer with little to no damage at all. As a matter of fact, the Earth could be placed in Venus' orbit—at about 62 million miles from the sun— with surprisingly little damage in the grand scheme of things.

> **Where can I see the pictures of the rings around Uranus?**

Oh sure, life as we know it would disappear, but the temperature on the Earth's surface would increase by only about 68°F— not enough to destroy the planet.

HAILING COMETS

When was the first recorded sighting of Halley's Comet?

THE FIRST KNOWN sighting dates back to 239 B.C., when astronomers of the day noted its presence in the night sky. But it wouldn't be called Halley's Comet until the 17th century A.D., when astronomer Edmund Halley noted that the comet reappeared about every 76 years.

How many people have been killed by falling meteorites?

THERE HAVE BEEN no recorded instances of anybody being killed by a meteorite.

How can I tell if a weird rock I found is a meteorite?

METEORITES ARE pretty rare. Here are some things to look for before taking it to a museum to get it checked out:

- Does the rock have a sooty-looking brown, black, or orange exterior?

- Does it seem denser or heavier than most rocks?

- Does it seem to be completely or partly metallic?

- Will a magnet stick to it?

- Does it look different from other rocks in the area?

- Does it have a holey texture like Swiss cheese?

If you answered yes to any of these questions, you might have a meteorite.

Where's the best place to find meteorites?

Do meteorites contain radiation or anything that is harmful to touch?
No.

ANTARCTICA. No other rocks appear on the surface of the ice fields, and the ice pushes meteorites to the surface, so they stand out.

WISE GUYS AND GALS

Where can I find a biography of Pythagoras?

YOU CAN'T. Not a good one, anyway. You can find information on the Pythagorean theorem and on the group of his followers (Pythagoreans) that kept his ideas alive for centuries after his death, but there are few written records on the Greek philosopher and mathematician. As a matter of fact, some people believe that all of the theories attributed to Pythagoras, including those regarding hypotenuse and the shape of the Earth, actually came from the brotherhood collectively and not from any one person. What we do know is that Pythagoras lived in the sixth century B.C. and his followers were still active throughout the fourth century B.C. Other Greek philosophers, such as Aristotle, commented widely on the group's discoveries and advances.

No matter who—whether an individual or the group—is responsible, what they proposed was astounding for their time. Pythagorean theories include the famous "the square of the length of the hypotenuse is equal to the sum of the squares of the lengths of the other two sides." They also reduced both music and astronomy to numeric patterns, and theorized that the planets, the Earth, and the moon all revolved around the sun.

What does the word calculus actually mean?

"PEBBLE," IN Latin. Pythagoreans used pebbles, lined up to form various shapes, to represent numbers.

What's the name of Isaac Newton's theory of gravity?

IT WAS published as *Principia Mathematica* in 1687. Interestingly, Newton wrote it at the persistent urging of well-known astronomer Edmund Halley—a colleague and good friend. When Newton finished it, Halley had the piece published with his own money.

How many Nobel prizes did Marie Curie win?

SHE WON TWO—and was the first person ever to do so. The first, for physics in 1903, she shared with her husband, Pierre Curie, and scientist Henri Becquerel for the discovery of radioactivity. The second was for chemistry in 1911, for the isolation of pure radium.

GOOD NIGHT, MOON

Why does the moon look so much bigger near the horizon than it does overhead?

THIS IS AN optical illusion based on the fact that you see the moon close to, yet clearly behind, familiar large objects like mountains and buildings. When the moon is high in the sky, the brain "sees" it as a smaller object not that far overhead (no matter what we logically know). When the moon is near the horizon, its proximity to large distant objects gives a comparison scale and makes us see it as being much larger (although our brain still cannot fully fathom how large and distant it really is).

Some scientists used to believe that the moon looked bigger at the horizon because light beams were being distorted by the Earth's atmosphere. However, that theory can easily be ruled out. If you use your thumb or a coin held at arm's length to "measure" the moon, you'll find that it's exactly the same size no matter where it is in the sky.

Why does the same side of the moon always face Earth?

IT DOES SEEM like a pretty strange coincidence that the moon would rotate at exactly the same rate that it revolves around the Earth. But of course it's no coincidence at all. When the moon was much closer to the Earth than it is now, the Earth's gravity distorted the moon slightly, so that it's somewhat egg-shaped. As a result, the pull on the moon is now slightly stronger on the pointy end, keeping it always faced toward us.

BREAKING OUT OF PRISM

Why are rainbows arch-shaped?

BECAUSE WE'RE standing on the ground and looking toward the horizon. If we were in the air or looking down from a mountain, we might see the whole rainbow...which is a circle.

What's the order of the colors in a rainbow, top to bottom?

RED, ORANGE, yellow, green, blue, violet. However, if you see a double rainbow, with a larger but fainter secondary rainbow outside the main rainbow, the colors will be reversed in the second rainbow.

When is the most likely time of day to see a rainbow?
Late afternoon or early evening.

EINSTEIN=MC2

I'm looking for an Albert Einstein autograph. How come they're so hard to find?

HE WAS STINGY about giving them out. As a matter of fact, he was known for charging people for them. He would ask for a dollar before signing anything to anyone. He gave the dollars to charity, but people still weren't comfortable asking, so there aren't many signatures around today.

There was one exception to Einstein's rule. Charlie Chaplin once commented about Einstein's fame, "I'm famous because everyone can relate to what I do, but you are famous even though no one understands what you do." When Einstein met Chaplin, he eagerly gave him an autographed photo for free.

Where can I see an explanation of the Pythagorean theorem?

Albert Einstein seems like the quintessential "absentminded professor," but was he in reality?

IT'S HARD to tell from the evidence—many of the stories told about Einstein could be fabrications to perpetuate that stereotype. What we know is that he was a daydreamer as a schoolboy—so much so that his headmaster informed young Albert's father, "It doesn't matter what field he goes into, he'll never make a success of anything." Although this turned out to be far from the truth, in college Einstein's first wife and his best friend reportedly took turns reminding him to do such basics as eat and show up for classes.

An instance that illustrates Einstein's lack of social understanding was when he met with young Queen Elizabeth and they shared a violin duet. He reportedly stopped midpiece to tell the young queen to quiet down—she was playing too loud. Stories like this abounded, and his reputation as absentminded and even slightly bizarre continued to grow. Part of this was no doubt due to his physical image, complete with a shock of wild hair, sleepy eyes, and tattered clothing. With the rising popularity of the motion picture industry at the time, his unruly image became well known worldwide.

Where can I see pictures of Einstein's brain?

After years of teaching and fame, just for the heck of it, Einstein took to going without socks. They were an "unnecessary complication," he said, but it furthered his spacey image. Still, there are a few far-fetched stories, like the one about him returning to his office and reading his own GONE TO LUNCH. BE BACK IN 10 MINUTES sign. Supposedly, he was found sitting outside, waiting for himself to come back.

Where is Einstein's brain kept?

FOR THE most part, it's still with the man who did Einstein's autopsy in 1955, Dr. Thomas Harvey, from Wichita, Kansas.

In 1978 the editor of the *New Jersey Monthly* gave a young reporter an assignment: find Einstein's brain, which was reportedly removed before the famous scientist was cremated. The reporter, Steven Levy, now a senior editor for *Newsweek,* went first to Harvey and in the doctor's study found two Mason jars filled with pieces of Einstein's brain. He broke the story, and groups of scientists from all over the world asked the doctor to lend them the pieces to examine. Dr. Harvey has never stopped lending out the pieces. As recently as the summer of 1999, a group of scientists from McMaster University in Ontario, Canada, found that Einstein's inferior parietal region—the part of the brain that's associated with mathematical reasoning and visual and musical understanding—was 15% wider than most people's brains. Harvey isn't just good for loans, though. He took the brain to visit Einstein's granddaughter in 1997, reuniting generations even after death.

For Steven Levy's thoughts on the experience of tracking down Einstein's brain, go to www.echonyc.com/~steven/einstein.html

FATHER OF INVENTIONS

What else, besides the electric light, did Edison invent?

AMONG HIS many inventions are the mimeograph machine, the phonograph, the movie projector, the stock ticker, a rock crusher, an electric vote-counting machine, the fluoroscope (the first X-ray machine), and a "rat paralyzer," which consisted of an electrically charged metal plate that electrocuted curious vermin.

Wasn't Edison deaf? How did he hear to make the phonograph?

HE WAS almost entirely deaf, but not totally. By the age of 13, he had only partial hearing in his right ear and his left was nearly as bad. Despite this, he still insisted on having the final say at the Edison Record Company on what music was recorded and released, and he was pretty grumpy about the fact that his invention was being used for sappy ballads and jazz. He was noted as saying, "I don't want the phonograph sold for amusement purposes. It is not a toy. It is for business purposes only."

FREEZE A JOLLY GOOD FELLOW

Which freezes faster: a cup of hot tea or cold water?

IF THE CUP of tea was made with boiling water, it will, in theory, freeze faster than the cup of water. Why? Because heating drives out any air bubbles that can slow down the freezing process.

Who is considered the father of frozen food technology?

ENGLISH AUTHOR and philosopher Francis Bacon was the forerunner of the great frozen-food scientists of the early 20th century, such as naturalist and author Clarence Birdseye. Bacon did many experiments with meat and discovered the undeniable connection between meat preservation and subfreezing temperatures. Tragically, his experiments killed him. While on a journey in March 1626, Bacon stopped to experiment with a dead chicken and some snow. Exposure led to bronchitis, which killed him a few weeks later.

MICROWAVE IT GOODBYE

How does a microwave oven work?

SIMPLY PUT, the microwaves cause water molecules inside the food or drink to vibrate at a rapid pace. The vibrating molecules rub against each other, and the friction rapidly creates heat.

Will microwaves kill you?

THEY SURE won't do you any good. Even small doses might do long-term damage, and larger doses can cause a dangerous buildup of heat, especially in body parts like eyes, which don't cool quickly. Having said that, though, it's also true that people stationed at microwave towers used to stand in front of the micro-wave generators to warm up. In fact, it was after a chocolate bar suddenly melted in the jacket pocket of one of them that the idea came to try using microwaves for cooking.

How are microwaves used—besides for cooking? They're used in cell phones and televisions.

Why does metal in a microwave create sparks?

MEDIOCRE HEAT conductors like water get hot when bombarded with microwaves; good conductors like metal get charged with a large electrical field. Eventually, it's enough to arc across air to a wall or some other conductive part inside the oven, creating a massive electrical spark.

BIOSPHERE AND THE UNKNOWN

They call that thing in Arizona Biosphere 2. Where is Biosphere 1?

"BIOSPHERE 1" is the Earth. Biosphere 2 is a human-made, enclosed ecosystem where four men and four women lived for two years, beginning in 1991. After this original group, another crew came in for six months in 1994. The $150 million structure was built to see how well a human-made and -maintained ecosystem would hold up—with the idea that such colonies could perhaps be set up in remote locations like Mars. Today the structure is open to the public for tours. A Biosphere 3 is in remote northern Siberia (uninhabited), and there may be a Biosphere J under construction in Japan.

What were some of the pitfalls the Biosphere 2 crew encountered?

A FEW TIMES the oxygen level dropped low enough to turn on ventilators, and food supplies were an issue because of lack of sunlight and insect problems on crops. Animals didn't reproduce as hoped, so meat was a rarity and the crew had to go on food rations. Crazy ants *(Paratrechina longicornis)* became a real problem as well. They clogged electrical outlets and sensors and were the suspected culprits in declining numbers of pollinators, such as butterflies.

Where can I see the inside of Biosphere 2?

ELEMENTAL, MY DEAR WATSON

Where did the term quark come from?

THE TERM was coined in James Joyce's *Finnegan's Wake*. The line goes, "Three quarks for Muster Mark! Sure he hasn't got much of a bark." The *quark*, as it came to be called in the realm of physics, was proposed independently by two renowned physicists, Murray Gell-Mann and George Zweig, in 1963. (Zweig called the mathematical particle a "kwork" or something like it. Gell-Mann adopted Joyce's quark.) Both suggested that quarks, grouped together, made up various parts of electrons and protons.

Quarks come in six types: strange, charm, bottom, top, up, and down. Each of these types comes in varying colors: blue, green, or red. The proton, as a basic example, is believed to be made up of three quarks—two up quarks and a down quark.

Where can I see the complete periodic table online?

Which basic chemical element is found most on Earth?

ELEMENT #8: oxygen. It makes up almost 50% of the Earth's mass and its atmosphere. The second most common element is #14: silicon.

I know "Homo sapiens" is shorthand. What's the full classification for humans?

KINGDOM: *ANIMAL*; phylum: *Chordata*; subphylum: *Vertebrata*; class: *Mammalia*; order: *Primates*; family: *Hominidae*; genus: *Homo*; species: *sapiens*. Present-day humans are further classified into the subspecies *Homo sapiens sapiens*.

Is oxygen the most plentiful gas we breathe?

NO, NITROGEN IS. Disregarding water vapor, which varies with humidity, nitrogen makes up 78% of all the air we breathe. Oxygen makes up about 21%. The remaining 1% consists chiefly of argon, with only extremely small amounts of other gases.

What is the Richter scale?

A LOGARITHMIC scale that gauges the magnitude of an earthquake's force. Invented by Charles Richter in 1935, it is measured on a seismograph machine, interpreting the data the machine picks up from the Earth's vibrations. Each number is 10 times more powerful than the previous number. For example, a quake that registers 8.0 is 10 times stronger than one that measures 7.0; 100 times more powerful than one that measures 6.0; and 1,000 times more intense than one that measures 5.0.

The scale is from 1 to 9 but is technically open-ended. Many factors influence what occurs during a quake, but the basic scale is as follows:

1.0	Detectable only by instruments
2.0	Barely detectable, even near epicenter
3.0	Felt indoors
4.0	Felt by most people; slight damage
5.0	Felt by all; damage minor to moderate
6.0	Moderately destructive
7.0	Major damage
8+	Total and major damage

TIME AND TIME AGAIN

Who invented time?

NO ONE invented time; it was merely discovered. Early humans were aware of time passing and at some point began marking it. Archeologists continue to uncover ancient civilizations that devised elaborate methods of keeping track of the movement of the sun and the stars. Stonehenge is one example. The earliest clock—a shadow clock similar to a sundial—dates back to 3500 B.C. The hourglass dates back almost as far. As cultures advanced, the mechanical clock was invented and then the pendulum clock. By the 18th century, more and more people had access to clocks and watches and were able to keep time more accurately themselves.

Today we use a 24-hour clock and have the world divided into 24 time zones. The zones start at zero at the original site of the Greenwich Observatory in Greenwich, England. We go by what is called the Scientific Standard of Time, based on the second, which is defined by scientists as "the duration of 9,192,631,770 periods of radiation" and in other circles as "one Mississippi. . . ."

Playing Around

ANCIENT GREEK ADOLESCENTS sacrificed their old toys on altars to Apollo and Artemis, as a sign they had reached the end of childhood. The Bible counsels that people should "put away childish things." But Jeeves suggests instead wrapping them carefully in their original boxes and calling them "collectibles."

TO ETCH HIS OWN

What is the powder inside an Etch A Sketch? Is it dangerous?

ACCORDING TO Ohio Arts, the manufacturer, no . . . but it sure would make a mess if you broke one open. It's aluminum that's ground fine so it will stick to everything it touches, with some small plastic beads added to agitate the powder and keep it from clumping together.

How does it draw? Each knob controls nylon strings that move a cone-shaped brass stylus. The stylus removes a thin line of powder from the inside of the glass, revealing the darkness of the inner compartment. (If you scrape away enough in a systematic way, you can actually see what the strings and stylus look like.) To make it difficult to damage, the glass is covered with a thin layer of plastic.

FAMILIAR NAMES

Who were Barbie and Ken named after?

THE DAUGHTER and son of the doll's creator, Ruth Handler. Imagine what life must have been like for them going through school . . . particularly poor Ken.

My sister remembers there was a big fuss about one of the Skipper dolls, but can't remember why. Can you help?

IF YOU'RE a plastic public figure, you have to expect some controversy. Barbie's little sister ran afoul of women's and religious groups as Growing Up Skipper, introduced by Mattel in 1975. When one of her arms was turned, she grew a quarter-inch taller and sprouted womanly hips and breasts like her big sister's. If only puberty were really as easy as that.

Barbie has had a few skirmishes herself, including one in which lumber workers threatened boycotts against Kmart if it didn't stop carrying a talking environmentalist Barbie who wished for a day when trees wouldn't be chopped down.

I saw a list of the 20th century's most popular toys in England, and one of them is Action Man. If it's so popular there, why hasn't it ever come to the United States?

IT WAS HERE before it was there. It's G.I. Joe. When the boy toy made its way to England, the name was changed because it sounded too American. I suppose there was a fear that, as in World War II, a dashing American soldier would seduce nice English dolls and either abandon them or take them back to the States as war brides.

Was Mr. Potato Head once a real potato?

WHEN THE famous potato sprouted in 1952, he was real. The plastic body parts were designed to be stuck into a real potato or any other fruit or vegetable. That was really pretty fun for kids, but there were some problems. For one, the potato would begin rotting and sprouting, making the once-benign vegetative visage into a malignant tuber. For another, the plastic parts had to be pretty sharp in order to pierce the firm flesh of a real potato. The real potato was replaced by an oversized plastic one, and the pins of the plastic eyes, mouths, and other pieces were rounded off to be child-safe. Another significant change in the portly potato's lifestyle: Pressure from surgeon general C. Everett Koop in 1987 deprived him of his pipe on the grounds that it glorified smoking to kids.

CONTACT SPORTS

What was the largest round of Twister ever played?

What's the story behind the original superball?

USING HUNDREDS of Twister boards taped together, the biggest game to date was held on May 2, 1987, at the University of Massachusetts: 4,160 people played.

Where did Nerf get its name?

AFTER HE successfully invented Twister, toy designer Reynolds Guyer decided to work on another game. He came up with a caveman motif that used foam rubber rocks to hide prehistoric coins. Unfortunately, the game idea was a loser. Guyer and his development team discovered that the the only good part of it was picking up the rocks and throwing them at each other. One day Guyer took scissors to the "rocks" to make them round, and invented a "soft, friendly" name for balls that you could throw at someone without threat of injury or lawsuit— Nerf. Within ten years, the Nerf line had expanded to include all sorts of nonlethal missiles.

FURRIN' POWERS

Who was the Teddy bear named after?

PRESIDENT Theodore Roosevelt. As the story goes, someone tethered a bear cub to a tree for him to kill on a hunting trip. When he refused to shoot the bear, he became a hero of sorts. Stuffed bears were made to commemorate the event.

Why were Furbies banned from the National Security Agency?

IN 1999, the jabbering little creatures were banned by the NSA, the Norfolk Naval Shipyard, and the Pentagon, based on the fear that the dolls would mimic top-secret discussions and, as a government source told the *Washington Post,* "people would take the dolls home and they'd start talking classified." A spokesman for Tiger Electronics, maker of Furbies, said the fears were based on "funny yet incorrect rumors," adding that, "although Furby is a clever toy, it does not record or mimic voices. The NSA did not do their homework. Furby is not a spy!" At least that's what they want us to believe.

CONSTRUCTION ZONE

Is "Lego" supposed to mean something—like "leggo my toys"?

IN 1934, carpenter-turned-toymaker Ole Kirk Christiansen held a modest contest among friends and employees to name his new toy company, offering a bottle of his very own homemade wine as a prize. After getting a number of entries, Christiansen decided he liked his own entry best: Lego, based on the Danish phrase *Leg godt* ("Play well"). He uncorked his wine and drank it himself.

Who invented Lincoln Logs?

THE SON OF famed architect Frank Lloyd Wright. While accompanying his dad to Tokyo, where the elder Wright was building the Imperial Palace Hotel, John Wright was taken with an earthquake-safe construction method. It was based on inter-locking grooves similar to those used in American log cabins. It occurred to him that miniature construction logs could make a good toy. Knowing the importance of trading in on famous names, he named his company John Lloyd Wright, Inc., and his new product Lincoln Logs, to tie in to the Abraham Lincoln–log cabin mythology. Unlike most toys that originated in the 1920s, Lincoln Logs have not gone plastic, but are still made of Oregon lumber.

DO NOT PASS GO, DO NOT COLLECT $200

Are the streets on the Monopoly game real streets from somewhere?

YES, ATLANTIC CITY. Or at least they were when Charles Darrow sold the game to Parker Brothers in the 1930s. If you're planning a trip to see the originals, however, you'll be disappointed to see that many of the game's upscale streets, like Pacific Avenue, are now pretty seedy; that Marven Gardens, misspelled in the game, is way out of town; that none of the railroads stop there anymore; and that St. Charles Place was replaced by a casino parking lot. There's still plenty of free parking spaces and a jail, though.

Is there a national Monopoly tournament? Yes, every four years.

What space is landed on most in Monopoly?

ILLINOIS AVENUE. It is followed by B&O Railroad, Free Parking, Tennessee Avenue, New York Avenue, and Reading Railroad.

Were the original Monopoly tokens different from the modern ones?

YES. IN the game's 1935 debut, the metal tokens were a flat iron, cannon, pocketbook, lantern, race car, thimble with "For a Good Girl" engraved on it, baby shoe, top hat, racehorse, and battleship. The houses were made of wood, and the hotels had "Grand Hotel" written on them. Currently there are 11 tokens: iron, cannon, thimble (without the inscription), shoe, top hat, battleship, horse and rider, dog, money sack, wheelbarrow, and finally, the race car—the token voted most popular by players in 1998.

STAYING WITHIN THE LINES

What makes that distinctive smell when you open a box of crayons?

IT IS A SMELL that nearly anybody can recognize blindfolded. It's stearic acid, which is the formal name for processed beef fat.

What Crayola crayon names have been changed?

"POLITICALLY CORRECT" alterations, reflecting the full spectrum of progressive and conservative thought, include changing the names of Flesh to Peach (because beige is not the color of all skin); of Indian Red to Chestnut (based on the misassumption that it had something to do with Native Americans when instead it is a color from India); and of Prussian Blue to Midnight Blue (because nervous Crayola officials feared that it sounded too much like "Russian" during the anti-Communist hysteria in the 1950s).

IT'S A SMALL WORLD AFTER ALL

What's the usual scale of dollhouses compared to real life?

1:12. It seems like a strange conversion (why not something more even, like 1:10, for example?) but it really makes a lot of sense, in the non-metric United States, anyway. Here's why: There are 12 inches in a foot, so if you want to scale something in our world down to dollhouse size, first determine its size in feet, then turn that number into inches. A 6 foot person here becomes a 6 inch doll. A 30 foot room becomes a 30 inch room. Simple!

Where does the miniature trucks' name "Tonka" come from? Is it Japanese?

NO, IT'S Minnesotan. In 1957, a group of school teachers decided to augment their meager incomes by manufacturing garden tools. After investing in materials, they decided that marketing the tools was going to be too difficult with the budget they had, so they abandoned their plans. To use up the leftover sheet metal and paint, they built a few playthings for children.

What's the first color in a crayon pack to be used up?
Usually black, followed by red.

One sturdy little dump truck looked like it had possibilities, so the teacher-entrepeneuurs showed it around toy stores and toy shows. "What do you call it?" someone asked. A pun came to mind from the name of nearby Lake Minnetonka, so the teachers called them "Mini Tonka Trucks." The company has since sold more than 30 million of them. Presumably the teachers were able to quit their day jobs.

Q & A FROM THE LETTER BOX

How many Q's come in a Scrabble game?

ONLY ONE. That's also true if you're trying to catch some Z's. There's only one J, K, and X as well. E, the most popular letter in life and Scrabble, appears on the most tiles: 12.

What's the highest score ever recorded in Scrabble?

ACCORDING TO the folks at Guinness Records, it's 1,049, set by Phil Abbleby in 1989. His opponent scored 253. The highest single-move score was Dr. Saladin Karl Khoshnaw's 392 for the word CAZIQUES (which means "native chiefs of West Indian aborigines"), set in a 1982 competition in Manchester, England.

Scrabble, by the way, was originally called Criss Cross. The game was invented by Alfred Butts in the 1930s during the big crossword puzzle craze. (Crosswords had just been invented and everyone was doing them.) Butts, justifiably sensitive to what a bad name can do in this cruel world, eventually changed the name to Scrabble and the rest is history.

FLYING SAUCERS

Is it true that Frisbees were invented by a pie pan company?

YES, BUT not intentionally. In the 1870s, William Frisbie opened a bake shop in Bridgeport, Connecticut. His pies came in metal pans with his last name stamped into them. At some point, Yale students discovered that if the pans were thrown like a discus, they would fly and hover.

None of this was known to Walter Morrison in the early 1950s, when UFOs were in the news. Young Morrison decided to try to create a flying UFO toy. He made a prototype in tin, then convinced the Wham-O company to sell his Morrison's Flyin' Saucer molded out of the new wonder material, plastic. On a campus promotional tour, Wham-O representative Richard Knerr brought a crate of the new toys to New Haven, and was amazed to find that the students were already throwing pie-plate discs and shouting "Frisbie!" as a warning. The Yale kids liked the lighter, more aerodynamic design of the Flyin' Saucers; Knerr liked the name Frisbie. In 1959, Wham-O changed its disc's name to Frisbee, and they began to all but literally fly off toy and sporting goods shelves.

UNDER A BRIDGE

Who designed the first troll doll . . . and why?

TROLLS ARE the leprechauns of Norse culture: ancient beings who guard treasure and love to play tricks, dance, and fornicate. In the late 1950s, an impoverished Danish wood carver named Thomas Dam couldn't afford a doll for his daughter, so he carved an ugly troll for her and gave it white hair. Dam told his daughter the troll would bring good luck. Sure enough, a toy store owner saw the doll and asked if her father would make more. The pinched and paunchy dolls became a worldwide fad in the early 1960s and then again in the early 1990s.

> How many possible hands of bridge are there? 635,013,559,600.

SHUT UP AND DEAL

Was the Bible really the first thing printed on Johannes Gutenberg's printing press?

NO. THE BIBLE was the first book he printed on his movable-type printing press, but before that he printed playing cards. Making playing cards was also one of the first jobs in Ben

Franklin's print shop; he was among the first to print them in the New World.

In poker, what is the "Dead Man's Hand"?

TWO PAIR, consisting of the black aces and eights. It's called the Dead Man's Hand because it's what Wild Bill Hickok was holding, along with a jack (some say queen) of diamonds, at the moment he was killed. Gunfighter Hickok made it a policy never to sit with his back to the door, but when another player playfully sat in his seat, Hickok broke his own rule. Unfortunately, it just so happened that this was the day drifter Jackie McCall came through the door with a gun. He shot Hickok from behind, and since then some superstitious gamblers dread getting aces and eights.

Isn't there some country that has round playing cards? Yes, India.

AND TO ALL A GOOD KNIGHT

How many possible moves are there in a game of chess?

ONE MATHEMATICIAN calculated that a game's first 10 moves alone could be played in 170,000,000,000,000,000,000,000,000 different ways.

What are chess pieces supposed to represent?

MODELED AFTER the ruler and military of sixth-century India, where the game is thought to have originated, the first chess pieces represented the sovereign, his main minister, and the army's elephants, cavalry, chariots, and infantry. By the 13th-century, the game was being played in Europe, where the minister was replaced by the queen, and the remaining pieces were bishops (political figures in royal times), knights, rooks (or castles), and pawns (soldiers).

In chess, why does the queen have so much power when the king can barely move?

ASK

Who invented the board game checkers?

CHECKERS is one of the world's oldest games, with a variation played in the days of the early Egyptian pharaohs (about 1600 B.C.). The game was mentioned in the works of Homer and Plato, too. About 800 years ago, checkers was adapted to the 64-square chessboard, and by the 16th century, it was essentially the same as the modern game. It is called *draughts* by the British and *dambrod* in Scotland.

Into the Mystic

ASTROLOGY, SPOON-BENDING, fire-walking, Ouija Boards, Magic 8-Balls . . . some things cannot be explained by mere mortals. Or can they? Some apparently mysterious things have pretty ordinary explanations, and vice versa. Sit still and clear your mind. There is magic afoot.

BENDING THE FLATWEAR

What's with bending spoons with psychic powers? Is it really possible?

IT'S ARGUABLY POSSIBLE, but there's no real evidence of it. In fact, it's a magician's trick that's very easy to fake:

1. Either start with a spoon with a thin neck or, behind the scenes, use both hands and bend the neck back and forth several times to weaken it.

2. In your performance, after you've shown that the spoon is straight, casually push hard against the bowl of the spoon with your thumb, concealing the handle loosely in your hand afterward. The spoon will look like it's still straight while you gesture and talk about the powers of the mind and such.

3. Since the bend is already done, you can now relax and concentrate on putting on a good show. Look intense and rub the spoon lightly with your forefinger.

4. After a long period of staring, sweating, and vein-popping, begin to slow-w-wly advance the handle of the spoon forward with your thumb, half a millimeter at a time. Your friends will swear that the spoon is bending right before their eyes.

5. Set it down and say, "Look, it's still bending!" and odds are good that nobody will contradict you.

How did the case turn out when professional spoon-bender Uri Geller sued magician James Randi?

RANDI IS A PROFESSIONAL magician who specializes in debunking claims of the paranormal. Since the 1970s, Geller has claimed to be able to bend spoons and start broken watches with his amazing psychokinetic powers. Randi said that Geller had "tricked even reputable scientists" with mere magic tricks of "the kind that used to be on the back of cereal boxes when I was a kid," commenting, "Apparently scientists don't eat corn flakes anymore." In 1991, Geller sued Randi for $15 million. Four years later, the case was dismissed as a "frivolous complaint," and Geller was ordered to pay almost $150,000 in court costs.

What is pyromancy?
Divination by reading the movements of a flame.

SILENCE, THE SPIRITS ARE ABOUT TO SPEAK

When was the Ouija Board invented?

FIRST OF ALL, let's knock down some of the Ouija myths. The board is not, as some have claimed, an ancient fortune-telling method first used thousands of years ago in Egypt or Babylonia. The first Ouija rolled off the assembly line a little more than 100 years ago. Its roots go back a few decades earlier to France, where interest in spiritualism was at the peak of a cyclical revival.

In the 1850s, someone in France, tired of depending on human mediums, invented a device meant to let anyone have a direct long-distance line to the Other World. That device was called a *planchette,* meaning "little plank." The planchette was an easy-rolling, heart-shaped piece of wood with, at the heart's point, a pencil. The way it worked was that one or two people placed their hands on it. When their hands mysteriously moved, the pencil traced a path, writing a message from Beyond.

When planchettes arrived in the United States in 1868, they became an immediate sensation as a parlor game, and millions were manufactured by toy makers. However, many people took their planchette's "messages" seriously and complained at the slowness and illegibility of the writing. So some game designers came up with the idea of a spiritual typewriter: a planchette with a helpful array of preprinted letters, numbers, and common words like YES and NO. Suddenly, the spirits could communicate at relatively high speed and clarity. The Ouija Board was poised to revolutionize the spiritual medium.

What does "Ouija" mean?

THE CHIEF INVENTOR of the Ouija Board, Charles Kennard, consulted the board to come up with its own name. The spirits spelled out "O-U-I-J-A," explaining that it was the Egyptian word for "good luck." That turned out to be wrong, but no matter: Ouija it was. Later, the spirits from Beyond played an even worse trick on poor Kennard: Despite his frequent use of the board, they neglected to warn him that his company was about to be taken away from him. His partners suddenly forced him out and turned the company over to his shop foreman, William Fuld.

Fuld immediately began rewriting the history of the Ouija, representing himself as the inventor and claiming that the name actually came from the French and German words for "yes": oui and ja. It's a myth that still appears in print. Fuld ran the company for 35 years, until he was struck by his own unforeseen tragedy: while supervising the replacement of a flagpole at the top of his headquarters, he fell several stories and died. Fuld's heirs ran the company until 1966, when they sold out to Parker Brothers. Sales continue to hold steady today. The boards sell especially well during times of crisis, such as wars.

How does the Ouija Board work?

THERE ARE THREE theories as to why a Ouija Board might work, when and if it does:

1. **The Spiritualist Theory.** Forces or spirits from beyond our world are moving the planchette. *Evidence for:* It sure seems like the thing is moving by itself, sometimes giving completely unexpected answers. *Evidence against:* Try using the board with both people blindfolded and see how well the "all-seeing spirits" do.

2. **The Ideomotor Theory.** You are moving the board's indicator, but don't consciously know it. "Unconsciously picturing what you want to happen can cause your muscles to make it happen," says psychologist Ray Hyman. "People think they're not doing anything and that some outside force is making it happen." It may be a mild form of self-hypnotism in which your hands move as if they're not in your control, meaning that perhaps the Ouija Board can be used as a shortcut to knowing your unconscious mind. *Evidence for:* While people are often surprised at a message, they just as often get exactly the answer they expected, whether good or bad. *Evidence against:* It's hard for people to imagine that they wouldn't know they're moving the indicator.

3. **The Somebody's-a-Big-Fat-Liar Theory.** This theory holds that both partners will usually deny manipulating the planchette...and that at least one is really lying. *Evidence for:* How many Ouija sessions have ended with the two partners struggling as if arm wrestling to spell out the answer each wants? *Evidence against:* Very trustworthy people have sworn convincingly that they hadn't deliberately cheated, yet still got messages.

REPLY HAZY, TRY AGAIN

What are the odds that you'll get a positive answer when you ask a question of the Magic 8-Ball?

"OUTLOOK GOOD," as the ball itself might say. There are 20 possible answers, and half of them are to some degree posi-

> **Where can I consult online oracles?**

tive. Of the remaining 10, 5 are negative and 5 tell you to try again later. The positives are OUTLOOK GOOD, YOU MAY RELY ON IT, MOST LIKELY, YES, YES DEFINITELY, IT IS CERTAIN, SIGNS POINT TO YES, WITHOUT A DOUBT, IT IS DECIDEDLY SO, and AS I SEE IT YES.

The negatives are OUTLOOK NOT SO GOOD, MY REPLY IS NO, DON'T COUNT ON IT, VERY DOUBTFUL, and MY SOURCES SAY NO. Finally, the abstentions are ask AGAIN LATER, CANNOT PREDICT NOW, BETTER NOT TELL YOU NOW, CONCENTRATE and ASK AGAIN, and REPLY HAZY, TRY AGAIN.

HOTFOOT

How can people walk across hot coals?

VERY CAREFULLY! Actually, there's no real trick involved, and you don't need to be spiritually evolved or fortified with meditation and fasting. Jeeves will tell you how it's done if you promise not to try this at home or anywhere else. First of all, successful fire-walkers use dry wood, not charcoal or stones, and let it burn for quite a while so the ashes can build up. Wood coals don't generate much heat, and as they get crushed underfoot, they get even cooler. The coals are raked very thin so that even though they're still glowing, there are spaces between them. Fire-walkers walk quickly and take only a few steps through the pit. Also, they often have wet grass or a small puddle of water at each end of the pit to put out any embers and cool the feet. Still, even in optimal conditions, some fire-walkers do get minor burns and blisters.

BELIEF IN THE UNBELIEVABLE

How did Nostradamus predict all those things?

JEEVES IS RATHER skeptical of the claims made for
Nostradamus, having read him in the original ancient French. It
has been suggested convincingly that, as a politically active
Protestant living during the Inquisitions, he was most often
talking in code about contemporary occurrences instead of trying to predict future ones. Regardless, his maddening obscurity
has been interpreted after the fact in dozens of different ways,
showing that if you're obscure enough, put no time limit on
your "predictions," and have thousands of people reinterpreting
and retranslating your words for centuries afterward, you can
be an amazing psychic, too.

How does astrology work?

THERE'S NO EVIDENCE that it does. There has been no good
study so far that correlates people's astrological signs with their
personality types or fates. So why does it seem that descriptions of your sign fit you so well, you may ask? It could be that
the stars have absolutely pegged our personalities. Or it could
be something else: Psychological studies show that people will
agree with nearly any personal assessment of their personality,
provided it is couched within a mild compliment. The same
people will usually also agree with a second statement similarly
couched, even if it directly contradicts the first.

Why does almost every type of medical treatment have people who swear it did them some good?

STUDIES OF THE "placebo effect" show that more than a third
of all patients will feel better if given medicines with no active
ingredients. In a 1955 study of more than 1,000 patients, the
condition of 35% was improved by administering a placebo. In
another study, researchers gave sugar pills to a large group of
college students and told them that half would be getting sleep
aids and the other half, mild stimulants. Of the students, only
two reported no change in their sleep patterns; the rest claimed

that they felt either a pronounced stimulant or narcotic effect. Why do placebos work? It's not completely understood, but one theory is that the patient's faith in a medical treatment may release brain chemicals called endorphins, the body's natural opiates, which relax the body and help it to heal.

Who was Nostradamus?

I saw a psychic who actually made his pulse stop when he went into a trance. How did he do that?

WELL IT COULD BE that he has amazing, supernatural powers that keeps his brain cells from dying without a flow of oxygen. But more likely, he's using an old fakir's trick. Here it is: Typically, the perpetrator allows you to hold his wrist. The pulse gets weaker and weaker until you can't feel the pulse anymore. Amazing! But note he doesn't suggest you listen to his heart. That's because stopping your pulse in one arm is easy and not too dangerous if done only for a short period of time. All you have to do is hide a rubber ball under your arm and slowly squeeze to block the artery.

How do psychics reproduce a drawing that someone else has drawn without showing anybody?

PERHAPS THROUGH psychic powers, but that would be the hard way. More likely, it's the same methods magicians use. It's another old trick, and there are lots of ways to do it, even without having a confederate looking over the person's shoulder. Some magicians will simply look at the indentation on the page, but if they want a sure bet, they'll use a piece of carbon paper or carbonless paper a layer below the top page to give an instant copy which they can glance at and then quickly duplicate. Basic shapes can also be discerned by watching the movement of the person's eyes and the end of the writing utensil.

How does water witching work?

A COUPLE OF observations:

1. You will always strike water if you go deep enough.

2. There are natural land features that are likely to indicate water at a reasonable depth.

Given those two facts, there's no evidence that dousing works any better than guesswork by a knowledgeable hydrological amateur.

WHETHER IT'S USED TO FRESHEN UP, bathe, or brush one's teeth, the bathroom is probably the most traveled room in every house—yet it's still considered rude to discuss it in polite company. Let Jeeves go boldly where no butler has gone before.

HOLD ON, YOUNG MAN—DID YOU REMEMBER TO TWIG YOUR TEETH?

Before toothbrushes, what did people use?

BEFORE ORAL-B, people used twigs, leaves, sand, fingers, animal bristles—you name it—to clean teeth. One of the earliest recorded toothbrushes dates back to Egypt in about 3000 B.C. It was a "chew stick"—a twig with one end frayed into bristles. The other end worked as a handle. Ancient Romans and 15th-century Europeans used a carved toothpick and sometimes a quill. Finally DuPont Chemical Company invented nylon in 1938. Not long after, Doctor West's Miracle Tuft Toothbrush became the first nylon-bristled brush. The first edition sold well, but often caused gum injury because the bristles were too hard. Toothbrushing finally became commonplace in the United States during World War II, when each military recruit was issued a brush.

When was toothpaste invented?

TOOTHPASTE has been around for thousands of years. One of the earliest was a mixture of wine and pumice. The Egyptians used it with a chew stick (see question above) some 5,000 years ago. From the early Roman Empire until 18th-century Europe and America, urine was a main ingredient in toothpaste, because the ammonia in it is an excellent cleanser. Ammonia (from other sources) is still a main ingredient in many toothpastes.

How did they figure out that fluoride prevents tooth decay?

ALTHOUGH ADDING fluoride to toothpaste and drinking water is a relatively new thing, scientists have noticed fluoride's effects since the early 1800s. The soil and water around Naples, Italy, is very high in fluoride, and as a result its residents historically have had little or no tooth decay. This was noted in 1802, and by the 1840s, fluoride lozenges were passed out in many European communities to fight tooth decay. By 1915, a few cities in the United States had begun treating drinking water with fluoride. By the 1950s, fluoride-treated water was cropping up everywhere, and Crest became the first toothpaste to add fluoride.

How come people didn't have many dental problems before fluoride?

THEY HAD horrible dental problems. Queen Elizabeth spent her whole life with the pain of deep cavities because she was unwilling to have her teeth extracted. George Washington lost his teeth to decay, one after the other, starting at the age of 22. His dentures almost destroyed his gums as well, and it is believed that by the end of his life, his tooth loss and dentures may have contributed to his deafness. Washington held his jaw jutted out so it wouldn't be so obvious that his teeth were missing; this posture probably did significant damage to his eardrums.

How many people have the oral herpes virus that causes fever blisters? In the U.S., about 80% of the population.

Not just that, but ignorance on the part of "dentists" contributed to an enormous tooth decay problem, even for people who might not naturally have suffered from it. White teeth were prized, so dentists began offering this luxury to those who would pay. They would first file down the enamel of the teeth with a metal instrument, then coat them with *aqua fortis*, a highly corrosive whitening solution that was essentially nitric acid. The treated teeth would be as beautiful as pearls for a short time, then would begin to decay.

Does "whitening" toothpaste work?

NOT MUCH, as far as anyone can tell. The truth is that age is the prime cause of yellow teeth. Anything that causes outside stains on teeth is easily removed by a regular cleaning at the dentist and oftentimes by regular flossing and brushing alone. But most discoloration takes place below the enamel and is a natural part of a tooth's aging process. There is plenty of evidence that using hard abrasives and corrosive chemicals on the teeth regularly can actually cause enamel loss and gum injury. It's important to have one's dentist advise the best solution to stained teeth.

LISTEN, MY CHILDREN, AND YOU SHALL HEAR . . . .

What did Paul Revere do for a living?

REVERE WAS most known for his work as a silversmith and engraver, but he was also a barber, as were many people in his day. And like most barbers of the time, he was also a dentist. He's said to have yanked a tooth or two from George Washington's mouth, and reportedly made at least one of the first president's sets of dentures.

THE CLEAN, SWEET SMELL OF SUCCESS

When was soap invented?

WRITTEN RECORDS of soap date back thousands of years to Sumeria, where plant extracts, vegetable oils, and alkaline salts were used to clean. Ancient Romans discovered animal fats worked even better for washing. Although soap's popularity waned in the plague-ridden medieval years (when bathing was considered unhealthy), it didn't die, and secret recipes continued to be passed down through soap maker's guilds.

Up until the early 1800s, most households made their own soap; only a small fraction of people bought it. In 1806, William Colgate opened a soap-manufacturing business and added perfume to his soap. It was a huge success. From there, other manufacturers got in on it, and the competitive bar soap industry began. In the 1970s, a whole new revolution with "deodorant" soaps revived soap manufacturers' rivalry for consumer dollars.

For a complete history of soap in general, try this site: www. sappohill.com/soaphist.htm

How does soap work?

THIS EXCERPT is taken from an article on soap at Encyclopedia.com:

> Soaps cleanse by lowering the surface tension of water, by emulsifying [liquefying] grease, and by absorbing dirt into the foam. Soap is less effective than detergent in hard water because the salts that make the water hard react with the soap to form insoluble curds (e.g., the ring left in bathtubs).

In other words, soap makes dirt and germs slip away.

What's the difference between soap and detergent?

REGULAR SOAP has two key reactions—one part has molecules that latch on to dirt and grease and shy away from water. They are insoluble and they come from fat. The other part of soap loves water and helps to rinse away most of the molecules that have surrounded the dirt, but not all. This is why soap leaves a film on surfaces.

Detergents are made up of short molecules that, when mixed with alcohol, seek out dirt and grease and surround it. The difference is that, without the fat of soap, detergents rinse completely away.

GOOD CLEAN FUN

How long should I wash my hands to get them really clean?

THE BIGGEST barrier to the spread of diseases like the common cold is consistent hand washing. It is said to take 20 seconds of scrubbing with soap and water before your hands are considered sanitary.

What are the origins of the bathtub?

FOR AEONS people have used stone, brick, or wooden tubs to bathe in, in or around the home. But two men significantly affected the bathtub as we know it today. John Kohler, a foundry owner in Wisconsin in the late 1800s, developed an enameled iron watering trough for animals. When indoor plumbing became popular, he attached his trough to four cast-iron feet and began selling it as a bathtub for the house.

How do I make soap?

A few years later David Buick, (the very same man who began the car company) became the father of the modern bathtub. Before he delved into the world of automobiles, he manufactured plumbing fixtures in Detroit. He patented a method of affixing porcelain to an iron surface, the same method used for bathtubs today.

How often should people bathe their bodies?

THE WHOLE POINT is to eliminate dirt, oils, and odors from the body to a socially and culturally acceptable level. If it doesn't dry out your skin, bathing once every day works well. If a bath every other day accomplishes these goals, then there is nothing wrong with that schedule, either.

Why does Ivory soap float?

IN 1881, a worker at Procter and Gamble forgot to turn off the machine that whipped a little air into the soap mixture. He ran the "ruined" batch through production and packaging anyway instead of pulling it. Consumers went wild. They loved the way the bar floated instead of sinking to the murky bottom of the bathtub. Procter and Gamble decided to keep the method and make it a selling point.

Why did they call it Ivory? Procter claims he took the name from a verse in the sermon he heard that Sunday. It was Psalms 45:8: "All thy garments smell of myrrh, and aloes, and cassia, and out of the *ivory* palaces whereby they have made thee glad."

WHAT THE MAKERS OF TUB CLEANERS DON'T WANT YOU TO KNOW

Why does mildew grow in grout but not on tiles?

MILDEW AND mold result from too much moisture on a surface. Tiles dry quickly, so they aren't prone to the problem. Grout won't grow mold or mildew, either, unless it has broken down enough to become damaged or porous. Mildew in grout is a good indicator that it's time to re-grout; the old stuff just can't keep moisture out anymore. Here's the irony: Products with bleach are the number-one cause of grout breakdown.

For mildew and mold problems, replace old grout before moisture seeps so far into the wall or flooring that it causes serious damage. To keep mildew and mold from coming back, make sure the tile and grout are wiped after each shower or bath and stop using products containing bleach and other harsh chemicals.

CLEANLINESS IS NEXT TO . . . SATAN

Is it true that leaders of the Christian church once ruled that bathing was a sin?

IT'S TRUE. In A.D. 500, the Christian church, seeing how the lewd Romans had thrived in their social hot tubs, decreed that exposing one's skin was a sin against God. As a result, bathing fell out of favor and people resorted to dousing themselves in perfume. The decree also led to the belief that bathing was how disease was spread: that the warmth and the water opened up one's skin to "pestiferous vapors" that caused diseases like the plague. Diseases flourished as a result of these attitudes, yet they simply furthered the belief that even infrequent bathing was the culprit.

During this era of bathroom history, bathing once a year was not uncommon. Instead of regular bathing, people wiped their bodies with pieces of dry white cloth. When they did get up the courage to bathe, they were very careful. They got plenty of rest both before and after the event. Then as soon as they were scrubbed clean, they quickly wrapped their bodies completely in cloth to block it from harmful diseases. This attitude lasted for over a millennium in some places. In fact, Benjamin Franklin was a pioneer in the 1700s for promoting bathing as a healthy activity.

ONLY SKIN DEEP

How do skin creams and bath oils moisten skin?

CONTRARY TO popular belief, oils and lotions don't sink into the skin. This is a good thing, since skin must present a barrier to such things as disease and infection. Human skin actually supplies its own natural moisturizer to keep itself from drying and cracking, but soaps, water, cold air, and dry heat can remove it. Lotions and bath oils lie on top of the skin, keeping outside elements from stripping away the skin's natural oil.

BALD AMBITION

Who invented shampoo?

SHAMPOOS MADE with detergents (which, unlike soap, rinse completely away) began making an appearance in continental Europe in the 1800s.

Do vitamins in shampoo work?
Not on hair—it's dead.

But in the United States and England, we owe a big thank you to a balding fire chief named John Breck. Breck was 21 in 1898 when he began losing his hair. This disturbed him and he sought medical advice to no avail. Desperate, he enrolled in chemistry classes at Amherst College in an effort to understand how he might stop his hair loss. This was where he learned about the shampoos used in European beauty salons, and he began to experiment with his own mixtures of oils and detergents. After receiving his doctorate, he ran a scalp treatment center, then teamed up with a beauty supply dealer and launched the John H. Breck Corporation in 1929.

Breck never did discover a cure for baldness, but he did introduce shampoo to the United States. In 1930, he introduced ph-balanced shampoo, which helps prevent hair and scalp damage, and in 1933, he created different shampoos to meet the specific needs of oily and dry hair. In 1946, his company began a long-running ad campaign featuring "Breck Girls"—pretty women with beautiful hair.

What does hair conditioner actually do?

IT COVERS the hair with a thin coating of either grease or a plasticlike substance. You may be wondering why people would do this just after using a shampoo to strip the oil out of their hair. There's a good reason: Hair is very jagged. Under a microscope, you can see notches all up and down the shaft. After we wash our hair, taking all the oils out, rough spots catch on each other and hairs stick together, forming tangles and making hair more susceptible to splitting and breaking. When conditioner is applied, it fills in these rough spots with a lubricating substance, smoothing out the hair strand. As a result, hair feels nicer, lies flatter, and is easier to brush and comb.

A CLOSE SHAVE

Who invented the razor?

NO ONE we know of by name. Razors of one kind or another have been around for ages: flint, shells, and hammered metal all have been used. Soldiers of ancient Rome shaved for battle so their enemies couldn't grab on to their beards. The ancient Greeks shaved daily—they liked their faces clean of growth. The Founding Fathers of the United States lived in a time when it was fashionable to pluck each hair individually with clamshell tweezers, although straight-edge razors were available (they'd been around for nearly as long as swords). The modern razor had its start with the French, who invented the "safety" razor, which prevented serious injury when shaving. In the 1880s, North America saw the T-shaped razor for the first time, and in 1895, King Gillette (his real name, not a title) gave the world the disposable razor blade.

When did women start shaving their legs and underarms?

NO ONE KNOWS for certain, but we know that ancient Egyptians pretty much shaved everything they could reach.

They were concerned about bodily cleanliness and—in a time without modern soaps and deodorants—realized that clean-shaven areas don't

> **Are there any special instructions for shaving your head?**

offer the same welcoming atmosphere to bad-smelling bacteria that hairy ones do. Shaving heads became an efficient way of dealing with both heat and hair lice. From there, it wasn't much further to simply go ahead and rid the body of the rest of its hair as well—whether on an adult or a child. Barbers were held in high regard and oftentimes were on the house staff of the very wealthy.

For centuries afterward, other Middle Easterners continued this practice. Eventually, for women at least, it spread to Europe and the Americas.

Didn't women used to shave off their eyebrows for fashion?

YES, THEY DID—and so did many men during the 1700s. They also removed the rest of the hair from their faces and foreheads, then wore extended hairpieces on their foreheads and press-on mouse-skin eyebrows. By the late 1700s, women (and some men) started shaving their heads completely so they could wear fantastically ornate wigs.

For other weird shaving habits of yesteryear, see www.quikshave.com/timeline.htm

Does shaving make hair grow in thicker and darker?

NO. GENETICS is the only thing that determines hair color and thickness, and no amount of shaving is going to make hair thicker. However, hair may *appear* to be darker after shaving. The longer hair is exposed to light, the lighter it may become. If hair is shaved, the new growth will reflect the true nature of the hair color prior to age and sunlight bleaching it out, so this may cause some to think that the shaving itself caused the darkening.

How do they get toilet paper neatly onto rolls? They make long rolls, then slice them.

ON A ROLL

Who invented toilet paper?

IF YOU'RE talking about the perforated rolls we know today, Walter Alcock did in 1879, in England. The Scott Brothers from Philadelphia, seeing its potential, brought toilet paper stateside and called it "Waldorf Tissue" to capitalize on the luxury hotel's name. They later changed the name to Scott Tissues, and the rest is history. Before Alcock's perforated rolls caught on, toilet paper was sold in loose sheets in England. Americans used the Sears catalog, among other things.

Is there an official right way to load a toilet paper holder?

STUDIES INDICATE that more than 60% prefer the toilet paper to come over the top, while 29% prefer a bottom line. The other 11% have no preference. The service industry over-whelmingly deems over-the-top the correct way to load a roll of toilet paper, because that way you can see the design printed on the roll. Furthermore, groping for toilet paper flush against the wall leads to premature wear on the painted surface.

Why do hotels fold the ends of the toilet paper in a V shape?

THE PRACTICE of folding the end of a roll is to indicate the cleanliness of a room's facilities. This was meant to replace the SANITIZED FOR YOUR PROTECTION paper loop that fit around the seat of the toilet, which was considered too much work for guests to have to remove. The fold on the toilet paper roll is meant to assure you that no one has used that bathroom since it was scoured.

EVERY MAN A KING

Why do some people call the toilet a "throne"?

"THRONE" IS simply a euphemism, and we have plenty of them for subjects that are considered unmentionable. Try hopper, johnny, janey, loo, potty, or privy. This particular euphemism—throne—is said to have been spawned by none other than Louis XIV, who often saw to royal business from his toilet, deeming it an alternative to his usual throne.

Did Elvis die in the bathroom?

YES. OTHER celebrities who have passed on in the same location? Judy Garland and Lenny Bruce, to name just two.

THE SCIENCE OF TOILETS

Does toilet water always flush clockwise?

NO. WHILE it is true that large bodies of water are affected by the Earth's rotation, there is no law of physics that operates on toilet flow besides the spiraling downward motion the flushing causes. Water-jet streams control the actual rotating motion, so if water is pumped in at a clockwise or counterclockwise tilt, that's the way it will go down. And no, there's no difference in rotation whether you're in the northern or southern hemisphere.

Was the toilet invented by Thomas Crapper?

NO. IN 1969, a writer named Wallace Reyburn wrote *Flushed with Pride,* a far-fetched "biography" of one "Thomas Crapper," who he said invented the flush toilet. The book was apparently meant by Reyburn as a joke, as was his next tome, *Bust Up: The Uplifting Tale of Otto Titzling and the Development of the Bra.* Unfortunately, a number of people took Reyburn's hoax as gospel truth, and you will still see both of these "inventors" erroneously credited in reference books and trivia games by writers who should know better.

Having said that, however, here's a twist: There is evidence that there really was a Thomas Crapper, who, although he didn't invent the toilet, manufactured toilets and accessories in the late 19th century. The evidence is quite convincing, consisting of old newspaper ads and so on, but one hesitates to take it at face value, considering past hoaxes and the too-good-to-be-true name. So, to sum up: There *might* have been a Thomas Crapper who sold toilets, but we can be absolutely sure that the invention of the toilet predated him by at least 200 years.

Who invented the toilet?

TOILETS WITH running water have been around for thousands of years. No one person can be credited with thinking up this efficient way to dispose of human waste. However, it is known that Sir John Harrington, a godson of Queen Elizabeth, created the first *flush* toilet in 1596. Queen Elizabeth was thrilled until Harrington wrote a book about his invention. The queen instantly became the butt of her countrymen's jokes, as it were. She was humiliated and had Harrington banished from her sight. Thus, flush toilets stayed empty.

In 1775, Alexander Cumming designed a "stink trap" for toilets that kept water in the pipe, preventing odors from wafting back up from the sewers—a substantial milestone in toilet history. Regardless, it was still a century before flushing toilets would replace the old standby, the chamber pot.

How much raw sewage does the average person create per day?
About 60 gallons.

Why is the handle on the left side of the toilet when most people are right-handed?

THE EARLY pull-chain flushers were placed on the left side of the tank so that people sitting could reach up and flush with their right hand. When handles replaced the chains, the flush mechanism, although lowered, remained on the left side of the toilet. These days, 66% of people flush when standing, using the left hand or crossing over with the right. Even some of the sitter-downers admit to crossing over and using their left hand to flush because it wrenches the shoulder to try to flush with the right hand while sitting. The toilet is thus one of the few devices in our modern world set up for lefties.

Where does sewage go?

IN THE United States, the water part of raw sewage is extracted, purified, and placed back into a waterway or on crops. The solids are sterilized and composted. Often they are then sold to fertilizer companies to package and sell back to the original owners.

NATURE CALLS . . . COLLECT

Where did pay toilets go?

YOU DATE YOURSELF. Although most people alive today don't remember coin-slotted lavatories, they were once quite common. The original thought was that making people pay for the "service" would encourage them to keep the toilet clean. But the opposite happened. People were so angry at having to pay to carry out basic biological functions that vandalism increased, costing more to fix than could ever be collected in dimes. Furthermore, women's groups declared pay toilets discriminatory because women had to pay to urinate, whereas men had the luxury of free urinals. Many courts backed this argument, and by the late 1960s, most coin slots had been removed. Today pay toilets are very rare indeed.

> **Where can I find a guide to etiquette for using urinals?**

WHO PUT THE "U" IN "PUBLIC TOILET"?

Why are the toilet seats in public restrooms open in the front?

IT MAKES them easier to clean. Why didn't this U-shaped trend catch on in home bathrooms? Probably because it reminds people of public restrooms, which is not a pleasant image for a private powder room.

IS THIS THE TRAIN TO FLUSHING MEADOW?

I ran across an old train sign that read "Don't use the toilet while train is in the station." Why?

UNLIKE TODAY'S vacuum-flushed train toilets, which lead to air-sealed storage containers for holding waste, toilets used to flush directly out of a hole in the bottom of the train car. While moving along in open country, flushing onto the track seemed a commonsense way of disposing of waste. However, it also made sense not to do this while the train was parked in a bustling station.

In Asia, travelers were often surprised to find that "toilets" in trains were just holes in the floor, so they could watch the tracks and ground below whiz by as they prepared to relieve themselves. A tad risky and definitely drafty.

Wild Animals

"WILD THING, YOU MAKE MY heart sing." From early childhood on, wild animals fascinate like nothing else. At least when we're safely behind glass, bars, or the video screen. Fangs and claws, scales, stripes, and spots bring people back again and again to zoos, nature preserves, and television documentaries.

IT'S SO THEY CAN HIDE BEHIND THE PENGUINS

Zebra stripes are supposedly for camouflage. Where in Africa do you find black-and-white striped terrain?

THE STRIPES of the zebra set it apart from other members of the equus family, and make it a natural for its home environment. "Picket fences in suburban neighborhoods?" you may ask. No, the zebra is quite camouflaged, even in its desertlike environment, through what is called "disruptive discoloration." The black stripes on white or yellow background break up the outline of the animal, preventing many predators from seeing the zebra at all. This is especially true during low-light times of day, when many of their natural enemies hunt.

I've never seen a domesticated zebra. Can zebras be trained?

ZEBRAS ARE quite easily trained. Their use as circus animals dates back to the ancient Romans, when zebras pulled two-wheeled carts for traveling performers. Despite their normally sweet, docile nature though, zebras have a vicious side. They are quite loyal and devoted to one another. If a predator attacks a member of a herd, the rest of the herd will circle the enemy and stare it down until it backs away. If an attack continues against one of its members, the group stands ready to bite and stomp the attacker.

LOST IN TRANSLATION

Why do they call it a "white" rhino when it's grey?

THE NAME comes from the Dutch word *weit,* meaning " wide." These large, bulky-but-quick animals have a wide, square muzzle that's specialized for grazing. But don't tell the plush-toy manufacturers! They've enjoyed decades of selling snow-white toy rhinos to unsuspecting consumers.

BLOOD, SWEAT, AND WATER

Is it true that hippos sweat blood?

NO, BUT THE falsehood is based on an oddity that bears mentioning. A hippopotamus has no oil or sweat glands on its entire body; it does, however, support a type of gland that kicks into action only when it gets excited or nervous. This gland excretes a reddish oozing liquid that is often mistaken for blood and coincidentally may function, in part, to scare off attackers.

Do hippos ever leave the water?

YES. A HIPPO'S specialized eyes and nose, located on the top of its head, help it stay almost entirely submerged for large portions of the day, and young hippos actually have a specialized tongue that lets them dive down and nurse while under water. That said, during the night these heavy, often aggressive beasts come sauntering out of the water to feed. In a line, they march out into the grasses, sometimes five miles, to fill their large bellies. They come back to the water in a traversing loop and repeat this pattern throughout the night.

COMPARE, CONTRAST, DISCUSS AMONGST YOURSELVES

Are the rhino and hippo related?

YOU'D THINK SO, wouldn't you? Both are large, stumpy-legged herbivores. The hippopotamus is second only to the elephant in the category of "heaviest land mammal"; the rhinoceros is third. However, they are not related. The rhino is actually a very primitive land-dwelling mammal. The hippo, in contrast, spends over half of its life in the water. And if you want to talk biology, the hippo's closest living relative is the pig.

What's the difference between anteaters and aardvarks?

IT'S EASY TO confuse the two, based on their all-termite diets and their notorious digging abilities, but that's where the similarities end. The South American anteater, a furry creature that walks on its knuckles in the front, has an elongated face and a long, tubular nose. It can grow up to six feet long, but its mouth is a mere one inch wide. When you think of anteaters, think of the wise-cracking cartoon character in the Pink Panther cartoon show.

The African aardvark, on the other hand, looks a bit like a cross between a wild pig and a rabbit, with a short but broad tail. *Aardvark* aptly means "earth pig." This creature is considered, scientifically, a *near-ungulate,* meaning it is closely associated with hoofed animals. It has claws, a stumpy neck, a hairless body, a pig-shaped nose, and upright ears. Its tail leaves a distinctive track. Seeing that the aardvark has very poor eyesight, the tail track is a detriment to it, for humans are its principal enemy. The aardvark moves quickly and briskly at night, hunting for food, and sleeps in burrows during daylight. Vacated aardvark burrows are considered valuable real estate by jackals, warthogs, snakes, blue swallows, and hyenas.

How do you tell the difference between a panther and a leopard?

YOU DON'T. The name "panther" doesn't apply to any one cat but is usually used to refer to leopards, particularly black leopards. However, sometimes pumas and jaguars are called panthers as well.

MANE ATTRACTION

Where does the expression "to beard the lion in his den" come from?

IT COMES FROM two separate stories in the Old Testament of the Bible. I Samuel 17:35 has David telling of how he confronted and killed a lion before he braved Goliath: "and when he rose up against me, I seized him by his beard and struck him and killed him." The den part of the phrase is taken from the story of Daniel being tossed into the den of lions, from Daniel, chapter 6. The two portions of scripture combined in people's minds and stuck over the centuries and is now used as a trite saying meaning that one must be brave in order to complete difficult tasks.

FACTS NEVER TO FORGET

Can elephants swim, or do they just sink?

AN ELEPHANT can't gallop, jump, or leap, but it can swim quite well. Water is bouyant and supports an elephant's immense weight. When an elephant makes it to water that's deep enough to submerse itself in, it will often swim for miles as part of a trek. That's not surprising. Consider for a moment the elephant's weight: An Indian elephant supports about 11,000 pounds of weight on its feet every day; an African elephant, over 15,000. An elephant

How much does an elephant eat per day? Several hundred pounds of food.

will choose floating and kicking over marching or running any day.

How long is an elephant's gestation period?

A WHOPPING 22 months. Imagine the cost in pickles and ice cream. An African elephant weighs between 150 and 250 pounds at birth; an Indian elephant, a little less.

Can other animals besides humans stand on their heads?

THE ASIAN ELEPHANT is the only other animal with this ability.

THE NECK'S BIG THING

How many more neck bones are there in a giraffe than in a human?

GIRAFFES HAVE no more and no fewer vertebrae than a human. They also have the same number as a mouse. All mammals except two—the sea cow and certain sloths—have exactly seven vertebrae in their neck. The giraffe has highly elongated neck bones, giving it its great height.

NEWS FROM THE UNDERGROUND

> **How far can a kangaroo go in one jump?**
> More than 30 feet.

What's a wombat?

"WOMBAT" is a common name for several different rodentlike, ground-burrowing marsupials from Australia. The largest type is the most prevalent and is often domesticated in Australia, as its docile temperament makes it a good pet. The animal has been killed or driven out of many areas, however, because it is thought to damage crops. Although wombats may be doing some damage, in actuality the damage is

> **Where can I see livecams of wild animals in Africa?**

probably from rabbits that inhabit abandoned wombat burrows. The wombat has been nearly annihilated in some parts as a result of this belief, and these cute and affectionate creatures currently hold a place on the endangered species list.

To hear what a wombat sounds like (a little like a motorcycle refusing to start or a professional wrestler with asthma), go to www.abc.net. au/archives/mammals.htm

BILLING AND COOING

What does a platypus look like? Does it make a sound?

THE PLATYPUS is a true freak of nature. Its body is egg-shaped and it grows to be about 14 to 20 inches in length. Barely classified as a mammal on a technicality—nippleless glands on the mother's belly secrete a liquid that the newborns lick off her stomach—the platypus has characteristics from more than one animal group. Like birds, it lays eggs. It also has a bill like a duck and webbed feet. At the ends of those feet, however, there are cat-like claws for digging in the mud for food. Like other mammals, the platypus grows a coat of fur. On the males, there are spurs inside the back legs that are poisonous. When frightened, the platypus growls. Normally, it uses a clucking noise to call out to other platypuses.

> **What kind of animal is a prairie dog?**
> A rat.

PICKPOCKET'S PARADISE

Besides Australia, where do marsupials live?

THERE ARE A number of marsupials in New Guinea and Tasmania, as well as in Australia. In addition, the Americas are home to two marsupial orders: the *opossums* and the *caenolestes*. Opossums are found throughout the United States and Canada. They are best known for their practices of hanging upside down from trees and freezing and "playing dead" when threatened.

Some might argue, though, that they're best known for the mess they make of people's garbage cans in residential areas. Caenolestes are found in South America and are commonly called "shrew opossums." They have elongated heads and tiny eyes that don't see well. They mostly live in densely forested areas on the ground, but can climb well when necessary.

SLOW CHILDREN

How many babies are in a litter of sloths?

A SLOTH GIVES birth to just one offspring per litter. The baby clings to its mother until it is old enough to take care of itself.

Is it true there used to be gigantic sloths in South America?

INDEED, THE GIGANTIC ground sloth, the mylodon, was very much alive and real and living alongside people during the Pleistocene period—or Ice Age—some 10,000 years ago. It only became extinct, most believe, as recently as 5,000 years ago. Unlike its modern-day counterpart, it had no tail, but other than being the size of an elephant, it was very similar.

THIS WAS *BIG*, BABY!

What is "megafauna"?

THE LAST ICE AGE is said to be responsible for the extinction of many large creatures—called "megafauna"—including the woolly mammoth and the mastodon. For

> **What did the extinct marsupial diprotodon look like?**

years, their fossils spawned mysterious tales about dragons, unicorns, and giants. Putting to rest these mythological creatures, serious study of the large mammals of the Ice Age began in the 1700s and continues today.

Megafauna from the Pleistocene epoch (Ice Age) included giant saber-toothed cats (including tigers), the woolly rhinoceros, the giant ox, giant deer, an enormous armadillo-like animal called a glyptodont, a giant vulture (with a wingspan of over 13 feet), a giant bear, a giant beaver, and a large camel.

How many wolves make up a pack?
Up to 20.

In Australia, specifically, lived a giant marsupial called the diprotodon, a giant flat-faced kangaroo, a marsupial lion, a large spiny anteater, and a gigantic, chickenlike, flightless bird. There have not been many extinct megafauna creatures found in Africa because large mammals—the elephant, rhinoceros, hippopotamus, and giraffe—never became extinct. Some believe it is because the weather patterns in that part of the world did not drastically change during the Ice Age.

What did mastodons eat?

THESE HERBIVORES became extinct as recently as 8,000 years ago, along with their Pleistocene cousins, the mammoths. Although mastodons had many similarities to both mammoths and elephants, they were different in one way: their teeth weren't flat, but bumpy, perhaps for better tearing and grinding. Mastodons ate shrubs, leaves, and grasses, and some experts say their favorite treat was the fibrous stalks and leaves of the water lily—remnants have been found in the digestive tracts of several well-preserved carcasses.

Which animal has the biggest penis?

THE SIZE of a whale's penis is, no doubt, not easily measured to exact inches. Beyond the obvious reasons, whales don't have erections exactly, but projections: the penis retracts and protrudes from its body, remaining the same size, but usually hidden except for intercourse in which case it's mostly hidden, too. But somehow those crafty marine biologists did it: the right whale's penis is the largest of all mammals', measuring over seven feet long. Its testes weigh no less than a ton. But of course, as we all know, in a loving relationship size doesn't matter.

"POP GOES THE ERMINE"

What's an ermine?

AN ERMINE is a weasel when it's white. A weasel, normally brown in color, sheds its fur and grows a new winter white coat, and subsequently undergoes a name change in most parts. Especially in the fur industry, where "ermine" sounds more glamorous than "white weasel."

TAKE A STAB AT IT

Does a porcupine shoot its quills at an enemy?

ALTHOUGH THIS is a common stunt used in cartoons, porcupines don't have projectile quills. As a last resort, after growling and spitting, a porcupine will turn backward and ram itself into enemies. Quills, like fishhooks, have barbs that make them very difficult to remove without causing a great deal of pain. It is, again, a porcupine's last line of defense. In general, porcupines are very docile creatures and easy to tame. So trusting, as a matter of fact, their number-one danger in life is being killed by humans. People eat them but more often use their hollow quills in rituals of magic and religion, as musical instruments, and as vials for gold powder or other precious liquids or powders.

DEPRECIATING YOUR CAR, ONE BUCK AT A TIME

What do you do if a deer runs out in front of your car while you're driving?

YOU BRAKE, stay calm, and try not to further endanger yourself, your passengers, other traffic, or the deer as you would in any other collision situation. But there are several preventative steps you can take to avoid running into deer in the first place. The first is being aware of the season. Deer are most prevalent in June (when young fawns are on the move) and from October through December (mating season). A good thing to remember during these times—and always—is to lower your speed in

How much sleep do koalas get per day? Up to 18 hours.

heavily deer-populated areas; if you see deer signs, heed them. And keep your eye especially keen during the dawn and dusk hours, when deer are most active. Most car-deer collisions happen during these low-light times of day. If you do hit a deer, some states allow you to keep the carcass. Whether you want venison for dinner or not, contact the authorities and alert them about the hit immediately.

I KNOW YOU ARE, BUT WHAT AM I?

What are groups of bears called?

IF YOU SPOT a group of bears (and you usually don't, except when Mama Bear is towing Baby Bear), you can safely say, "Look! A sleuth of bears!"

You can have more interspecies fun with other animal-group names: for example, a *clowder* of cats, a *gang* of elks and a *mob* of emus. Foxes come in *skulks,* and gorillas in *bands.* Cobras group in *quivers,* and groups of crows are called murders. Ponies, apparently, *string,* and rattlesnakes *rhumba.* It's hard to catch a *wisp* of snipe, but a *pitying* of turtledoves happens more frequently. Starlings grouped are called a *murmuration,* and swans, a *lamentation.* You may not want an *unkindness* of ravens in your yard, but how about a *tiding* of magpies?

Do most baby animals have special names?

MOST OF THEM have been classified. While cats have *kittens,* bunnies do too, and beavers have *kits.* Eels have *elvers,* elephant seals have *weaners,* and fish have *fry.* Sheep can have *hogs,* but usually we call them *lambs.* Kangaroos have *joeys,* rhinos have *calves,* and so do whales and elephants. Aardvarks and dogs have *pups.* Baboons and chimpanzees have *infants.*

Hodgepodge

RATHER THAN WILLY-NILLY discarding the short odds and sods that didn't fit neatly into the nooks and crannies of this book, Jeeves has decided to toss them higgledy-piggledy into this hodge-podge of a chapter.

A WORD IS A WORD IS A PHRASE

Where does the phrase "Let's get down to brass tacks" come from? And why are the tacks brass?

THERE ARE a couple of theories about the origins of this phrase, both from England. The first comes from Cockney rhyming slang, which uses rhymes instead of the intended word: "the weep and wail" instead of "jail," for example, or "my struggle and strife" for "wife." Some say "brass tacks" was a rhyming substitute for the word "facts," alluding to the meaning of the phrase: getting to essentials.

> **Where did the expression "crisscross" come from?**
> "Christ's cross."

A different theory: Brass tacks, instead of tacks made from copper or another metal, were used to measure bolts of cloth back in days of old because they don't rust and wouldn't mar the fabric. When a customer was ready to measure up and pay the clerk, it was time to "get down to brass tacks."

What does "Mind your p's and q's" actually mean?

MINDING ONE'S p's and q's means, simply, "being circumspect." The origins of the phrase most likely come from the two letters' similarity to each other: Young children just learning to write often put a "p" for a "q" or vice versa. Two other, more whimsical explanations should also be noted. The first is that the phrase reminded bartenders in English pubs to correctly tally up their customers' pints and quarts. The second hails from Louis XIV's France, when dance masters would suggest to their pupils they mind their p's (*pieds,* meaning "feet") and q's (*queues,* meaning "wigs") when dancing.

> **Is there a name for when a phone number spells out a word?**
> It's called a *numerym.*

What's the difference between idiots, morons, and imbeciles?

THESE WORDS were originally designed as legitimate medical classifications to differentiate among different levels of mental retardation. Those classified as morons have the emotional and mental capacity of nine-year-olds; imbeciles react as five-year-olds; and idiots as two-year-olds.

Where does the word kindergarten come from?

IT'S GERMAN, meaning "garden of children." Educator Friedrich Froebel coined the term, but only after trying to coin another one: *Kleinkenderbeschaftigungsanstalt.* Although its meaning was clear—"institution where small children are occupied"—its pronunciation was quite a feat. Public rejection of the term persuaded Froebel to make the switch to *Kindergarten.*

What is ikebana?

THE TRADITIONAL Japanese art of flower arranging, which emphasizes balance and form. It is traditionally done by anyone from artists to samurai as a form of Zen meditation.

What does the Japanese name for Pac-Man mean?

THE WORD is *paku* and it means "eat" in Japanese.

Where does the word heroin come from?

IT COMES from Bayer officials who thought the new painkiller would be an effective substitute for morphine, "nonaddictive" yet effective. They celebrated its power by putting "hero" in the name and sold it over the counter.

How many times does the word "Sunday" appear in the Bible?

Zero.

Is Greek a Romance language, since it's very romantic sounding?

NO, A ROMANCE language is not determined by love but by whether it is based on Latin, the language of the Romans. French, Italian, Portuguese, Romanian, and Spanish are Romance languages...actually in *both* senses of the word.

What motto is inscribed in the lobby of the CIA building in Langley, Virginia?

"AND YE shall know the truth, and the truth shall make ye free." It's from the Bible.

HOORAY FOR HOLLYWOOD

What is Tom Cruise's real name?

THOMAS MAPOTHER IV. He dropped his last name and the IV and now uses his first and middle names.

Were the Three Stooges brothers?

MOE, CURLY, and Shemp were all Mrs. Howard's little boys. Larry Fine and a succession of replacements for Curly after he died were not. They were some of the most prolific film stars, appearing in some 200 different films (most of them 20-minute "two-reelers").

What was Tom Selleck's first film?

THE STORY goes that Mae West spotted Selleck in a Pepsi commercial. She personally had him cast as The Stud in her 1970 film *Myra Breckenridge*.

In the movie *The Wizard of Oz*, what was written on the side of the balloon that was used to escape from the Land of Oz?

OMAHA STATE FAIR.

Did Alfred Hitchcock have a nickname or was he too stuffy?

HE HAD SEVERAL. His folks called him Fred. His schoolmates and friends called him Cocky. He referred to himself as Hitch.

How big were Fred Astaire's feet?

FRED ASTAIRE'S shoe size was a pretty average 10½. His height, however, sometimes caused problems. He looks tall on-screen because he was very thin and angular. In reality, however, he was quite short—5' 8"—and sometimes needed his dancing partners to take off their high heels for dialogue scenes. Ginger Rogers, at 5' 5", was shorter than Astaire, but in order for Astaire to appear much taller, she would lower her heels. Ann Miller, at 5' 7", danced in ballet slippers so that she wouldn't tower above him.

Astaire is rumored to have also been uncomfortable with the size of his hands. They apparently looked so large and his fingers so long that he kept them turned sideways to the camera or audience so they could see only their edges. Watch for it the next time you see an Astaire film.

Where did the writer get the name James Bond?

Bond was a writer of bird books.

To see photographs of Fred Astaire's shoes, try http://themave.
com/Astaire/FAport3.html

Was Bruce Lee ever on television before he got famous in martial arts?

YES, HE played superhero Green Lantern's sidekick Kato in the late 1960s.

Who were Frances Gumm and Frances Butts?

THE REAL names of Judy Garland and Dale Evans, respectively.

BEST $35 DOLLAR LOGO EVER

How did Nike come up with its name and logo?

IN 1972, the Blue Ribbon Shoe Company turned to the art department of nearby Portland State University for a student who could design a distinctive logo. Carolyn Davidson was chosen, and she set about the first real job of her career. Company founder Phil Knight asked for something both functional and stylish. He wanted what Addidas had: a distinctive logo that was also part of the support of the shoe. He wanted the logo to "reflect movement and speed." Davidson produced a series of designs, including a broad stripe with a hole in the middle that was only briefly considered. She suggested Knight put support in the shoe itself and leave the logo to reflect movement only. Knight wasn't pleased, but settled on the fat check-mark design anyway, deciding it would grow on him. Davidson billed the company $35; the logo turned out to be worth millions.

The Nike name comes from the Greek goddess of victory and was given to the shoe a few days after the logo was approved. The name was chosen from a list of possibilities largely because it was short enough to fit on the back of the shoe and still be readable.

MY GREAT-GRANDFATHER UNLOADED TEA, AND ALL I GOT WAS THIS LOUSY T-SHIRT

What are the origins of the T-shirt?

THE TRUTH is that the t-shirt has been around a long time, and no one knows its exact origins. Following are two popular theories. One idea is this: Men working on the docks at Annapolis, Maryland, in the late 1600s unloaded a great deal of tea. The simple shirts they wore became known as "tea shirts," later shorted simply to "T-shirts."

> **How many T-shirts does the average person own?**
> 25.

The second theory comes from across the pond, in the Royal Navy. Navy men wearing the equivalent of tank tops offended the British Royal Family who insisted they cover their arms enough to hide their armpits. The shirts looked like "T's" in comparison to the old tanks and so were dubbed "T shirts."

IN STYLE

Do clothing designers ever go "too far"?

THEY SOMETIMES do and sometimes big-name designers have to eat a little crow. Take the example of designer-extraordinaire Karl Lagerfeld in 1994, with a slinky black dress made for Chanel's seasonal line-up. Lagerfeld, feeling a little artsy, decided to embroider decorative Arabic writing on the front of the dress. Unfortunately, he didn't know that what he thought was a love poem was actually from the Muslim holy book, the Koran. Uproar ensued in the Muslim community, and Lagerfeld issued an apology for his apparently honest mistake. The dress was pulled from the line-up, and all pictures and video of the dress on the runway were destroyed.

> **Which color necktie is the best seller?**
> Blue sells best, then red.

Where did the top hat come from?

IN 18TH-CENTURY England, hats became more fashionable as the practice of wearing huge wigs died out. Most historians believe the top hat originated in London with John Etherington, the owner of a fashionable men's hat shop. The story goes that Etherington designed this far-out stovepipe contraption and wore it on his way home from work. The extra-high hat caused so much of a stir that a brawl erupted among spectators. Orders for the hat came pouring in.

A BIT OF HERSTORY

How old was Joan of Arc when she was put to death?

NINETEEN. She first began hearing voices and having visions at age 13. By the time she was 17, she was wearing men's clothes and leading armies into battle.

TO YOUR HEALTH!

How much more likely is a smoker to die from lung cancer than a nonsmoker?

SMOKERS ARE 20 to 30 times more likely to die from lung cancer than nonsmokers.

What kind of doctor is Jack "Dr. Death" Kevorkian?

HE WAS a pathologist before he was legally forbidden to practice medicine.

NAVEL DESTROYER

Is it dangerous to pierce your own belly button?

HERE ARE some facts you might want to consider before proceeding. There is always risk when you have

> **Where can I see interesting tattoos?**

any part of your body pierced. It is minor surgery and should be treated as such. With navel piercings, you are at a higher than average risk for infection for two reasons. First, the area you're perforating naturally receives a certain amount of friction. An earlobe, by contrast, doesn't rub against clothing or other people on a regular basis. Friction often leads to irritation of the wound and prevents proper healing.

Second, the navel is a receptacle for sweat and dirt from the upper body. Navels are already prone to infection even without holes, because they sport wrinkles, crevices, and a certain amount of depth, making them prime real estate for multiplying bacteria. When you pierce your navel, you statistically have better than a 40% chance of getting an infection in the time it takes for the wound to heal. Even after the piercing has healed the first time, you are still at risk for future irritation and infection.

POTPOURRI

When was the adding machine invented?
IN THE late 1880s. It was developed specifically to help with taking the U.S. census that took place during that period. It significantly reduced counting time for the Census Bureau.

What could make you legally lose your citizenship in the United States?
YOU CAN'T serve in another country's army, be convicted of treason, or vote in another country's election. You also lose your citizenship if you formally renounce it.

How much were workers paid for digging the Erie Canal?
IN THE 1820s, canal workers got 37 cents to $1 a day. This was for a 10-hour day, and they were expected to work six days a week! They also got up to a quart of whiskey each a day, given in a series of four-ounce shots starting at 6 a.m. What's surprising is how straight the canal is, considering.

What can babies do that adults cannot?

BESIDES GETTING people to tend to their every need by alternately crying and being cute? They can breathe and swallow at the same time without choking. People lose that skill when they're about seven months old.

In which month do newborn babies weigh most?

NOBODY KNOWS why, but babies born in May average about seven ounces heavier than those born in other months.

Is the American billion really different from the British billion?

YES. AN AMERICAN "billion" is 1,000,000,000 (a thousand million), but a British "billion" is 1,000,000,000,000 (a million million).

About the Authors

JACK MINGO is the author of 15 books including *How the Cadillac Got Its Fins, The Whole Pop Catalog,* and *The Couch Potato Handbook.* He has written for countless publications—*The New York Times, Washington Post, Boston Phoenix, Reader's Digest, Wall Street Journal,* and *Los Angeles Times,* to name a few.

ERIN BARRETT is the author of a kids' trivia book from Klutz Press; has written for magazines and newspapers, such as *Icon* and the *San Jose Mercury News;* and has contributed to several anthologies, including the *Uncle John's Bathroom Reader* series.

Together, Jack and Erin have also designed numerous electronic and online games. They live on the Bay in Alameda, California, with three children and a canoe.

Still Curious?

Jeeves is always at your service at **Ask.com**. So bring *your* most intriguing queries and be ready to learn. Browse the Answer Point, our interactive forum allowing users to share their questions or their expertise. And sign up for your own Personal Jeeves to receive daily updates on news, sports, horoscopes, or any other topic that suits your taste.

Just ask.